TO SUMBURGH

FAIR I.

ORKNEY
ISLANDS

PAPA
WESTRAY   N. RONALDSAY

WESTRAY   SANDAY

ROUSAY
EDAY
ORKNEY   STRONSAY
HATSTON
STROMNESS   KIRKWALL
OLD MAN
OF HOY   WIDEFORD FM.
SCAPA   FLOW
SWOMA   S. RONALDSAY
PENTLAND FIRTH
DUNNETT HD.   STROMA
DUNCANSBY HD.
THURSO

WICK

Robert A. Barr,
49, Wilson Av.
Troon

KINBRACE

DORNOCH FIRTH

MORAY FIRTH
TON   LOSSIEMOUTH
CROMARTY   BANFF
NAIRN
DALCROSS
INVERNESS
HUNTLEY

GRANTOWN
KINTORE
DYCE
ABERDEEN
BANCHORY

Air Road
To
The Isles

*Captain and Mrs. Gwen Fresson before leaving Inverness
for London in G-AAWO, 1948.*

AIR ROAD
TO
THE ISLES

The Memoirs of

Captain E. E. Fresson, O.B.E.

Illustrations by John Blake

DAVID RENDEL LTD.

Printed and bound in Great Britain by
Bookprint Limited, Crawley, Sussex

Contents

Foreword	vii
Author's Preface	ix
Chapter One	1
Chapter Two	41
Chapter Three	62
Chapter Four	70
Chapter Five	82
Chapter Six	103
Chapter Seven	124
Chapter Eight	145
Chapter Nine	166
Chapter Ten	176
Chapter Eleven	184
Chapter Twelve	212
Chapter Thirteen	224
Chapter Fourteen	237
Chapter Fifteen	254
Chapter Sixteen	268
Index	274

Foreword

by Eric Linklater

In the *Shorter Oxford Dictionary* a pioneer is defined as 'one who goes before to prepare the way; one who begins some enterprise, course of action, etc.; an original investigator, explorer, or worker.' These descriptions, excellent as far as they go, fail to indicate that the pioneer may also, like the artist, be a true creator. It is necessary to be aware of this before trying to form a balanced view of the initiatives undertaken and the results achieved by that remarkable man who in the north of Scotland, where he became famous, was generally known, not by some nickname or familiar Christian name, but as *Captain* Fresson.

This curious fact is some indication of the unusual respect that he enjoyed in those sparsely populated parts between Inverness and Shetland, between Inverness and the Western Isles. Fresson was a pioneer in that he explored the possibilities of establishing air services between the north of Scotland and its adjacent islands, and he was also the creator of new habits of life, a new comfort in life, because his aeroplanes brought to a people, who had previously travelled at the fastest by horse and gig, the thrills of hurtling through the air at a hundred miles an hour or more. And the natives of the outlying islands took to that brand-new form of transport with alacrity.

Fresson had served his apprenticeship to flying during the first Great War. Then in China, with overtones of considerable courage, he experienced and survived both commerce and service with some of the monstrously dictatorial Chinese war-lords of the 1920s. When he came home he was still a young man, and to the great benefit of all who were living in the far north of Britain he saw that the aeroplane could usefully supplement the railway train and the steamer. He began his service with a minimum of capital but a maximum of vision, with a sufficiency of knowledge and an experience capable of growth. Initially his resources were slender. I remember the earliest years of Highland Airways, and a day when, his only commercial machine having developed some engine fault, Fresson hired an even smaller aeroplane and a pilot who had never been north of Inverness before. In those days there were no modern aids to navigation, such as radio, and when we ran into fog we were soon lost. But suddenly we came down into a patch of fortuitous sunlight, and below us were the Highland Railway and the name – all too clearly legible – of a little wayside station. Hastily we turned, and a hundred feet above the bright steel lines flew towards Inverness.

Fresson writes feelingly of the difficulties of flying without aids to navigation or foreknowledge of the weather. There was the particular summer hazard, north of Helmsdale, of dense cloud which sometimes lay only a couple of hundred feet above the sea, and it was necessary to fly between the wrinkled water and that low white ceiling. I have flown with him in such conditions, and I remember the confidence with which he navigated the narrow shelf of visibility above Sinclair Bay and the Pentland Firth. They looked as strange and unfamiliar as the coastal waters of New Zealand when Captain Cook first sailed them; but Fresson, like Cook, had a genius for finding his way about.

The aeroplanes that were the mainstay of Highland Airways were small biplanes of exceptional virtue called D.H. Rapides. Fresson and his regular pilots flew them daily through the violent, unpredictable weather of the northern and western isles. They were hardly ever storm-stayed, and they never had a serious accident. Their maintenance men were few in number, but expert and devoted to their task. Fresson flew mail and newspapers to the farthest isles with a punctuality and regularity that have never been surpassed, and not always equalled, by the great organisation that took over the service he had established. He and his pilots flew throughout the war, and soon after the return of peace Fresson was deprived of his livelihood. Over the routes that he had pioneered flew the larger machines of B.E.A., and in the earliest years of its existence the Scottish service of B.E.A. was much less efficient than the service of the man it had ousted. Fresson got no reward for his good work, but was treated with conspicuous shabbiness.

In addition to his genius, he was a friendly, agreeable man with a great deal of interesting conversation. But the bureaucrats may have found him difficult to deal with, for he was proud and independent and had grown accustomed to having his own way. He was in all ways an admirable man, but he could sometimes be as unpredictable as the weather through which he flew. Once, I remember, I drove to Kirkwall in a great hurry, without having booked a passage, and pleaded with Fresson to take me to Inverness. He said, 'I am flying a full load of mail, but if you like to lie on top of the mail bags, you can come.' After we had crossed the Pentland Firth he turned and shouted, 'I hope you won't mind if I go out of my way a bit. I've got very interested in fulmar gulls, and for the last week or two I've been counting their nests.' Then, to my horror, he drove his aeroplane along the top edge of the Caithness cliffs, weaving in and out, with his head over his right shoulder and his right hand scribbling notes and details of what he saw. But his D.H. Rapide behaved as if it were an extension of Fresson himself. He had a host of devoted friends, and machinery gave him perfect obedience.

It is a remarkable story which I have the honour to introduce. With the simple honesty of his genius, Fresson tells precisely what he did, and how it was done, and it is my privilege to speak for the people of the Highlands and Islands of Scotland, and express the gratitude of all those whose lives he enlarged and whose comfort he increased. He was benefactor as well as pioneer, and he created, not only Highland Airways, but a legend that will endure.

Author's Preface

When I first discovered the Orkney Islands in Gipsy Moth 'Ah-WO' on Sunday, 19th April 1932, it was like flying into another land. The population appeared different in some intangible manner. My passenger, and owner of the Moth, Miss Helen Pauer (whose home was in Trentham, Staffordshire) was of the same mind after half an hour's talk with the crowd which surrounded our small plane that afternoon – 'itching to touch and prod it as if it was made of solid wood', as Miss Pauer naïvely put it at the time.

My instant impression of the Orcadians was their desire to be of assistance, and on my second visit some months later I found the same pleasant trait in the people with whom I came in contact. It was not really surprising, that feeling of strangeness which smote the visitor who descended from the sky that Sabbath afternoon, because we learned later that the population of Orkney and its neighbouring islands eighty-six miles to the North – Shetland – were of Norse descent.

That first journey of exploration was to earn me many years of close contact with the Orcadians, and so I had the opportunity of establishing a firm friendship with the people of Orkney. I found it more difficult to get close to the population of Shetland, with whom I came in contact a few years later. They appeared far more reserved in themselves and in their habits; for instance, it took very much longer to wean the population from surface transport to air, whereas the Orcadians took to flying as a duck does to water. However, once you made a friend in Shetland, he was your friend for life, and that was very noticeable to me when I made a return visit to the two islands after an absence of fourteen years.

In writing an historical account of past events, it has been my endeavour to quote actual facts and in some instances express my reactions to certain happenings. It has also been my intention to avoid anything that might wander into the realm of fantasy or inaccuracy. So I hope that in dealing with the activities of Aberdeen Airways, which subsequently crystallised into Allied Airways (of which my good friend Mr. Gandar Dower was the owner), he will not hold it against me when I describe the events as they occurred in the internecine war which he and I fought over a

ix

period of thirteen years. There was little doubt that his operations, along the routes I had established and in which I was first in the field, caused Highland Airways Ltd. many heartaches, as the population in the area simply did not justify the existence of two companies in competition. We were at an added disadvantage as we did not possess the finance to fight a war of attrition. We were accordingly forced into tying up with big business which eventually superseded our local authority. However, those heartaches are of the past and were erased from my mind when it became my unhappy lot to take over Mr. Gandar Dower's firm after the State had grabbed the fruits of our combined labours for which we had worked so hard over the years. I am happy to say that we are friends now in adversity and I often have the pleasure of calling at his attractive residence overlooking one of the parks in London, always receiving a real 'Scottish welcome'.

With regard to my more drastic references to the State Corporation which grabbed our livelihood, I make no apology. Their actions were callous and quite un-British. It should, however, be clearly understood that the British European Airways I chastise refers to the Corporation which existed in 1947–48, when it was ruled by the personnel of the wartime A.T.A. organisation, who applied wartime 'know-how' to commercial operations which were doomed to disaster from the beginning. When Mr. Peter Masefield became chief executive, B.E.A. was reborn and became a businesslike organisation. Before long, under his management and leadership, the huge losses of the previous years were turned into a profit. That high standard has been perpetuated by his successor Mr. Milward (now Sir Anthony Milward), and it is common knowledge that the present day B.E.A.'s Continental operations are a model to its competitors. The same goes for the London-Glasgow route on which I frequently have the pleasure of travelling. I bear no ill will to the B.E.A. of to-day. They were not involved in the regrettable happenings of 1947–48 recorded and described in the last chapters of my narrative.

Inverness, 1963.   E. E. F.

CHAPTER ONE

I first became interested in aviation in 1908. At that time, Blériot, Henri Farman, Voisin and others were conducting experiments with their home-built planes while the famous Wright brothers, Orville and Wilbur, were giving advanced exhibition flights in France with their biplanes.

Early in the summer of 1909 I was spending my holidays at Minster-on-Sea in the Isle of Sheppey and one day when cycling through the countryside on the east end of the island, I found myself at Leysdown marshes. Two early air pioneers, the brothers Short, had built themselves an air-shed on the flat marshland and were constructing an aeroplane of their own design. There was also a group of enthusiasts trying to teach themselves to fly and I watched a few making quite long hops. I was greatly interested and cycled back day after day to watch the experiments. Among the more successful was Moore-Brabazon – later to become Lord Brabazon of Tara – who succeeded that year in winning the *Daily Mail* prize of £1,000 for successfully making the first circular flight in an all-English aircraft, the Short biplane No. 2. Also there were Frank McClean, the Hon. C. S. Rolls (later killed when gliding in to land at the Bournemouth flying meeting), Maurice Egerton and J. W. Dunne. The latter designed and built the first tail-less biplane which was inherently stable. A young man working with Mr. Dunne became, many years later, a famous aircraft designer and constructor – his name was Richard Fairey.

On 26th July 1909, flying made its big impact on me. Crossing Blackfriars Bridge that Monday morning I observed a *Daily Mail* poster carred by a sandwich-board man. In large type it presented the startling headline – **Blériot flies the Channel.** I was thrilled, like many other people, over such an important event, which portended considerable changes in our insular position.

There had been extensive excitement throughout July 1909 as Hubert Latham with his beautiful Antoinette monoplane had been waiting for favourable weather at Calais to make the first crossing by a heavier-than-air machine and so win the prize of £1,000 offered by the *Daily Mail* for the first aviator to fly the English Channel. Latham made his first attempt on Monday, 19th July, but was forced down into the sea by motor failure. While the Antoinette was being reconditioned for another attempt, Louis Blériot arrived at Calais determined to make a desperate bid to get across the Channel before his rival. He was suffering and in great pain from a badly burned foot and ankle – the result of a crash. He walked on crutches and had to be lifted into his plane. At 4.30 a.m. on Sunday, 25th July 1909 Blériot was called by his mechanic.

"It's a fine morning, Monsieur, the wind has abated, shall I get the monoplane ready?"

Blériot gave the order, dressed with difficulty and made his way out to the flying field. His mechanic helped him into the small single-seater Type XI monoplane. He was soon airborne, and headed towards the English coast. The plane was fitted with a 25 h.p. Anzani three-cylinder motor which had to be run flat out to keep the small monoplane in the air. Half-way across the 20 miles of sea the motor began to overheat and appeared likely to seize up, but luckily Blériot was saved by a heavy rainstorm which cooled the red-hot cylinder heads, thus enabling him to reach the cliffs of Dover. Unfortunately he was forced to land downhill and his history-making machine was damaged. A piece of the airscrew blade is hanging as a souvenir in the Royal Aero Club premises in London today.

The flying bug had now bitten deeply into me and I began trying to teach myself the rudiments of flight by building numerous models. My parents were then living in the pretty little country village of Wickford, on the London-Southend railway. Opposite their house, 'Whyteways', was a large field which I used for flying tests. The kitchen table served as a bench and I worked into the small hours of the morning building my models. A few hours' sleep and I was up at six o'clock to carry out flight tests in the field, before catching the nine o'clock express train for London. At that time I was employed by a London firm of Far Eastern merchants, in the engineering section, with a view to taking a post in China.

Many models were made and written off and it was at least six months before I really got one to fly well. I was greatly excited over my first success and the whole family had to line up in the field to watch a demonstration. I felt they also deserved a share in my success, for their sleep was constantly disturbed by the noise I created in my midnight carpentry sessions.

During 1910 there were a number of air displays in Britain which were well attended by the French and British aces. Blackpool, Lanark and Doncaster were a few of the most important meetings

which were crowded with paying spectators anxious to see an
aeroplane fly. It was at Hendon airfield, belonging to Mr. Claude
Grahame-White, one of Britain's first French-taught pilots, that I
saw my first aeroplane fly. Designed by a Mr. Barber, it flew tail-
first and in consequence was known as a *cana d* (duck). Powered by
a 35 h.p. Green four-cylinder water-cooled motor, Mr. Barber's
machine would circle Hendon airfield time and time again, flying
most gracefully at fifty feet or so.

With the advent of the 50 h.p. Gnôme rotary motor in 1910,
flying advanced very quickly and long cross-country flying became
the order of the day in France. Long-distance flying in England was
also beginning, for in April 1910 Claude Grahame-White entered
for the London to Manchester flight for which the *Daily Mail* had
offered a prize of £10,000. Grahame-White had learned to fly at
the Blériot and Henri Farman schools in France.

On the morning of Saturday, 23rd April 1910, Grahame-White
took off from Wormwood Scrubs and reached Lichfield 117 miles
away. During refuelling the Henri Farman biplane was blown over
by a squall of wind which suddenly arose. Hurriedly the plane was
returned to London for repairs so that an early re-start could be
made. In the meantime Louis Paulhan, a young Frenchman, also
had designs on the *Daily Mail* prize. As soon as he heard of Grahame-
White's bad luck, he forthwith packed up his new racing Farman
and came to England. Paulhan's plane did not reach Hendon, his
starting point, until Wednesday morning, when Grahame-White's
damaged aeroplane was ready for flight. Grahame-White had
decided that as the wind was gusty he would wait until the calm
hours of the morning before making a fresh start, and turned in to
rest. Like Hubert Latham a year before, his sleep was disturbed by
the unwelcome tidings that his rival had started. He immediately
set off in pursuit and actually caught Paulhan up and passed him,
when engine trouble forced him to land. That was Paulhan's opportunity, for before repairs were finished, came the crushing tidings
that the Frenchman, starting at half past five in the morning, had
reached his goal and won the coveted £10,000.

In the summer of that same year, the famous *Circuit de l'Est* was
flown. That brought at least a dozen aircraft across the Channel to
Hendon aerodrome on the English leg. I was out early in the
morning, a beautiful sunny day, to see the departure of those pilots
for the Continent. I have a vivid recollection of the then famous
French pilot Vedrines taking off in a Morane monoplane. He was
off the ground in 60 yards and went into a steep climbing turn to

3

the right over the sheds. The performance of the Morane mono-plane, with its Gnôme engine, was astounding. All the competitors left like clockwork and landed safely in France, and yet, only one year before, Latham and Blériot were struggling just to make the Channel crossing.

The following summer of 1911, which incidentally was the last but one that I was to have in England for seven years, the round-Britain race was flown. A large number of entries were received for the race and the competitors left Brooklands on the afternoon of 22nd July for Hendon, the first sector. They would stay over until Monday, 24th July, before starting the race in earnest. Among the starters were the usual famous names – Beaumont (Blériot mono-plane), Vedrines (Morane monoplane), Valentine (Deperdussin monoplane), S. F. Cody (biplane St. Paul's specially built for the race), C. H. Pixton (Bristol biplane) and a further 26 entrants, a number of whom did not start, or at any rate did not get further than the Hendon/Harrogate sector. The course was 1,010 miles and was won by André Beaumont in twenty-two hours thirty minutes flying time. He was closely followed by Jules Vedrines over the whole course, with James Valentine some way behind them. It was Wednesday when the winners arrived back at Brooklands, the third day after leaving Hendon.

At the time of that race I was staying with my cousin Mrs. Amy Troldahl who lived at Hexham-on-Tyne. Her son Bob was some years younger than myself and equally interested in the Air Race and we decided to be at Gosforth Park, Newcastle-upon-Tyne, on Monday morning in time to see the arrival of the leading com-petitors. They were scheduled to arrive at Gosforth, having landed at Harrogate en route, at nine in the morning. We were up before six, caught an early train from Hexham into Newcastle and boarded a tram for Gosforth Park. We sat on top and so had a clear view of the sky. It was a beautiful sunny morning but very hazy.

Approaching Gosforth I suddenly spotted a Blériot monoplane high in the sky gliding down towards the Park.

"Look Bobs, look up there," I shouted, pointing, "can you see it? A Blériot monoplane. I'll bet that's Beaumont – dead on time."

It had only just passed nine o'clock. We jumped off the tram outside the Park gates, paid our entrance money, and raced to find the landing spot. We got there out of breath to see Beaumont lying under the wing of his monoplane resting, while mechanics were

4

filling up with fuel and oil. Another mechanic was checking the
motor and aircraft. Beaumont had flown from London in the record
time of 4 hours 20 minutes, half the time taken by an express train
in those days. A few minutes later a shout went up 'There's another
plane coming in'. On landing it turned out to be Vedrines in his
Morane monoplane. He had covered the distance in 4 hours 11
minutes, but had spent more time on the ground at Harrogate than
Beaumont. They both got away for Edinburgh after a very short
stop.

We waited for another hour before the third competitor, James
Valentine (Deperdussin monoplane), arrived. He filled up and was
away within 20 minutes. By then, a choppy wind had got up
and I remember seeing the Deperdussin rocking badly after take-
off until altitude was reached. He disappeared from sight in a few
minutes, heading North. Bob and I waited around until lunch time
and as no further competitors arrived we decided to get to town for
a late lunch before returning to Hexham. We learned later that the
other competitors were scattered all along the course, some with
engine failure and many hopelessly lost. It had been reported by
the first three to arrive that the visibility was not good, and unless
a pilot could fly a compass course, it was hopeless. There were no

5

specially designed aero compasses in those days and the land compass was exceedingly difficult to operate owing to vibration and difficulty in swinging – the French pilots were far ahead in that technique. They were constantly making long inter-city flights on the continent whereas our pilots contented themselves by flying around aerodromes at flying meetings, no doubt influenced by the cash returns offered.

That race made a great impression on me and I was determined that one day I would learn to fly. It was not until six years later that my chance came, when I joined up with the R.F.C. in Canada.

At the end of July Mr. Simpson, our managing director at the office, told me that I was to be transferred to the company's Shanghai branch the following November. I was given a list of special kit required for very hot summers and extremely cold winters and told to make all preparations to travel.

Early in November I left Liverpool Street Station for Harwich. My parents, uncles, aunts and brother came to see me off and bid me godspeed. I was about to take the trans-Siberian route to the Far East; but first of all, I was to visit some steel works in the Rhineland to pick up one or two agencies for the Shanghai branch of our company. I would then go on to Berlin to spend a week's holiday with some German business friends. They lived in the fashionable part of Berlin and gave me a wonderful time.

I left that city at ten o'clock at night for Warsaw and Moscow. When I awoke next morning we were near the Eastern German border with Poland where we ran into snow-covered country. I had to change trains at Warsaw because the Russian gauge track was wider than the German. I had half a day to spend in Warsaw and took the opportunity of visiting the Cathedral to see the great composer Chopin's grave. After lunch, I was driven in a droshky through the Warsaw ghetto to the Russian departure station, some four miles distant. I was terrified. The ghetto occupants looked as if they would cut anyone's throat for a few pence and the droshky driver seemed just as bad. There was nothing to stop him delivering me to the wolves had he felt so inclined. In that case, I would never have been heard of again and not missed for weeks or until the time I was due to arrive in Shanghai. However, my fears were not realised and the droshky driver delivered me safely to my train. I let out a terrific sigh of relief.

I spent three days in Moscow at the Metropole Hotel. The snow lay thickly in the streets and I was driven from the station in a droshky on sledge runners. The horse had a large hoop over its head with a small bell attached which jingled as we glided over the snow. What a magnificent hotel that was in the days of the Czar's reign. The splendour of the receptions and dinners held there and the glistening of the women's magnificent diamonds and jewellery had to be seen to be believed. I will never forget pre-Bolshevik Russia.

I boarded the train for Harbin in the evening. The journey was to take ten days, and we were to pass through Ekaterinburg where the Czar and his family were butchered some seven years later. From there the long rail haul took us through Omsk and Tomsk and on to Irkutsk. I found the going very hard at first, as I could not sleep owing to the noise. It was three days and nights before I eventually got to sleep. From then on, however, I had no further trouble and slept soundly from sheer exhaustion. I was only 20 and my journey was looked upon in those days as a great adventure. The language problem was difficult, if one did not speak French or Russian. Fortunately, I knew a little French and German which got me by. On the train, I became acquainted with an Englishman who had been in China for a number of years and was returning from leave in England. It broke the monotony having another person to talk to. He also knew the ropes and shepherded me along the 7,000 miles of rail travel. He told me there was a plague epidemic in Manchuria and China and advised me of the precautions to take.

After leaving Irkutsk, the train had to wind its way around the southern shore of Lake Baikal. There must have been 100 miles or more of tunnelling and sharp curves around that rocky shore. We were constantly pitched from side to side. The moon was shining and occasionally I would catch a glimpse of the lake which looked very beautiful in the moonlight. Later in the season, in the depths of winter, when the lake was frozen to a depth of many feet, the railway engineers would lay a track straight across the ice from shore to shore, thus saving many miles and hours of tortuous travel. When we awoke next morning we were climbing up the Trans-baikalia plateau. We arrived at Chita before noon where we refuelled and replenished the dining car victuals. On the morrow, we entered Manchuria after crossing the great Khingan Mountains. It was not long before I began to realise what an eastern plague meant, for the train began to pass long mounds adjacent to the railroad track several hundred feet long, some eight to ten feet high and many feet wide, under which the plague victims were buried en masse. It frightened me and I remember wondering how long I

7

would be obliged to live out there under such unpleasant conditions.

After being on the train for ten days, we ran into Harbin around eleven o'clock in the morning. That train was proceeding to Vladivostok and so we had to change over to the South Manchurian Railway. As there was no direct train to the seaport of Dairen, we were obliged to stay the night at the Railway Hotel in Mukden. It was all very strange to me and I felt a long way from home. Next morning we embarked on the train to Dairen and after rolling through undulating country all day, reached our destination around tea time. We were told we would have to stay a night at the Yamato Hotel (Japanese run), as the Shanghai steamer which plied across the Yellow Sea would not depart until next morning. That night I went to a local Japanese cinema, which in those days was very crude and I got badly bitten by fleas, which forced a hasty retreat to the hotel long before the very inferior film came to an end.

We sailed next morning in brilliant sunshine. The steamer was fast, making 20 knots, but rolled like a barrel. It was not long before most of the passengers were down below, but I managed to weather it that trip, although on a subsequent one, many years later, I succumbed to my first attack of sea-sickness. The Yellow Sea is comparatively shallow and the wind soon whips up a terrific swell. The name Yellow Sea is very well chosen as the water is a dirty, muddy yellow colour.

On arrival in Shanghai, I ran right into the 1911 revolution, which ended a dynasty and changed China into a republic. The killing and bloodshed I witnessed for the first few months was a fearful introduction to a new country for a young man. I was taken under Stanley MacNider's wing, and I rapidly learnt the wide difference between living in rural England and the Far East. He had a flat in the Kukiang Road and entertained on a large scale. At such parties, one met the business people who counted. During the day I was tutored into the business routine at the office. I gleaned many things in a very short time in Shanghai. I stayed there until the end of January 1912, and by that time had obtained a good grounding in the company's procedure.

In February 1912 I was sent up to Hankow where the revolution was still raging. Junks used to come drifting down the Yangtze, which was a mile wide at Hankow, full of dead refugees. They had been machine-gunned from the shore. If you tried to walk outside the Concessions, you just had to step over the dead every few yards. It was a frightful state of carnage which affected me considerably. By the summer, the situation became more normal,

8

and I fell into the way of life, boxed up in a few square miles, 600 miles from the coast. Our only connection with the outside world was the river steamer, which took three days to make the journey between Hankow and Shanghai.

I could write a separate story of my next five years in China. I was very interested in my work which took me over many thousands of miles of the interior. There were no roads in China then and I was kept busy travelling the hard way, mostly on foot. It was nothing for me to walk 20 miles a day for several days on end. Then there were the rivers; I had a sampan converted by installing a 5 h.p. single cylinder De Russet motor, which would take me hundreds of miles inland serving the constructional units of the Canton-Hankow Railway sections.

The war came in August 1914, and I signed on to join the first Volunteer Contingent, leaving Shanghai in October. In September, I contracted typhus fever, and all but died of it. I was laid up in the Hankow Roman Catholic Hospital until the middle of November, and it took me several months longer to regain my strength. In the meantime, the first Contingent had sailed for Britain. Very few of those volunteers came out of the war alive, so perhaps the typhus saved me instead of claiming me.

When I was fit, our Consul put me on the 'indispensable' list, and I was not allowed to offer myself as a volunteer for other Contingents which sailed. It was not until the early part of 1917 that I managed to get the restriction lifted, and I left for home, via America and Canada, to join up on my own. I sailed on the *Tenyo Marru* from Shanghai to Honolulu and San Francisco.

I spent a month in California touring the country on a Red Indian motorcycle which I bought over there. I made it a good holiday as I thought it might be the last I would ever have. On arrival back in San Francisco, I joined up at a Recruiting Station for the Army, passed the medical board and was to go back next morning to be sworn in and receive the 'King's Shilling'. That night, some friends in Los Angeles phoned me. "Come back right away," they said, "an R.F.C. officer has just arrived, recruiting for the Royal Flying Corps."

I had told them that I was anxious to get into the R.F.C. I ignored my interview of that afternoon with the Army boys, and left next morning at half past four on my motorcycle for Los Angeles – 400 miles away. The roads in those days were mostly dirt-surfaced and the trip over the mountains approaching Santa Barbara was tough going and slowed me down so much that I did

9

not arrive there until six o'clock that night. I had to ride through three small rivers which were unbridged, and got thrown into the water in the middle stream when the front wheel hit a big stone. On reaching Santa Barbara I was thirsty, hungry and dead beat. I went into a coffee bar and drank at least six large cups of coffee with my meal and then went along to the beach to have a sleep before tackling the remaining 100 miles. Unfortunately, the coffee worked against my tiredness and I was unable to sleep. So at three in the morning I started off for Los Angeles, arriving there at around six-thirty. I went to my friends' house. They were all asleep at that hour, but there was a hammock swung on the veranda, which I slipped into. That was where they found me at eight o'clock in the morning, dead to the world.

My friends were English. He was a Doctor Frances, and had emigrated to the U.S.A. some years before. He was married to an Englishwoman and had a family. They owned a very pleasant house on the outskirts of Los Angeles. Dr. Frances got in touch with the R.F.C. officer who was staying at one of the principal hotels and made an appointment for me next day. I was duly ushered in and presented to a Captain Paul Arbon. I was put through a lot of questioning when he suddenly enquired where I was educated.

"Framlingham College," I answered. He looked up, surprised.

"What years were you there?" he shot at me. I told him.

"What year were you in the Remove form?" he countered.

"Around 1903," I replied.

"My God! I've placed you," he said; "I remember you now."

He mentioned the name of a cousin of mine, Roland Fenn, who was also in the Remove. He went on talking about several anecdotes and my mind began to focus back 15 years. Suddenly, I recalled him. A medium-height boy with black hair, very unassuming, who kept much to himself.

There was no further questioning; I was 'signed in' on the dot as a candidate for the R.F.C. in Canada, and given a steamer and rail ticket to Toronto where I was to report for a medical examination. I stayed in Los Angeles for a week and we met frequently. Paul was very well-to-do, having invented certain improvements in oil drilling gear. I took him back to the Frances home and introduced him. They were amazed over such an extraordinary reunion and asked him to stay for dinner. It then transpired that a near relative of Mrs. Frances had also been educated at Framlingham, another extraordinary coincidence!

A few days later I sailed from Los Angeles for Vancouver. I left my trusted Indian motorcycle with the Frances family who promised to look after it for me until the war was over. If I survived, I planned to return to my job in China (which was open for me) via America and I would call at Los Angeles to see the Frances family again and make arrangements to have my machine shipped to Shanghai. Which is precisely what happened, for not only did I survive the war, but I did return to my job in China, via Los Angeles.

I travelled up to Vancouver and spent a few days there before proceeding across the Canadian Rockies to Toronto by train, which carried an observation car. The scenery was a stupendous sight, and I have never met its grandeur anywhere in my subsequent travels, which have been fairly extensive.

I stayed over in Banff Springs Hotel for a couple of days, before continuing on to Toronto. On arrival there I booked in at the King Edward Hotel and presented myself next day at Royal Flying Corps Headquarters, handing over Captain Arbon's confidential letter which he had given me for the authorities. After the usual form-filling activities, they sent me along to the medical section for a report on my physical fitness to undertake flying training. I thought I was in first-class condition but the doctor examining me thought otherwise. He told me my blood pressure was phenomenally high and he was unable to pass me unless I could reduce it. I could not believe my ears, I had always been very fit and then I thought of the typhus fever three years before. I told the M.O. about it and said in despair,

"Just fancy coming all the way from China to join the R.F.C. to be told I was medically unfit." The M.O. was a really decent sort and when he heard where I had come from, he asked me how long I had been in Toronto.

"I've just arrived – left Los Angeles a week ago and been travelling most of the time since."

"Ah!" he ejaculated, "that may be the cause of your trouble."

"What! travelling?" I asked.

"Yes, railroad travel can be hard on the bloodstream. Go back to your hotel, starve yourself and take Epsom salts for a couple of days, three or four times a day and keep quiet. Then come back and we'll have another go."

I don't think I have ever spent such a harassing two days in my life. Magnesium sulphate is not exactly an exotic diet, but I kept strictly to orders and presented myself on the third day for another test. I asked for the same medical officer, and he greeted me with

11

"How did you get on? Don't fret, that will only make matters worse." So again the arm band was pumped up, one – two – three times – the M.O. saying nothing. At the third go, I thought my doom was sealed, but almost simultaneously the doctor said,

"Fine, the salts have done the trick."

A day or two later I went before a board, and was accepted as a cadet and posted to the R.F.C. Officer Corps at Toronto University for preliminary training, which consisted of route marches and living in uncomfortable conditions in a tent, sleeping on the hard ground on a groundsheet until my bones ached so much that I could hardly stand. On top of that, Army rations helped to make life more miserable. Reporting at the University that evening, I drew my kit. They told me to be down on the campus at nine o'clock sharp next morning for a parade. Unfortunately my watch, unknown to me, was a few minutes slow, and I was three minutes late. There they were, at least 50 other cadets all lined up on parade, with a bawling Irish sergeant addressing them. As soon as he saw me he let out a howl.

"Are you Cadet Fresson?" he shrieked.

"I'm very sorry, Sergeant . . ." I began – I was not allowed to finish my explanation.

"Look at him," the Sergeant bellowed, "thinks himself a bleeding officer already. Fall in quick, and remember don't be late on parade again."

The rest of the Cadets enjoyed the scene immensely at my expense. Actually, at heart Sergeant Higgins was not a bad sort. I caught him up after the parade and explained what had happened. He just laughed and told me I would soon get into the swing of things. By that remark, I assumed I was excused. We spent six weeks at the University, mostly on route marches and a discipline course. After two weeks of marching, one of my ankles became so sore that I developed a limp. Sergeant Higgins coming up from behind, spotted me limping along. Each step was painful but the only sympathy I got was a loud

"Hey! You with the oceanic roll, pick 'em up!"

There were titters from my fellow cadets. I still went on limping, I could do nothing else and every step for another two miles was agony. Eventually Sergeant Higgins called me out of the squad.

"What's wrong with your foot?" he asked, a little more humanely. I told him.

"Have you been to see the M.O.?" he asked.

"No, not yet."

"Well, the sooner you go the better for you."

So with that I duly reported at medical headquarters, had the sore dressed and was excused route marching for a week until the wound had healed.

I got to like Sergeant Higgins. Under the rough exterior of a disciplinary instructor, he had a heart of gold. He was efficient at his job and just the man for breaking in raw recruits, who had to be taught the difference between civilian life and hard military discipline.

Eventually, the next move came and we were sent down to a place called Longbranch on the edge of Lake Ontario, some 15 miles out of Toronto on the Hamilton Highway. There we also lived in tents but with the comfort of camp beds, only two in a tent, and an excellent dining hall in a corrugated iron barn. We attended lectures and radio instruction, with a certain amount of drilling in between. The winter had now set in and it was bitterly cold. We took our baths by smashing the ice on Lake Ontario and washing ourselves down in the freezing water. The whole course was to make one tough, but the part I hated most was sentry-go at nights. Two of us were seconded for three nights at a time, and we shared sentry-go at the main gate on four-hour shifts. Being on the main road there were plenty of motor cars passing by at night, and how I used to envy the occupants.

It was now beginning November and the snow was not far away. I was posted for flying training to the airfield, Camp Borden. I started my flying instruction the day after my arrival in a Curtiss JN-4 two-seater aircraft powered by a 60 h.p. O.X motor. The plane just flew at 40 m.p.h. and its all-out speed was about 55 m.p.h. so there wasn't much to play with. It also meant that the motor was running at 85 to 90 per cent of its power output and so was very unreliable. Forced landings were consequently the order of the day. Between that first Thursday and next Saturday afternoon I received four and a half hours' instruction. On the Saturday afternoon, as dusk was falling, my instructor, Lieutenant Speakes, got out of the front cockpit and said "I guess you're good enough to go solo. How do you feel?" To the best of my recollection, I answered

"I'm not so sure, but if you think I am competent, I'll have a go."

"Just keep her straight on the take-off and you will be all right," he replied – "Good luck!"

It was five minutes to five on 13th November 1917. I was frightened and I do not mind admitting it. I thought:

13

"No wonder they are killing so many cadets, with so little instruction."

(The death rate was as high as one to two a day.) Then I said to myself:

"You have just made a circuit on your own with Lieutenant Speakes, so why not again: and isn't this the moment you have been waiting so long for?"

With that, I set my teeth, opened the throttle, zig-zagged a little until the tail came up, and I was quickly off the ground and climbing. I remember making a left-hand circuit at 500 feet and following a dried-up stream back to the airfield, dropping off height for the turn in and making a first-rate landing not so far from the perimeter of the airfield. Lieutenant Speakes came running up to me. "Well done!" he said, "that was a very good first landing." I was very pleased with myself. I had at last attained my ambition of becoming a pilot. Next day our Cadet course was ordered to Camp Everman, Texas, for further training.

Snow was beginning to fall in Ontario Province and to avoid converting our aircraft to skis the R.F.C. authorities had come to terms with the U.S.A. to lease us an airfield in Texas. We were packed up and ready to go in two days' time and we left by train on 15th November. That was a long journey of over 1,000 miles. It took us three days to reach our destination, and except for a long stop at Little Rock, Arkansas, which enabled us to march around the small town for much needed exercise, we were cooped up in a crowded troop train.

We got quite a shock at Camp Everman. The airfield was by no means completed, we had to live in tents and the only meals one could obtain were from very badly organised camp catering. Flying started soon after our arrival. I was given another half-hour's dual by a Lieutenant Halliwell and I made my second solo in Texas on 21st November. Texas around Forth Worth was very flat country and the sun usually shone every day. The planes were not furnished with compasses and as the countryside was featureless it was very easy to get oneself hopelessly lost. It was therefore wise to fly by the sun's position and by the layout of the railroad system which formed a square to the west of Camp Everman. I found this method accurate because I wandered quite a way from the airfield as time went on and always got back by hitting one of the railroads running into Fort Worth which was within sight from the air of Everman airfield. Some weeks before we moved from Camp Borden an advance party of mechanics had been sent ahead to prepare for aircraft maintenance, in order that flying instruction might begin with the least delay, on arrival of the cadets.

At weekends, we were allowed into Fort Worth itself and to be properly dressed, cadets were required to wear white bands on their forage caps, which indicated they were *ab initio* air pilots under instruction. It soon became evident to us that we were being ostracised by the opposite sex and however hard we tried, we could make no headway socially. To make matters more galling, the air mechanics were in great demand and would sail past us accompanied by the beauty of the town, with wide grins on their faces. This situation went on for a week or two, before we got wise to what was happening. By then we had got to know some of the business men of the city and we discovered through them that, before we had arrived, the air mechanics had spread the story around that they were the flying pupils and that shortly a bunch of guys would arrive with a white band round their forage caps. This white band they said served to indicate that the wearers were under medical treatment and should be strictly avoided – anyway, they added as a *coup de grâce*, they are only the mechanics. We had to give it to those boys, they had certainly put it across us, and we set to, to discuss ways and means of putting this smart trick straight. Almost at once, the answer was solved for us by a ruling of the camp commandant that in future, the population of Fort Worth would be allowed on Sunday mornings to watch the flying at Everman Airfield. In those days, flying was a rarity, and of great public interest, so the response was terrific. A large crowd turned up the first Sunday morning and the ladies to their amazement saw their so-called 'Pilot Cavaliers' in grubby mechanics' overalls attending to the aeroplanes while the tainted 'White Caps' were doing all the flying. From that moment on, the cadets had it all their own way and the trick the mechanics had played, boomeranged severely upon them.

We had some new instructors at Fort Worth, among them the celebrated dance instructor, Captain Vernon Castle. He was very interested in me when he learned I had come over from the Orient to join the R.F.C. Being so famous, he naturally had many influential friends in Fort Worth and my entrée to social life was complete. My flying training at Camp Everman continued for five weeks which brought us up to Christmas Eve. I went north to Buffalo and Niagara on the Lake, to stay with friends over Christmas and New Year, returning to Fort Worth and to a new airfield of aerial gunnery, on 9th January.

At Hicks Airfield on the other side of Dallas, we received a concentrated course in camera work, firing at silhouette targets on the ground, and towed-target gunnery. The tests having been completed satisfactorily, we were shipped up to Toronto, and eventually joined the next overseas contingent and entrained for Halifax. That was a nightmare journey. It took four days, the ground was feet deep in snow and the temperature was below zero. We were placed two in a narrow train bunk which made it virtually impossible to sleep and to make one's life more unbearable the water system was frozen solid. That meant no washing and very little food. One day we stopped at a wayside station to let the Halifax-Montreal express through. I joined one of our instructors and another cadet for a walk along the platform to watch the express arrive. Our instructor, Captain Mackenzie, hailed from Scotland and wore the service kilt. The express pulled in and the Restaurant Car stopped right alongside us. How our mouths watered to see the passengers enjoying their afternoon tea in luxurious comfort. There were two elderly ladies at one table and one was pointing at Captain Mackenzie. The kilt was evidently intriguing them. Mackenzie took great umbrage at being the object of their inquisitive study; without warning, he turned, faced the two old ladies, and pulled his kilt right above his head. He was one of the tough kilties who did not wear trews. The two old ladies, held up their hands, gave one shriek and ducked. Captain Mackenzie walked on murmuring,

"I hope that satisfied their curiosity."

The other cadet officer and myself were buckled up with laughter. We had never seen anything so funny as the look of outraged horror on the two old ladies' faces.

We arrived in Halifax, frozen, dirty, hungry and in low spirits after a four-day nightmare journey. The town of Halifax was in a bad state. A month before, on 6th December 1917, an ammunition ship had blown up, flattening a great part of the town at a terrific cost in life. There was one hotel left to which we repaired and where we were able to get superficially cleaned up and have a decent breakfast. We were then escorted to the docks and boarded the s.s. *Megantic* of the White Star Line. We were nonplussed with what we saw. A beautiful dining room laid out with spotless white linen and staterooms fit for the rich. What a contrast to our cadet camp life and long, uncomfortable journey all the way up from Texas. At Toronto, we had been given our commissions as fully qualified pilots and so we were travelling first class, with the troops and non-commissioned officers below. We suffered no illusions as to what might befall us on the way over the Atlantic to Liverpool, our port of destination. The U-boat warfare was at its height, and we were heavily escorted with destroyers. On two occasions, we could see the destroyers break formation and tear off to a certain section of the ocean, and the huge explosions which occurred from their depth charges shooting high columns of sea water into the air indicated that there were U-boats around. We were however lucky, for we did not suffer any casualty to our convoy; but it was a funny feeling waiting for what might happen, especially in the middle of the night. My friend Walter whom I met on the trip up to Vancouver was with another contingent on the s.s. *Olympic*, ahead of us. They had great excitement as their ship rammed a U-boat, cutting it in half; the two ends of the submarine appearing on each side of the liner, so it was said. One or two ships were also lost in the convoy. Walter Pawson and I parted at Liverpool. He was posted to an airfield in Hampshire and I to one in Norfolk, Narborough. Shortly afterwards, I learned that Walter killed himself, trying to land in a field near some house in the country, where he was keeping a date for afternoon tea. He apparently undershot the hedge, striking it, and the plane turned over, crushing him in the process.

After more instruction at Narborough, I was posted to a small airfield at Holt in Norfolk where we carried out coastal patrols for U-boats slinking down the North Sea. Our planes were fitted with wireless telegraphy, but we could only transmit and not receive. I was very excited one day when, picking up a ship convoy steaming south towards the straits of Dover, I spotted a U-boat stalking the convoy. It was submerged and to the rear of the ships which were steaming along quite unaware of the danger lurking beneath the waves. I at once tapped out a message on my wireless to base, reporting the situation, and they in turn contacted the naval authorities. I learned some time afterwards that the U-boat had been destroyed by depth charges.

On 1st April 1918 a great change was effected in the set-up of the Royal Flying Corps for its identity and that of the Royal Naval Air Service were merged to become the Royal Air Force. At the time, it did not make much difference to us and life went on as usual. After some months on coastal patrol, I was transferred to Duxford airfield some ten miles south of Cambridge, as an instructor. We were the first squadron to take up duty on that airfield. I flew over from Thetford with my belongings in the back seat of an R.E.8 biplane and my bicycle strapped to the side of the fuselage with the wheels resting on the lower wing. The arrival caused great excitement among the mechanics when I taxied to a stop outside the hangars. They had never seen anything like it before.

In the early part of the summer, the war nearly claimed me as a victim, not through any effort of the enemy, but by a large scale attack on me by the virulent Spanish 'flu which raged through Britain during 1918. To make matters worse, a repeat dose of malaria which I caught two years before in Hankow smote me. I was very ill in the R.A.F. hospital in Hampstead for a number of weeks and for two days it was touch and go whether I would recover. It was not until the late summer that I was fit for flying duties again. There had been a suggestion that I was to be transferred to the Independent Air Force which was operating from the Nancy district in France, but in view of the severe illness from which I had just recovered, the authorities sent me back to continue instruction at Duxford.

I was demobilised in June 1919. In July I was married to Dorothy Cumming whom I met at friends of mine in Hitchin the year before. The reception was given at my parents' home in Wickford, and the ceremony was performed in the old village church in the parish of Runwell, next door to Wickford. We went to Devon and Cornwall

18

on a three-week holiday in my little Swift cycle car powered by a 7 h.p. two-cylinder water-cooled engine. On my return to Cambridge we left by air for Skegness. Prior to my marriage, I had contracted with the Cambridge School of Flying to carry out a two weeks' joy-riding tour from the beach of that seaside resort, with a converted three-seater Avro 504K. We flew up one evening passing over my old airfield at Narborough in Norfolk and then Kings Lynn and out over the 15 sea miles crossing of the Wash. Half way across the motor stopped dead on us. Although we were flying at 3,000 feet, we were too far from shore to reach dry land on the glide. It looked as if we were going to have a long swim or be drowned in the process when suddenly I noticed the petrol feed pressure gauge was reading zero. As I was flying from the front seat I was unable to reach the auxiliary hand pump which was situated in the rear cockpit. I let go the controls and leant over to the rear and shouted to my wife Dorothy to lean forward. She responded quickly and I pointed out the pump handle and told her to keep pumping until further notice. As I sat down in my own seat the engine came to life while we were in a pretty steep dive. We had lost a lot of height by the time I got the plane flying level again for the altimeter only read 700 feet. My wife had to keep pumping until we reached our destination half an hour later. It was very tiring work from the awkward position she was sitting in. However, she saved our lives by doing it.

By the time we arrived at Skegness, it was getting dusk. I had no time to go looking for the field which the Cambridge people had hired for us as a parking place, so I put down in a favourable-looking patch just outside the town. Unfortunately, there were one or two bulls grazing that green sward and as soon as the plane came to a standstill, the bulls made ready to charge the intruder in their midst. I jumped out, tore off my leather flying coat and waved it at them. They hesitated a moment and beat a retreat. But, after a moment of furious tail wagging, they reformed and charged again. This time, my flying coat did not frighten them and I was obliged to jump back on the plane to avoid being tossed. It looked as if our Avro aeroplane was about to be completely destroyed by the angry beasts, when fortunately, the farmer and his cattleman arrived on the scene. They drove the bulls into another field and we descended and got acquainted with one another. In those days, an aeroplane was a rarity and so the farmer welcomed us both and apologised for the plight we found ourselves in. After picketing the Avro down for the night, I explained to him that we had rented a field on a certain farm but owing to darkness setting in so quickly we had had to make a quick landing. He said he knew the owner and would take us out next morning and show us the field and introduce us to him. We drove to Skegness in his car and checked in at our hotel for the night. I was kept very busy for the next ten days, flying off the beach and taking several hundred passengers up for an aerial view of their town. It was a great novelty, for almost no one in the civilian population had flown in those early days of flying.

Towards the end of the month, September 1919, the rail strike of that year descended upon us before we had completed our flying tour. The authorities would not allow us to draw any petrol and so I had to cease giving pleasure flights. To make matters worse, I could not even obtain sufficient petrol to take me back to Cambridge. After five days matters were getting extremely awkward for us. I had to get the plane south by the end of September owing to our impending sailing for New York on our return to China.

At first the civil authorities would not yield to my pleas but at last they gave way on one condition – that we would carry the several days' collection of mail to Cambridge and deliver it to the postmaster there. It was not clear in my mind where I was going to stow the mail as I could not leave my wife behind and she occupied most of the stowage room in the rear cockpit. However, I compromised and said I would carry as much as there was stowage room for and on that basis petrol was made available for the return flight.

By the time we had finished loading the mail, my poor wife was surrounded by mail bags but she stuck it, in great discomfort for the one hour and twenty minutes we were in the air. On that return flight we observed many convoys of lorries on the main North Road carrying urgent supplies which the railways would have normally carried. There was none of the softness shown to strikers who held up the national services in those days, as is the case today.

I still possess the receipt of the Cambridge Post Office for the mail sacks delivered to them on 30th September 1919, which was probably the first official air mail carried in Great Britain not as an organised stunt.

We sailed for New York in the middle of October from Liverpool and from there we crossed the country by train and at Seattle we boarded the steamer for Yokohama and Nagasaki. A year later to the day, my wife died from typhoid fever in a Shanghai hospital, leaving me with a small daughter three months old.

While in America I had been given an introduction to a high-ranking Japanese Naval Air Officer in Yokohama. He invited me to visit the Yokosuka Naval Air Station, some 30 miles away. The Station Commandant was anxious for me to lecture the Cadets on air fighting and armament. He said his Cadets would be most interested to hear first-hand knowledge from the Western Front. The Japanese Naval Authorities were using a locally designed float biplane built at the Yokosuka station. It flew very well, but I noticed a most curious feature with the wing bracing. Biplanes had the wing bracing wires, which carried the load when the aircraft was airborne, duplicated and the wires which carried the weight of the wings when the aircraft was on the ground were single. In the case of the Yokosuka biplane, they had it in reverse, namely single flying wires and duplicated landing wires. That was a very dangerous design error. On enquiry, I learned several aircraft of that type had broken up in flight in a way which they could not account for. I mentioned to the Station Commandant the error in design and the danger of flying aircraft with insufficient bracing of the wing structure while in flight. He was amazed at my report and I received a letter from him later saying that the design had been corrected and thanking me for the valuable advice I had given them.

After I had been back in Shanghai for a year, a Major Willie McBain, an ex-R.F.C. pilot, imported a 160 h.p. Armstrong Whitworth biplane, and levelled out a small airfield at his farm on the Hungjao Road, some ten miles from the Shanghai Bund. I assisted in the erection of the aircraft and he made the first test flight. Major McBain flew the plane a few times but tired of it quickly. I think he met with opposition from his wife. Anyway he didn't like the small airfield which was unsuited to a plane of that power. I however continued to fly it for hire and reward and business was brisk giving joy rides over Shanghai. I flew up to the Heng-li regatta some 50 miles north-west from Shanghai and up the Soochow Creek, with a photographer and took the first aerial pictures of that annual event, which was an affair of some magnitude and run on the English Henley lines. Eventually, I had an engine failure just after taking-off with an old friend of mine, Donald Leach. There was nowhere to make a forced landing and I had to crash land the plane on rough ground covered with Chinese coffins, surrounded by split bamboo poles sticking into the air. The machine was in fact impaled on them, and Donald and myself narrowly missed becoming speared. Neither of us was injured but the plane was almost a write-off. I immediately set to work to reconstruct

it in the bamboo hangar we had erected at the Hun-Jao farm.
In less than six months it was ready to fly but we had no spare
airscrew. The importation of aeroplanes and spares had recently
been forbidden by the Peking Government, and the two new airscrews I had ordered from home were lying in bond at the Shanghai
Customs. We were refused a permit to import, so some other method
of obtaining those airscrews had to be thought out. In the end we
shipped them to British Territory in Hongkong and got a friend to
wrap each airscrew up in a bundle of sugar canes and sacking
and reship to Shanghai by one of the native crew on a local coastal
steamer. When the ship arrived, we hired a sampan to go alongside
the steamer lying at the jetty, at night. The two bundles of supposed
sugar cane were then lowered over the side to the sampan, and
brought ashore. Within a few days the plane was tested, and flew
better than ever. I was frequently quizzed how I came by those airscrews. I evaded the question by saying we had made one ourselves.
That explanation was accepted but I don't think believed.

A year later the local Shanghai War Lord bought an Avro 504
with a 90 h.p. Renault engine and as he came under Peking jurisdiction managed to obtain a permit from the Peking Government

to import it. Having got delivery of the crates they were unable to erect and test the plane. I was approached as the Chinese knew I had erected Major McBain's aircraft. I agreed to do the work for an impressive fee, and eventually tested the plane on the Kiang Wan military parade ground, some 400 yards in length but with bad approaches. However it was sufficient for that type of plane, and I completed the contract in quick time and pocketed my fee.

Shortly afterwards, my firm transferred me to Hankow so I had no further contact with aircraft until 1924. Towards the end of 1923, I was approached by the Chinese regarding the establishment of an aircraft factory at Tai-Yuan-Fu in the Northern Province of Shansi, a very mountainous country, and bordered on the north by the famous Gobi Desert. I was invited by the Governor Yen Shih Shen to visit him in his capital, Tai-Yuan-Fu. That involved a rail journey of some 1,100 miles. To get there, I had first to travel by train via Nanking, cross the Yangstze River by launch to Pukow and then entrain for Peking. From Peking I had another train journey 140 miles south on the Hankow-Peking railway, to a little country station named Shih Chia T'swang, which was the junction for the railway running up to Tai-Yuan-Fu. There was a lot of inter-provincial fighting going on in that area. One of the local War Lords was trying to take a neighbour War Lord's territory and it was advisable to keep clear when these outbursts of inter-necine fighting erupted. I felt I had to take a chance as it was important that I should be in Tai-Yuan-Fu as quickly as possible. In any event, it would not be the first time that I had become mixed up in one of the many civil wars which were then going on in China, and been shot at.

I left Peking one winter's night. There were no proper coaches and I had to travel in an open truck. It was freezing and I was bitterly cold although I dressed in my flying kit, leather flying coat, flying helmet and fur-lined gloves and boots. The Chinese were swaddled in cotton wool-lined garments, and seemed accustomed to travelling in open trucks under freezing conditions. The night dragged on and in a few hours we passed through Pao-Ting-Fu, some hundred odd miles down the line, which boasted a military airfield and training school. The train crawled along at around 30 miles an hour. It was a beautiful starlight night and the moon shone brilliantly but I was far too cold and hungry to appreciate the heavenly beauty. We arrived in Shih-Chia-T'swang around one in the morning and I promptly made for the local Chinese hotel by the station to wait for the connection on to Tai-Yuan-Fu next

B

morning. I got a room on the first floor, and after some hot tea well lined with whisky I had brought me, I turned in to sleep. I was utterly exhausted and was asleep very quickly, but, it was not for long. I was suddenly awakened by utter pandemonium. There was heavy machine-gun firing and mortars cracked sharply above the noise, people were shouting and screaming with fear. As I got out of bed to see what was going on, the window glass was shattered by bullets which hit the wall just above my bed. I promptly ducked, grabbed my pillow and blankets and got underneath the bed. I could hear running, the crunch of heavy footsteps up the stairs, and cries of terror as Chinese guests were being dragged from their beds by the Chinese soldiers. Then, executions commenced outside the hotel as political prisoners were put to death, by beheading. My bedroom door was suddenly burst open and I could see heavy boots stump into my room from floor level.

The owner of those boots did not, fortunately for me, take the trouble to look under the bed although I could hear the wardrobe being flung open. As suddenly as the searcher arrived, he departed, and I spent the rest of the night huddled up on the floor. The firing went on all night and only died down at sunrise. I noticed many bullets had splattered the walls of my room, when I eventually crawled out from beneath the bed next morning. By breakfast time, as all had been quiet for an hour or two, I ventured down the stairs. The sight outside the hotel was a horror, the dead were lying all over the place with several executed bodies minus heads lying around. Eventually, I found a Chinaman connected with the hotel, who told me that the town had been attacked by a rebel army who were looking for persons of rank in the Army who were holding the area in that part of country. Such raids in those days were so commonplace that the train for Tai-Yuan-Fu was ready to depart at its scheduled time of 10.00 a.m. When I left, the hotel staff had recovered their equilibrium and were cleaning up and getting back to a normal day. The Chinese were very stoical about such raids. Needless to say, I was mighty glad to get away with a whole skin.

I hadn't had much sleep that night, so made up for it on the six-hour journey through the mountains to Tai-Yuan-Fu. I had a good view of the wonderful Chinese Wall built hundreds of years ago by the Manchus. I booked in at the principal hotel in Tai-Yuan-Fu and sent an emissary to let the Governor know I had arrived. A reply came back asking me to visit him next morning.

That interview was a long one, and I had many difficult questions to answer, technically and otherwise. Eventually the Governor said that he was prepared to sign a contract for me to build three proto-type aeroplanes. If they flew successfully, I was to obtain a contract for 50 more. That was something really worth going after, for I reckoned to make a thousand pounds on each plane. With the signed contract in my pocket, I returned to Shanghai by the same route as I had come and was fortunate in making a connection with a northbound train from Hankow at the junction Shih-Chia-T'swang, for Peking, thus avoiding another night's stay there, for which I was truly thankful.

As soon as the deposit was paid into my bank account in Shanghai, as called for by the contract, I resigned my position with the company I was working for. Lists of equipment and materials were compiled and forwarded home to my suppliers, the Aircraft Disposal Company Ltd., in Kingsway, London. Major Jack Stewart was the manager and I dealt through him.

I knew of a German engineer in Shanghai who had some ex-perience in aircraft construction. He was out of work so I managed to obtain his services. That was a bad day's work for me as will be seen later. I gave him the layout of the aircraft I had in mind and we got down to designing a plane based on the stressing of the Armstrong Whitworth biplane which Major McBain had imported. We used all the measurements and sections, but re-calculated the centre of gravity which would place the two cockpits behind the main planes instead of the passenger sitting beneath the top wing, as was the case with the Armstrong Whitworth. We knew of a first-class Chinese carpenter and woodworker and tied him up under contract. His name was Loh.

While the general arrangement drawings were being made in Shanghai, I returned to Tai-Yuan-Fu, to arrange for the con-struction of the workshops we would require and which would be sited within the Tai-Yuan-Fu Arsenal. It was on that trip that I met the Arsenal technical adviser. He was an Englishman by the name of Wright and he was an expert mathematician. He gave us great assistance in calculating stresses. As soon as the workshops and equipment were nearing completion, and the engine test bench completed, I sent for the German engineer and carpenter Loh. In the meantime, the first order I had sent home for aero-engines, timber and steel sheeting, had arrived at Shanghai. As I have said, the Peking Government had clamped down on all aircraft or spares being imported into the country unless required by the Central Government in Peking. Even Governor Yen with the influence he held in Peking could not get them to budge and give us a permit.

25

So everything had to be made on the spot. We could not, however, make the aircraft wheels or instruments. We managed to import these accessories as motor car parts, and they came through without any trouble. Welding equipment was bought in Shanghai, and by the late spring of 1924 we were ready to begin construction. The 160 h.p. motors were imported as motor-boat engines and on arrival in Tai-Yuan-Fu, were put on the engine test bench and given a run in, ready for installation. By the beginning of September, the first plane was nearing completion and ready for motor installation, when a disturbing report reached us. A French firm was endeavouring to sell Governor Yen some Breguet aeroplanes, and one was on its way by rail with a French pilot for demonstration. It was essential that our plane flew first, otherwise the subsequent order for 50 machines might be in jeopardy. We eventually got our aircraft to the airfield I had surveyed and had constructed some six miles to the North of Tai-Yuan-Fu. It had an 800 yards run which was a large airfield for those days, but as the altitude of the airfield was close on 4,000 feet above sea level, I expected the take-off would be quite a bit longer than at sea level. The body of the aeroplane was pushed along the dusty road on its wheels by coolies and the boxed wings, port and starboard, carried out separately to the bamboo hangar which had recently been erected. The final assembly of our aircraft was begun just as the French machine arrived on the aerodrome. That afternoon I had been engaged in welding a fitting, without any eye shield. That night my eyes began suffering badly from burning. I was obliged to stay in bed in the dark. After I had been confined to bed for several days, news was brought to me that the Frenchman was nearly ready to demonstrate his plane. I cursed myself for my folly in omitting to use a shield and getting myself laid up at that crucial moment. I was a week in the dark before the doctor would let me out and on that day the Frenchman made his test flight at noon. A few more hours and I would have managed to get the first flight. I went in to lunch heavy hearted, and feeling far from hungry, I was so upset. Within an hour my German engineer brought me the news that just after the Frenchman had taken-off and risen to 100 feet or so, his motor cut dead. He stalled his Breguet biplane and it crashed; he was killed and the machine a complete write-off. That finished the Breguet affair, and a gala day was called a few days later for the testing of our home-made plane.

The Governor and his ministers would appear on the airfield in the afternoon for the demonstration flight. There was great excitement in the town. There had been a lot of propaganda from the Chinese–French camp that our plane would never fly, and the Governor was anxious that these rumours should be given the lie. There were some Ministers in his 'Ya-mun' that I suspected of being in the pay of our would-be competitors, and they were present in the Tuchun's retinue hoping that we would be humiliated.

The motor started up first go and after being warmed up on the chocks, I waved them away and commenced to taxi the 800 yards to the south end of the field as the wind was blowing from the north. The spectators did not appreciate what was happening. They had never seen an aeroplane before and as my plane waddled down to the south end of the airfield they started up a cry – "The great bird cannot fly". Roars of mirth followed and by the time I had got to the end of the field and turned into wind, the poor Governor was also convinced he had been sold a pup. I took my time, quite unconscious of what was going on; tested both magnetos on the motor to be sure they were functioning properly. I then opened the throttle wide.

I was tense. "Would the plane fly?" I asked myself.

If so, I decided to fly low for a few hundred yards to test the controls, land and then start the run again for a higher flight. To my pleasant surprise, our locally made plane roared off the ground in a little more than 100 yards run, which at that altitude, was incredible. I levelled out, and I did not need to wait to know that she was flying normally although a bit tail heavy. As I came up alongside the grandstand, I pulled the stick back and the plane climbed at a sharp angle passing the Governor at not less than 400 feet and still gaining height. I felt a great exultation. We had succeeded and the big order which would rope me in 50,000 pounds must surely follow. I learned afterwards that when the crowd saw the plane suddenly in the air and starting to climb, they let off a big sigh of wonderment – eyes were gaping and the Governor's ministers who were on the French band wagon looked completely mortified and angry. The Governor was enraptured. I cruised around Tai-Yuan-Fu for 10 minutes at 800 feet. I brought the whole population out to see the 'Fey Jchee' (Flying Engine). I could see their heads turned skywards. After several circuits I returned to the airfield. I was anxious to see how the landing would work out. It would be heart-rending if anything went wrong and the plane got damaged just as success was ours. The approach was made on a very flat glide and the landing effected almost in front of the Governor and his ministers. The plane was faultless in its handling and controls. When I reached our hangar, a message was waiting for me, that the Governor wished to see me right away. He told me how pleased he was and that he wished me to call on him next day, at his 'Ya-mun'. Naturally, our own camp was greatly excited at the success of the many months' hard labour. We had a good look around the motor; there were no oil leaks and everything appeared in order, so I decided to make another flight with full tanks, which gave a range of six hours. I wanted to know the stalling speed, and flat-out speed of the machine, also the climbing characteristics with full fuel load. I took-off again at twenty minutes to five, this time with Loh our carpenter as passenger, and flew for two hours around the neighbourhood, to give the motor and installation a good testing. During the flight, I came to the unpleasant conclusion that the plane with a passenger was very tail heavy. Even using full tail trim, I was unable to trim the plane for level flight. The motor was too far back and needed moving roughly eight inches forward and that meant redesigning the engine bay. This alteration could quite easily be incorporated in the remaining two aircraft, which we had not as yet begun to assemble.

Two days later, I made a flight to the Hwang Ho River (Yellow River) 150 miles west and returned, non-stop. The flight took three and a half hours and was flown over mountainous country, where a forced landing would probably have been fatal. The Governor accepted the prototype after that flight and we began to make and plan arrangements for mass production and setting up a flying training school for Army officers.

Before long however, dark clouds began to appear on the horizon. A German representative of the Junkers company in Germany suddenly appeared in Tai-Yuan-Fu. No doubt he had read the newspaper report of the successful flights of our locally made aircraft. Within two weeks or so I learned he was spending a lot of time at nights with my German engineer and then my friend General Li, the Director of the Arsenal, told me that the Junkers representative had asked for an appointment with the Governor Yen Shih Shan. Through General Li, I was kept informed, and it soon appeared that my engineer had gone over to the Junkers camp. To combat that bit of double-crossing, I immediately made enquiries to obtain a British engineer to take on the mass production order I had been promised, and I have little doubt that the Governor would have kept his promise had this arrangement been put into practice. There is an old saying, 'It never rains but it pours', and that was surely applicable to my case, for without warning Communist-organised student riots occurred in the Nanking Road, Shanghai, and the British police were forced to open fire, killing a number of students. That sent a wave of anti-British feeling over China and was taken up by the students and agitators in Tai-Yuan-Fu. One afternoon a day or two later, I was in the inner courtyard of my room in the Chinese hotel where I was staying. This was connected by a narrow passage with the front of the hotel; suddenly my servant came running to me in an excited state:

"Master! Master!" he said in Chinese, "there is a mob of loafers outside the hotel wanting to know where you are. They mean to kill you!"

He had scarcely finished speaking, when I could hear the howls of the mob outside demanding from the Chinese owner to be told of my whereabouts. There was no other exit but the front entrance, so I was cornered like a rat in a trap.

"What is it that these people want with me?" I asked my boy.

"Master," he answered, "they say you are an 'Ing Gwer Ruen' (Englishman) and that your people have shot Chinese students in Shanghai. They mean to kill you," he repeated.

What was I to do? I had to think quickly. I could hear the shouting and fury of the mob, while they ransacked the front part of the hotel. There was no escape. I would have to try and bluff my way out. The courtyards in Chinese buildings are interconnected by narrow passages. The passage connecting my courtyard was not more than two and a half feet wide. That meant only one Chinaman could get down at one time. I had two automatic pistols in my room, holding 16 shots. Quickly I grabbed a chair and placed it at the entrance of the passage and waited. Within a few minutes, the mob broke into No. 1 courtyard and started for my passage. I fired one shot over their heads. They came to an abrupt halt.

"Who's your leader?" I shouted in Chinese. "I want to speak with him. Any Chinaman entering my passage will be shot dead."

A great murmur went up. I sensed they had received a shock. The leader came forward.

"Stand in front of the passage," I told him. He did so.

"Now," I asked, "what do you want with me and why are you breaking the hotel up?"

"The English police have shot our students in Shanghai," he answered, "and we mean to kill you."

"But I was not in Shanghai when the police shot your students," I answered. "What has it got to do with me? I am here as a guest of your Tuchun to build aeroplanes. Why insult your Tuchun's guest?"

29

He spoke rapidly to the mob. Before he could speak to me again, I told the leader

"Go home and leave me alone. If you try and force this passage, there will be another 16 dead Chinese. Are you prepared to pay such a price just to kill me? And don't forget, the Tuchun will certainly behead you, should I be harmed."

That created a problem for him. Chinese custom made a guest almost sacred. He turned round and harangued the mob. I could only catch bits of what he said. He spoke the local dialect which was very different to the Mandarin dialect which I knew. The leader said no more. Suddenly, they turned and left the hotel. By that time the sweat was pouring down my face. How lucky, I thought, I could speak Chinese and that the mob's leader understood Pekingese dialect. After they had gone, I went to look at the front of the hotel. It was smashed to pieces and would take a lot of repairing. I immediately got on the telephone to General Li at the Arsenal and told him what had happened. He said he would come down to see me. He did, and went to see the Tuchun (Governor).

There was no further disorder. The military were out in force. Next morning the Tuchun sent for me. He said how very sorry he was that I should have been insulted and in such danger in his Province, and that the culprits would be punished. They were – several heads came off – after that there was no further trouble.

The next move in the German camp came shortly afterwards. One morning I saw our plane in the sky over Tai-Yuan-Fu. I rushed out to the airfield and found the Junkers pilot was flying it. He had obtained permission from someone in the Yamun (Local Government Office). I was furious and went back to General Li. He was annoyed and very sorry for me. He then told me that my very 'loyal' German had come to an arrangement with the Junkers agent, and that they had the Governor's ear. The Junkers representative was able to promise the Governor the whole support of the Junkers factory and he promised they would turn out the aeroplanes cheaper than I had quoted. Even then, I don't believe Yen Shi Shen would have let me down. He was however, greatly disturbed about the recent rioting, and felt he could not be responsible for my safety, more especially as the troubles in Shanghai had by no means died down. In the end he gave me a considerable sum in compensation, and asked to be freed from the mass production contract. I could see his mind was made up and it was no use arguing, so with a heavy heart I was obliged to accept his offer.

I had spent almost two years under the greatest discomfort, cut off from my own race, and working round the clock to get that contract for the 50 aircraft. Mechanical success had come my way and I had taken a big chance in flying an untried aeroplane of local design and succeeded only to fail through no fault of my own. That was early 1926.

Twenty-two years later, history was to repeat itself with me, as the continuing chapters will show.

I returned to Tientsin, and stayed for a while with R. H. Rowlatt, who had been my boss during my early days in Hankow. He was very upset at the raw deal I had received and the grave disloyalty of the German I had befriended in Shanghai who, as I have said, at the time I employed him was out of work and on his beam ends. I returned to my house in Shanghai and had a holiday. I was very tired, but a month's relaxation in a civilised town soon put me right.

In the spring of 1926, I received particulars of the first de Havilland Moth which had recently made its maiden flight, and was about to be mass produced for the flying clubs in Britain and the Colonies. In Mukden, General Chang Tao Lin was building up an Air Force. Most of his aeroplanes were of French design. I had a contact in Mukden, a General Sutton, who had designed a new type mortar, which the Mukden Arsenal were producing in quantity under his supervision. I wrote to him and sent him the particulars of the D.H. Moth, asking if he would make enquiries as to such an aircraft finding favour in the Mukden camp. He answered and advised me to come up to Mukden. He told me General Chang Tao Lin's son was in charge of the aviation side, and would be interested to discuss the question with me.

I had another friend in Mukden also, a Mr. Butchart who was Mukden manager for the Jardine Engineering Company in Shanghai. He also had contacts with the local Government. The first few nights I stayed in the Mukden Station Hotel which brought back memories of November 1911 when I first stayed the night there waiting for a train connection to Dairen. Chang Tao Lin's son, the 'Young General' as he was called, was impressed with the D.H. Moth layout and the simplicity of the Cirrus I motor, also the price. I suggested that he should order half a dozen to try out in his training school. They were using the French Caudron biplane which was a very good little plane with the wartime 80 h.p. Renault Vee-type engine. However it cost more to buy and operate than the Moth and I hoped this might be a selling point. I stayed up there three weeks but could make no progress in tying the 'Young General' down to an order. I fell back on Sutton, who made some enquiries behind the scenes. He learned that the 'Young General' was tied up tight with the French authorities who it was suggested were making financial concessions, and Chang's financial advisers were unwilling to risk any possibility of upsetting the French Legation. A year or so later, I learned that the 'Young General' had got over his financial difficulties with the French authorities, and had ordered six D.H. Moths. I never heard whether they arrived. But if they did, I had again missed the bus by a short hop, for the second time. There accordingly seemed no purpose in pushing the subject any further so I returned to Shanghai and in the autumn left for California, on my way home, to see the Ryan Aircraft Company in San Diego, who were in the process of making a monoplane for a flier named Charles Lindbergh for a proposed non-stop Atlantic flight from New York to Paris.

My daughter's godmother, a Mrs. Newton, lived in Los Angeles. She also had a very nice summer house at Oceanside a few miles north of San Diego. I went to stay with her after spending a few weeks in Los Angeles. I had ideas of making a goodwill flight which was the rage those days, from Yokohama to Singapore, on a sales mission, and I wished to tackle the Ryan Aircraft Company to see if they would be interested and would provide the aeroplane. Mrs. Newton had a friend who knew one of the Ryan brothers, and he drove me in to San Diego one day and introduced me. They were interested in my idea but were at the moment so wrapped up with the Lindbergh plane that they had no time to consider anything else until they had completed the *Spirit of St. Louis*. This was the name Lindbergh had given his plane in honour of the city which helped to finance his famous flight that was soon to thrill the whole world.

I was taken down to their airfield, and after my log book was inspected they invited me to fly one of their monoplanes powered by a 200 h.p. Wright Whirlwind radial motor. I was greatly taken with the high-climb performance and its handling. The longitudinal trim was quite a different cup of tea to the Tai-Yuan-Fu plane.

A day or two later, I was in the Ryan factory picking up information when Charles Lindbergh arrived. We were standing by his plane at the time, with Mr. Ryan directing certain constructional details; he introduced me as an interested aviator from the Orient. We talked about Tai-Yuan-Fu and its outcome and his forthcoming Atlantic fight. I thought at the time that he was quite mad to contemplate a flight across the Atlantic in a small single-engined aircraft of only 200 h.p. I felt sure it would be the last we would ever hear of him once he had left Newfoundland, and I was not the only one who felt that way in San Diego. I sensed that the Ryan brothers were also sceptical but of course would not commit themselves. I was to meet Lindbergh again seven years later in Inverness when he flew in from the U.S.A. by the Northern route with Mrs. Lindbergh in a Lockheed float-monoplane, as I will record later on in my story.

The outcome of my visit to the Ryan works was negative for the time being, as I have said all their thoughts were concentrated on the Lindbergh plane, and it would be some months before that aeroplane was completed. There was a General Strike on at home and I was not anxious to be caught up in that, so I returned to Los Angeles and met up with a man who had a Travel Air two-seater plane at Santa Monica airfield. I went on a number of cross-country trips with him, which gave me an extremely interesting insight into Californian topography. By October, the strike at home was over and I left for Britain having decided to drop the 'Ryan Goodwill Flight' proposition.

The boat train from Liverpool was met at Euston Station by my mother and small daughter, who was so shy that she seemed to find the platform of particular interest. That was March 1927.

Two months later, in May, Lindbergh flew the Atlantic. I was laid up at my mother's house in Kenton, north of London, with 'flu, but itching to get down to Croydon to see the Atlantic hero arrive there after his Paris visit; however the doctor would not let me out of his sight. The frail plane I saw in San Diego six months before had actually stayed in the air for over 33 hours and Lindbergh, with inadequate instruments, had flown about half of that time in cloud. I think it still remains the epic flight of aviation history and of an order of courage that has yet to be matched.

The political situation in China was going from bad to worse with the Japanese, and I decided that I would not return there. So, in 1928 I joined Berkshire Aviation Tours, operated by Mr. F. J. V. Holmes. He ran a joy-riding circus with headquarters at Shrewsbury in Shropshire. I remember seeing an advertisement in the aviation magazine *Flight*. It ran something like, 'Wanted, a pilot for the season, with experience of Le Rhône and Clerget motors'. As I had that experience from my war training and had given joy rides at Skegness at the end of the war with an Avro 504K with a Clerget motor, I applied for the job and got it.

33

I motored up to Monkmoore airfield just outside Shrewsbury, and signed on. I was then shown around, and as we came to the gates which allowed the planes to be moved across the road to the flying field from the hangars, I was introduced to my prospective engineer, Bert Farminer. The poor chap was down in a deep hole digging for the erection of new gate pillars. I thought at the time that it was a peculiar job for a licensed air engineer to be at, but I soon got to know that in that organisation, or in any joy-riding organisation for that matter, one had to be a jack of all trades. I spent that summer joy-riding in Shropshire, Lancashire, and then up in Scotland at Dumfries and then Renfrew.

At Renfrew on the Saturday afternoon of the King's Cup air race I made 114 landings and take-offs. The place was packed with would-be customers wishing to fly. I was staying with a private family near the airfield and I returned to the house in my overalls soaked in castor oil from the Le Rhône rotary motor, for my late tea. I was sitting on the bed when they brought it in to me, as I was too tired to go into the dining room. The next thing I knew, it was four in the morning, the tea untouched and cold; and – horror of horrors – the bed soaked in castor oil off my overalls. Next morning was an awkward one, for I was not at all popular with my hostess. However she behaved very nicely when I told her how much flying I had done the day before.

After that, we moved to the beach at Ayr, where we flew for over a week. It was tricky cross-wind take-offs and landings the whole time. I was then transferred south, to work Shropshire and Yorkshire. While flying at Leeds, I met Lance Rimmer, Berkshire's chief pilot. We saw quite a bit of each other after flying duties and before I left at the end of the season we had agreed to form a joy-riding company of our own for next year. I was to raise the finance, and he would become joint director and bring the 'know-how'.

That winter, we arranged to purchase two Le Rhône-engined Avro 504K planes from the old Beardmore Flying School at Renfrew which had closed down. We were to collect the Avros early in the year. My engineer, Bert Farminer, was willing to join us and with the help of an old friend in Cambridge, Bertram Chater who was an accountant, the North British Aviation Company Limited was floated in January 1929 with headquarters at Hooton Park airfield, an old-time World War I air base. We rented part of a hangar there and to my surprise and pleasure, found there was a small flying club with a clubhouse, who were glad to admit me as a member.

34

In January, I went up to Blackburn Aviation Company, Brough, to carry out my R.A.F. Reserve training on a twin-engined Kangaroo. It was a curious machine, designed at the latter end of World War I for coastal patrol work, and looked a weird object standing

on the ground. On the cross-country flight at the end of the course I had to fly to Grantham. On my return I landed at R.A.F. Station Digby for lunch, where my youngest brother Noel was undergoing his training for a commission. The Kangaroo was an object of great interest. Apart from its peculiar look, twin-engined aircraft were an unusual sight in those days, and the senior officers were anxious to find out all the details. A large number of the R.A.F. personnel collected to witness the take-off after lunch. The two 260 h.p. Rolls-Royce Falcon motors gave a healthy roar as I opened the throttle full out. After a very short run the big plane was soon climbing and heading north for the Blackburn Training School at Brough alongside the River Humber.

In the first week of February 1929, Lance Rimmer my partner, our engineer Bert Farminer and myself motored up to Renfrew near Glasgow to collect the two Avros we had purchased from the Beardmore Aviation Company. After testing the planes in the air, it was found necessary to change one of the motors. It was a back-breaking performance as there was no lifting tackle available to lift the 330 lb. motor. The operation had to be done by the three of us manually. We struggled, cursed and sweated trying to lift that engine five feet into the air and into position, while Bert bolted the motor to the face plate attached to the fuselage. After three attempts we finally succeeded.

The following day, 5th February, after further test-flying, we departed for Hooton Park airfield 180 miles away. We flew in formation and Bert Farminer ferried the car back. I well remember the trip for it was a great excitement possessing one's own aircraft and starting an air business. It was a perfect day and the flight was completed in two hours and forty-five minutes. The only section of the flight I disliked was the sea crossing from Barrow-in-Furness to Fleetwood. I was, by habit, distrustful of rotary motors; they had a nasty habit of packing up when least expected and 20 miles of water did not inspire confidence under such circumstances. However we were flying at 3,000 feet with a slight following wind, so were soon across and home. Several weeks were spent in thoroughly overhauling the planes and motors which appeared in good condition, and it appeared that we had obtained a good bargain at £200 per aircraft.

The North British Aviation Company Ltd. began operations at Huddersfield on 29th March 1929. After two weeks' brisk business we returned to St. Helens, famous for the Pilkington glass works. We were visited by members of the Pilkington family who were extremely interested in viewing their home, Rainford Hall, from the air. They had many flights with me and during the period, I was invited to the Hall for lunch. I kept the engagement by flying over in the Avro and landing alongside the kitchen garden. The incident caused much local interest. After that occasion I made several visits while we were flying at St. Helens and after I had returned to Hooton base at the end of the season. To wind up our visit, one of the Miss Pilkingtons flew with me to Kendal when we moved on two weeks later.

On the second Sunday, the last day at St. Helens, the famous comedian Dave Morris arrived at the flying field and booked one of our planes to fly him to London that afternoon. He was required to attend a court case in London next morning and when that was finished, we were to fly him up to Huddersfield in time for him to take part in the evening performance at the local theatre. It was decided that I would take the flight and we set off at four o'clock in the afternoon in fine weather. There was a slight headwind which slowed us down and we were obliged to refuel at Coventry which delayed us further. So, by the time we reached Aylesbury it was almost dark. I chose a field on the edge of the town as near the railway station as possible and made a good landing in the twilight. It was not long before help arrived from the owner of a house close by who kindly offered to run Dave to the station, when the situation had been explained to him. I picketed my plane down quickly and went in with Dave Morris to see him off and make arrangements for the morrow. It was decided he would meet me at the de Havilland airfield at Stag Lane at two o'clock next day. Huddersfield was 155 air miles from London and as the Avro's cruising speed was 60 m.p.h. in still air we planned to arrive no later than five o'clock. We would arrange with a garage to send a taxi to meet us and Dave Morris should have been in Huddersfield town with an hour to spare; but things did not work out that way. I was at Stag Lane airfield before lunch and one of the D.H. engineers went over my motor ready for the afternoon flight. While that was being done I went into the clubroom for some lunch. Who should I run into but Cyril Murrell, an Aerofilms Ltd. camera operator. During the period we were forming the North British Aviation Co., we came to an arrangement with the Aerofilm company to charter our aircraft whenever we were flying in a district where they had filming contracts. Over lunch Cyril told me he had two or three days' work in Huddersfield and when he learned I was flying up that afternoon he suggested he should join the flight and I would stay in Huddersfield and carry out his air-picture contracts with him. A further advantage was that he would navigate for me by map reading from the front seat in the rear cockpit. To do that he tied a loop of rope like a rein – to each of my arms, he retaining the loop end in his lap. All he had to do then was to pull on each rein as he would in the case of driving a pony and trap. It worked fine and I was relieved of map reading and flying the plane at the same time which was hard mental work.

Dave Morris arrived on time and we were airborne by two o'clock. He was delighted to have company and readily agreed to Cyril Murrell coming along. All went smoothly until half way to Nottingham, when we ran into a strengthening gale which slowed our ground speed down to 30 m.p.h. At that rate, and especially should the wind get stronger, we would never reach Huddersfield before the theatre opened. I beckoned to Cyril to lean over to my cockpit so that I could converse with him. We agreed our friend Dave would stand a far better chance if we landed at Nottingham

37

and engaged a high-powered car to rush him the last 60 miles to Huddersfield. Cyril put the proposition to Dave Morris and he agreed to it. A fast car was out at the airfield within quarter of an hour. We bade Dave goodbye and good luck. He told us when we met him next day, that he arrived at the theatre just a quarter of an hour before the show was due to begin.

I left St. Helens to join Captain Rimmer at Kendal in Westmorland. Miss Pilkington and her sister joined me on that flight. They sent their car up to bring them home. They were delighted with the experience of their first cross-country flight.

We were kept very busy during our fortnight's stay at Kendal, for there were many people who were anxious to see Lake Windermere from the air. Our next port of call was Dumfries across the border. The night before we were due to depart my sister Christine arrived on the night train from London, so that she might fly up with me the following day to visit friends who lived in Dumfries. It was her first long-distance flight. She was lucky. The day was sunny and there was not a cloud to be seen in the sky. The view crossing over the Cumberland mountains and the Lake District was magnificent and the colouring had to be seen to be believed. We crossed the border after we had passed over Silloth and flew out over the Solway Firth to the Scottish border. It was not long then before we were circling Dumfries preparatory to landing at Mr. Wylie's farm at Tinwald Downs. Our plane was spotted by my sister's hostess and they were soon out at the airfield to greet us and take us back to town in their car. The middle of June found us flying at Penrith and our next engagement was at Groomsport, Northern Ireland, situated on the coast at the top end of Belfast Lough. We had a job getting across the Irish Sea. We carried no compass in our aircraft so we had to see the coast on the other side, before we lost sight of the Scottish coastline. We arrived at Port Patrick, south of Stranraer, which was our jumping-off point on the Scottish coast and found the visibility down to five miles out to sea. We were obliged to return and landed in a field alongside the lighthouse. We pegged the aircraft down and got a lift into Stranraer, where we spent the night. The following day, visibility was a little better, but we still could not see the coast of Northern Ireland. This was a dilemma, as we were advertised to fly that afternoon. We waited till after lunch but conditions remained the same. Rimmer and I just stood and glared vacantly at one another. Suddenly I remembered the relay races we used to run at school. Why not apply that system to our problem?

"Look, Rimmer," I said, "with the present visibility around eight miles, we ought to be able to get across if we both fly out together until we begin to lose sight of the Scottish coast. One of us then circles keeping the coast in view. The other continues on his course by keeping the circling plane on his tail. If the Irish coast becomes visible before the rear plane is lost sight of, then the first plane commences to circle. The rear plane will then follow on – join the first plane – and both fly on together. If the Irish coast is not picked up by the first plane, then he returns to the rear plane, and back we go to Port Patrick."

"By Jove!" Rimmer said, "that's a brainwave. Let's try it. I'll go on while you circle and you wait for me to signal."

So that's how we did it. Rimmer began circling roughly five minutes after leaving me, which in terms of distance represented about six miles. I joined him as quickly as possible, and all of a

sudden the Irish Coast could be discerned through the haze. Slowly the outline of Belfast Lough came into view and we were over Groomsport within ten minutes, to be greeted by a large crowd. It was an uncomfortable sensation crossing that 25 miles of sea. There was no shipping to be seen and I should say there would have been very little chance of rescue had either of us gone down.

We began flying as soon as we had unloaded the planes, and were kept busy until nightfall. During our three weeks' stay we took a lot of money at that town. I remained with Captain Rimmer for ten days, when I left him to carry on for the holiday period so that I could fly at Donaghadee, another seaside town a few miles down the coast. After three weeks, I returned to Scotland to give a flying display at Stranraer. That time, I had the sea crossing to do all alone excepting that I had my engineer in the back seat. We both had blown up car inner tubes around us to act as lifebelts in case of trouble. We arrived on 24th August and on the 26th towards the end of the day, I had the misfortune to damage my plane while taking off over the telegraph wires. I had passed the point of no return when I got caught in a vicious downdraught. I could see that I was not going to clear the wires so tried to duck underneath them. The undercarriage caught the top of the hedge and brought me down in the field on the other side of the road. The passengers and myself were unhurt but the plane was badly damaged and had to be railed back to our headquarters at Hooton Park for repair.

After the damaged Avro had left Stranraer by rail, I went back to Hooton to collect one of the two Avros we had bought as spares. Its registration was G-EBGZ and that plane lasted me until the end of the 1932 season. It flew as far north as the Orkney Isles.

The following year 1930, we changed our operational policy, and split up into two 'Schools' as I had learnt the know-how of running the business. By that means we doubled the territory covered and, what was more important, our receipts. The year 1930 saw me up in Scotland on my own, and proved a decisive point in my career.

CHAPTER TWO

I have frequently been asked what made me think of starting an air service to Orkney. The answer to that is that I didn't think about it. The need suddenly presented itself to me whilst I was touring the extreme North of Scotland and Orkney during August and September 1931.

On 13th April of that year Miss Pauer and myself left our head-quarters, Hooton Airfield in a Moth on a site-hunting tour for the coming joy-riding season. The Moth I was using was the latest type powered by a Gipsy I engine made by the de Havilland Aircraft Company at Stag Lane, Edgware, London. It was owned by Miss H. Pauer, a lady who had flown frequently with us when we were flying at Trentham the year before. She became a most enthusiastic aviatrix and commissioned me to find her a suitable aircraft on which she could learn to fly. The registration of the Gipsy Moth was G-AAWO. The last three letters AWO represented a Chinese name 'Ah-WO', so we christened the Moth by that name and had Chinese characters painted on the side. I gave Miss Pauer instruction at our Hooton airfield base, situated in the Wirral peninsula, Cheshire, which was within easy reach of Trentham by car. Sometimes she would join us on tour and would fly from place to place when I ferried the Moth, which she had generously loaned me for performing the aerobatic displays each weekend. In return, we housed the Moth in our hangar at Hooton during the winter months and serviced it for her.

Without that aeroplane, I could not have made the survey of the northern air routes and, incidentally, created the public interest which resulted from my comings and goings by air in Inverness and Orkney.

Our first port of call was Walsall and from there we worked our way north arriving at Nairn in the North of Scotland on 18th April. We had planned to work the extreme North of Scotland including Kirkwall in the Orkneys during the summer months as those places had never seen a joy-riding aeroplane before and breaking virgin territory was usually highly profitable.

Taking off from Nairn the following day, we flew up to Wick, and after circling around the south of the town for a while, found a suitable field to land in at a farm named Barnyards adjacent to the main road running south to Helmsdale and Iverness. Having had a word with the farmer, who went out of his way to help us, we made arrangements with him to guard the Moth from the crowds which soon gathered to have a look at the unusual sight of an aeroplane. One of the spectators kindly offered to drive Miss Pauer and myself to the Station Hotel in Wick.

We left Wick at lunchtime next morning, Sunday, and flew north over the famous motoring hotel at John O'Groats and out over the Pentland Firth. It was a fine day, slightly overcast and visibility as far as the eye could see. As we came up with the Island of Swona, I became conscious of a large number of sunken vessels on the starboard side. I spoke with Miss Pauer over our intercom about the phenomenon and neither of us could hazard a guess how those vessels came to be there. Later, we learned they had been deliberately sunk during the War, in order to block the channels into the Scapa Flow naval anchorage. On reaching Kirkwall a few minutes later, we circled around looking for a likely joy-riding field. I spotted one or two likely places on the north side of the town.

Kirkwall on a Sunday looked strangely deserted and we selected a field near the Balfour Hospital on the Scapa Pier road alongside the town boundary for a landing. After a dummy run in to test the approach and surface of the field, a smooth landing was effected. We had been battling a fairly strong northerly wind over the Pentland Firth and as the wind had been backing most of the morning I suspected bad weather was on its way in, so I wanted to complete the business on which we were engaged as quickly as possible. In no time, the town of Kirkwall came to life and the field was crammed with interested sightseers. Within a matter of minutes, a cultured voice behind me enquired

"Can I be of any use to you?"

I turned and found a man of middle height and pleasant demeanour, he introduced himself as the surgeon for Orkney, and his name was Ian McClure. I thanked him for his offer and explained my wish to locate a suitable flying field for operating a joy-riding air visit for the summer. He appeared deeply interested.

"I've my car here," he said, "come along and I will show you around. Have you any particular site in view?"

"Yes, I saw several during our search from the air", and I pointed the fields out to him on my map.

I set off with my new-found friend, leaving Miss Pauer in charge of the Moth. Already, many boys were trying to clamber up on the lower wing to take a look at the inside of the cockpit. Fortunately several onlookers offered to help her, so I figured I could safely leave. On our way, surgeon McClure told me he had been in the R.F.C. during the war, so we had something in common. I told him I was in a hurry owing to possible deterioration in the weather and also that we had to return to Newcastle-upon-Tyne that evening. So he hurried me around and I pin-pointed one or two fields that I thought were possibles, and we quickly made our way back to the Moth.

Thanking Mr. McClure for his kindness and saying I looked forward to seeing him again in August, we herded the crowd with difficulty to one side of the field, and I took off into a good 30 miles per hour northerly wind towards the houses at the north end. I was a little nervous that we might not clear the obstacles as the run was not very long and slightly uphill, but I need not have worried, for 'Ah-WO' roared off the ground half-way across the field. With the wind behind us we reached Wick in a little over 15 minutes and landed to fill up with petrol which I had arranged with the local garage that morning to deliver to the farm.

I had spent the first part of that morning in going over the motor very thoroughly and so it was decided, in order to save time, to make the 60-mile sea crossing to the Banffshire coast and carry on straight over the mountains to the Firth of Forth. With a strong wind on our tail, we reached Newcastle-upon-Tyne in 2 hours and 40 minutes, touching down at Cramlington at six-thirty in the evening. Dusk was beginning to fall as we reached Newcastle.

Next day we returned to Hooton on a direct course to Keswick in the Lake District, and due south to Liverpool and Hooton on the other side of the Mersey. In a little over a week, we had covered 800 miles and settled most of the joy-riding sites for the season. It would have taken three weeks to have done the same work by surface transport, if not longer.

I opened the season with a visit to Kendal, Westmorland, on Sunday, 26th April and worked my way north via Cockermouth and Keswick to Hornsea, Yorkshire. While there, I took the opportunity of carrying out my annual R.A.F. training on seaplanes, at the Blackburn School at Brough. Hornsea was within a half hour's flight of that place. The course lasted ten days, and I was able to carry out joy-riding at Hornsea over the week-end.

During the early part of my training, I was flying over the North Sea, when engine failure forced me to alight on the water, about three miles off the seaside resort of Cleethorpes. It was a hot sunny day and the time was around eleven in the morning. I dropped anchor in about 50 feet of water and got back into the cockpit to await rescue.

43

An hour went by and then another and still not a sign of any boat. The sun was extremely hot and I was getting thirsty. There was nothing I could do except pray that an off-shore wind did not get up and blow me further out to sea. The anchor was only a small one and I did not expect it would hold against a strong wind. By the time three hours and then four had gone by, making the time three in the afternoon, I was really getting alarmed. I had no means of signalling and it was quite possible that I would not be found. The motor was as dead as a crushed cockroach, so I could not taxi towards the shore. To add to my discomfort, I was beginning to feel very hungry and my thirst was unbearable with the sun beating down on me pitilessly.

All of a sudden, a noise broke the lapping of the water against the plane's floats. I looked up and there was a motor-boat coming towards me.

"Thank God," I said to myself, "help is at last at hand."

I scrambled down on the floats to greet the motor-boat skipper and to see he did not damage the plane with his boat. As he drew near, I could see it was full of females evidently on an excursion trip out from Cleethorpes. They were all waving to me and to my dismay, the skipper started circling the Blackburn Dart seaplane several times and then sheered off and made for the shore. I yelled at the top of my voice for help, and beckoned him back, but he just kept on his return journey. I got back into the cockpit and tried to figure things out. It was four o'clock and it would be dark in a few hours. What was I to do? Things were really getting desperate. Anyhow the boat skipper knew I was there so perhaps he would notify the coastguard.

Shortly after that, another sightseeing motor-boat faired up on me. Evidently, the first boat had told his pals and they were running excursions at good profit, for the holiday makers to have a look at such an unusual spectacle. Again the boat started circling, although I shouted and waved for the skipper to come alongside. He also went round me two or three times and made off towards the shore, his female passengers waving like the other lot did. Surely I thought, they are not going to let me perish, they must surely know something is wrong. The uncertainty was wearing me down, and oh! what I would have given for a pint of beer. I had never been so thirsty in my life. I was completely helpless and could only return to the cockpit and wait. Five o'clock had passed and no sign of any further boats.

It looked as though I was going to spend the night at sea and if my anchor parted company with the bottom and I started to drift, I was in for a sticky and painful end. I was sunk in apathy at the thought and did not hear the approach of another boat until it was right on me. I suddenly looked up and there was a powerful motor launch fairing up to the plane. This time there were no passengers but two or three people near the wheel amidships. They hailed me to get down on the floats and catch a rope. Then I knew that it was a relief launch come to my rescue. The time was shortly after six p.m. As the boat came alongside, I recognised my instructor from Brough Seaplane Base, Lieutenant Woodhead. What a relief! I had been on the water for seven hours. I was soon on board and the seaplane roped on tow and we started back for Hull, over 20 miles away.

Woodhead told me that the motor-boat skipper on the first trip had reported my plane down on the water to the coastguard and he had hurried down to Hull to pick up the launch and tow me in. The skipper of the pleasure cruise had said he was frightened to come too close to me, in case he damaged the plane by collision. Woodhead asked me what had happened. I said

"Give me a drink first, and I will tell you. My tongue is sticking to the roof of my mouth I am so thirsty."

"Sorry old chap," he replied, "there is nothing on board to drink. You'll have to wait until we reach Hull."

That was two hours and it seemed twenty! At last we arrived and I said to Woodhead

"Get me to the nearest hotel, as soon as possible", which he did.

Never have I tasted such fine beer as I did that night. Over dinner I told Woody, as he was known to us, about the forced landing. How I was cruising down the coast at 3,000 feet when suddenly there was a terrific bang from the motor and it stopped dead on me. He told me I had done a very fine job landing that plane on the water with a dead motor. We had an excellent dinner at the hotel and then boarded a car to return to Brough.

Next day I learned that the engine had partially seized up so no wonder it had stopped. I did not forget that experience for some time to come and never wandered so far out to sea on future flights. If there was to be another forced landing it would be near the shore!

From Hornsea we went on to Whitley Bay, Kirriemuir, Nairn and arrived at Grantown-on-Spey on 7th August. On the Saturday night in the hotel where I was staying, a wager was made between a young man who fancied himself with a fast sports car that he could win a race with my Avro from Grantown to Nairn, if I gave him half an hour's start. I worked the flying time out quickly in my head, and took him on for the sum of twenty pounds. The only condition I made was that the wind remained appreciably the same as it was that day.

The contest began next morning at eleven. It was a fine Sunday morning. We agreed that the finishing point at Nairn would be the entrance to the field at which I had been flying the week before. One umpire remained at Grantown and the other had left for Nairn. Promptly at eleven our motorist friend departed in his sports car with a roar.

A few minutes before I was due to take off, my engineer swung my propeller and by the time the half hour arrived, the motor was warmed up and I left the ground dead on time. At 2,000 feet I could see the coastline and was accordingly able to steer a straight course without a compass. I caught up with the sports car within three miles of Nairn and had been on the ground a few minutes when my sporting friend arrived. He graciously conceded me to be the winner and handed over his wager. The finish was a very close one and the race was therefore, all the more interesting and most certainly a very novel one. We repaired to the Marine Hotel, Nairn, for lunch and then set off back to Grantown-on-Spey to carry out a heavy Sunday afternoon's joy-riding.

46

Tuesday, 18th August, we were due to depart for Wick, our next port of call. I detailed my groundsman to take the heavy luggage up to Wick in our service car. We took-off at five in the afternoon in brilliant sunshine in Avro G-EBGZ. The plane was heavily loaded. My ground engineer occupied the back seat and the rest of the luggage was stowed in front of him. In addition there was a ladder some six feet long tied to the port wing inner interplane struts; that was used for assisting the passengers in and out of the rear cockpit.

Crossing over Nairn, we headed out to sea, picking up the Suther-landshire coast at Golspie and then altered course up the coastline for Wick. As we neared the cliffs at Helmsdale the weather began to change, clouds began to form, forcing me down from 2,000 feet to 100 feet over the water.

I was not aware in those days of the weather phenomenon which at times embraces the Helmsdale area, surrounded as it is by moun-tains to the landward side, when cloud forms under certain atmos-pheric conditions. I became well acquainted with it later. It is very local and does not usually extend more than ten miles up the coastline. The cloud spills down the mountains and over the cliff tops, which are some 300 feet high, leaving a passage of around 100 feet clear over the sea.

As I was unaware of the conditions, caution was necessary. We did not carry radio or cloud flying instruments; in fact they did not exist. We did not even have a compass aboard. I was unaware of what lay ahead and about to turn back into the sunshine, when I spotted a field at the base of the cliffs, two miles north of Helmsdale and promptly sat the Avro down on it.

We were barely out of the plane, when people came rushing towards us; among them was the farmer upon whose ground we were tres-passing. He shook me by the hand and welcomed us,

"You are the first airmen to land in these parts. Aeroplanes are quite unknown hereabouts."

I explained the cause of our impromptu landing and he asked us up to his farmhouse for tea. On the way he explained that the low cloud which was bothering us often occurred but added that it was very local and ten miles north where the mountains terminated, the weather would improve.

With that assurance and after having enjoyed our tea and being introduced to Mrs. 'Farmer', I decided to push on. We took off down the hill and downwind towards the sea with plenty of room to spare. I dropped down over the water to 50 feet or so, and could see the mist half-way down the cliff for a mile ahead. We scuttled along fearful that the fog would suddenly merge with the water. Without a compass and blind-flying instruments, envelopment in cloud would mean loss of direction and control, and could easily cost us our lives.

I prepared to turn back at the slightest worsening of visibility, but it did not occur. It appeared very weird with the oily sea beneath and the dim light caused by the cloud almost on top us, and the jagged cliffs rising sheer into the mist on our left. After ten minutes or so of tenseness, the farmer's words came true for the fog started to rise and the visibility to improve. In another five minutes we were clear and the sun could be seen shining on the sea ahead.

Soon we were dropping down to land on our prearranged field at Wick after one and a half hours' flying time from Grantown-on-Spey. After we had pegged the plane down for the night and cleared the usual crowd which had gathered on the field, an onlooker kindly took us down to the town in his car, and dropped us at the Station Hotel.

We began operations next day with a publicity flight over the town which incorporated a few aerobatics. At midday, the 'boots' from the hotel and a pal turned up for a flight around the town. I gave them a free trip for his good services. On landing he told me he came from Kirkwall and enquired what a return flight to Kirkwall would cost him. As I had to fly over there during my stay in Wick to select and license the field for my visit to Kirkwall in a few weeks' time, I quoted him a low price. He accepted on the spot and we took off at once.

As on my previous visit, I was intrigued by the host of sunken ships at the east end of Scapa Flow. They were all shapes and sizes and were blocking all the sea channels into the Scapa anchorage. It was a remarkable sight and my passengers were most interested. We landed some 35 minutes later in a field some three miles out from Kirkwall on the Deerness Road. The usual boat and road journey would have taken six hours at least via Thurso, so that was a saving of roughly five and a half hours for a 35-mile journey.

We had barely scrambled out of the plane when a man came running across the field from the road.

"Has anyone been hurt in the crash?" he enquired.

We looked at him in amazement.

"What crash?" we asked.

He looked blank and said, "Haven't you crashed?"

"Not as far as we know," we answered, "take a look at the plane."

"I'm so sorry," he said, "I've never seen a plane before. Can I be of help?" he asked.

"If you would take us into town, we'd be most grateful."

"Jump in," he said, and off we went. On the way in, we told him that he had just witnessed an historical event. He looked a bit puzzled, and asked what we meant.

"These two gentlemen are the first fare-paying air passengers to arrive in Orkney from Wick and they will make the return journey after lunch all within a little more than an hour of travelling time. Think what that means compared to the usual surface journey."

He goggled a bit, but I think it sank in. The date was 22nd August 1931. I wonder if that man is still alive, if so I'm sure he will remember.

Our arrival in Kirkwall created quite a stir and the representative of the local newspaper *Orcadian* lapped up all the news we could give him. This newspaper was owned by James MacKintosh who became dedicated to my later efforts in establishing airline connections to the south. He was a tall man, somewhat portly and when roused had a fiery temper but he was also blessed with a geniality and loyalty to myself in the super task which was to come. His columns were always at my disposal no matter how many I required. I remember an occasion in 1934 when he got word that there were two passengers arriving at Wick by the south train, too late for the scheduled service. He told me that I had to fetch them. As he was acting as our agent on a voluntary basis, I gracefully made a special flight over to Wick. I could not find the passengers anywhere and our Wick agent knew nothing about them. So after hanging around the airfield for half an hour, I returned to Kirkwall empty.

Mr. MacKintosh was awaiting the plane at the airfield. When he saw me step out, he went purple in the face.

"Why haven't you brought the two passengers?" he enquired indignantly.

"Because they were nowhere to be found," I replied.

"Of course they weren't," he bawled, "the train didn't get in until five minutes after you left Wick."

"Well," I said, "I've made one empty flight, I can't go across again."

By this time, I thought he was going to have an apoplectic fit. He went purple in the face and shouted,

"If you don't get them, you can look for another agent."

With that he slammed the clutch of his car in and the car leapt forward, nearly knocking me into the ditch.

By gum, I thought, I can't afford to lose him and the publicity of the *Orcadian,* so I climbed into the plane and returned to Wick for the elusive passengers. I duly found them waiting at the airfield and brought them back to Kirkwall. James MacKintosh was his usual self next day.

I gave the *Orcadian* plenty to write about our forthcoming barn-storming visit and it was well advertised without cost, long before the happy day.

While at lunch in the Kirkwall Hotel, the first person who came to see me turned out to be surgeon Ian McClure, who it will be remembered had helped me on my previous Moth visit with Miss Pauer, by motoring me around the countryside looking for a suitable landing field. After lunch, he again very kindly placed himself and his car at my disposal, until a field was found about a mile out of town, on the Stromness Road. It belonged to Hatston Farm. I found the farmer and booked the field for August. His name was Ritchie and a very nice person he turned out to be. Ten years later, Hatston Farm was incorporated in the Naval Air Station from which planes took off for the bombing of Norway and patrolling the North Sea for U-boats and enemy aircraft.

On our return to town, I met the Provost and some town Councillors who were more than ordinarily interested judging by the number of questions they asked about the first mainland-Orkney flight with the fare-paying passengers whom I had flown over that day.

The return flight took 30 minutes and on landing, I found a number of passengers waiting for flights. The return Orkney flight soon got around the town and my friend the 'boots' and his pal were a matter of great interest. Certainly, I could not have wished for better advertising agents.

Sunday was always a busy day for us, and Wick was no exception. The field was crowded and the flights went on incessantly until after dark. As usual, I was flying by the aid of car headlights for landing and take-off.

We drew our petrol supplies from a garage near the Station Hotel situated alongside the river. It was owned by a Colonel Robertson. He was greatly interested in the passenger flight to the Orkneys and I got to know him very well. He went out of his way to assist us. He thrilled the locals by accompanying me on the exhibition flight which I had been hired to carry out at the Wick Annual Gala. It was, I believe, his first flight and he was put through every aerobatic it was possible to do on an Avro 504K and that was quite a lot. He got a great ovation on landing which was very well deserved for a first effort.

We made three more trans-Pentland return flights during our

Wick visit. After ten days, we moved over to Thurso. Our flying field was a mile from Scrabster Pier from which the trans-Pentland

steamer *St. Ola* sailed daily to Stromness and Scapa under the command of Captain Swanson. During our visit, we often used to fly passengers out to sea, circle the *St. Ola* and then return for another load. These flights caused great interest and excitement, for already our trans-Pentland passenger flights from Wick to Orkney were being talked about in Thurso and the implications for the future were being mooted in bars and hotels, also no doubt in private houses.

Our first Sunday was a fine day. We had a grand crowd waiting to fly and to see the exhibition flight later on in the afternoon. The crowds were swollen by people who had come in from the villages to the west as far away as Tongue. I was kept going until well after dark. Passengers appeared to like seeing a town lighted up from the air and we never seemed to lack for night flyers. Our operations appeared to impress the Thurso inhabitants, and there was little doubt that there were many potential passengers for the coming week.

I was staying at the Royal Hotel, and during the week the proprietor, Mr. James Wilson, introduced me to a Mr. Peter Angus who represented one of the large wholesale firms in Edinburgh. Apparently he had heard about the Wick Hotel 'boots' flight and said he was anxious to be the first Thurso-Kirkwall return passenger, and the first commercial traveller to call on his customers in Kirkwall by air. We arranged, weather permitting, to leave at noon the following day, have lunch at the St. Ola Hotel, and he would make his business calls in the afternoon and fly back in time for tea at Thurso. It was a clever move on his part. The publicity was immense and he did big business in Kirkwall. We landed at the field at Hatston at 12.45 p.m. and on arrival at the hotel, he introduced me to Mrs. Stevens the proprietress, who became a helpful and trusted friend in days to come.

Mr. Angus was very impressed with the trip across the Pentland Firth. I don't think I ever met anyone so alive to the potentiality of commercial flying in the North of Scotland. He literally became a travel agency for me later on when my plans began to develop in terms of commercial air transport.

We left at four in the afternoon, landing at the Thurso field 30 minutes later. That night Peter was in great demand by his fellow business friends. They all wanted to know how he had got on.

"First rate," said Peter.

The publicity was great, being the first business man to make his calls by air. The return fare of ten pounds had been more than worth it in orders, and extra ones at that, which he had received as a result of his 'air publicity'.

Towards the end of the first week in September, we moved over to Kirkwall. The Air Ministry licence had come through for Hatston. As in the case of Wick and Thurso, there was no lack of customers, and our visit laid the foundation for future events. Mr. Angus had suggested to me that a trans-Pentland air service would be a great boon to the travelling public, and I had also been thinking in and along the same lines. In fact, it became obvious. A modern plane could fly the cross-Pentland journey of 35 miles from Wick to Thurso to Kirkwall in 20 minutes. The steamer took four to five hours. The Pentland Firth could be very rough, the air could be much smoother. Providing the traffic density was sufficient, an air ferry just couldn't go wrong.

I hadn't been in Kirkwall a week when on arriving back at the St. Ola Hotel after flying had ceased, I was invited into the private room and introduced to the deputy town clerk and several business friends. After a generous supply of liquid refreshment, they enquired if I was thinking of inaugurating an air ferry service across the Firth. "We've been impressed by the flights already made," they said.

They went out of their way to warn me about the stormy winter crossings in the steamer *St. Ola*, and how ill the passengers became in bad weather. I was impressed. Other people were thinking along the same lines as Peter and myself. I said I would think it over and we might have another meeting before I left for the south.

During the many up and down flights made during the next few days, I constantly turned this matter over in my mind. The more I thought about it the more the simple axiom dawned on me that 'where there were routes which involved sea crossings, air travel had great possibilities'. There were no internal airlines in those days to obtain any comparison from, but I felt sure that I had hit on something which had great potentialities.

With such thoughts in my mind, I met the boys again and told them that I was prepared to explore the possibilities, but of course the overriding consideration was the raising of finance to float an operating company. Up-to-date aircraft would be needed and air-fields would have to be constructed. That would cost a lot.

"How many of you would subscribe to such a venture?" I asked.

They all had excuses as to why they couldn't subscribe. And then a voice chirped up,

"Why not make your base Inverness, and fly the mails up which arrive by train from London and the south in the morning? After lunch you would fly the mails south to catch the London express and Glasgow and Edinburgh trains. That would speed up the mails some twenty-four hours."

We were now getting into a much bigger issue but with more attractive commercial possibilities. With a mail contract, I thought, a regular load would always be available and with the mail, why not the newspapers?

In my mind, the matter was clinched. I would go south, ask for an interview with the Director of Postal Services and contact one of the national daily newspapers. Should I be successful in obtaining such support, I would have a good lever to raise finance to float an air company.

In my mind there was little doubt that the days of barnstorming were coming to an end. Most of the towns in Britain had had their fill and in two or three years my livelihood would cease; and that is just what happened to those left in that type of flying.

There were a number of further charter flights across the Firth to Thurso, which appeared to be the natural mainland terminal owing to the train and steamer service operating from that port. From an operational point of view, Wick would be the better port for an air service operating Inverness to Kirkwall, as it lay directly en route, and, in addition, it was the major town in Caithness.

Before returning South we spent four days at Stromness and during that time there was a further demand for flights to Thurso and back. It was becoming quite a habit but I called a halt at the last one which was the thirteenth. I am not naturally superstitious, but I jibbed at that one. The Avro 504K was not suitable or really safe for so many sea crossings. The motor had been worked hard all the season and if that one engine failed in the middle of the Pentland Firth, it would have been certain death for my passengers and myself in the usually rough sea and dangerous currents. Even with life-saving equipment, it was most unlikely that we would be picked up in time as ships were not that numerous. I believe the passengers understood when I explained the danger to them of tempting providence too far. I had acquired what I wanted in the dozen flights I had made, namely, intense interest in air travel between the mainland and the Islands. A serious mishap at that stage would undo all that had been gained.

Curiously enough next day and on the thirteenth Pentland crossing, engine trouble occurred, on my way to Thurso and Dalkeith, where I was next booked. The engine spluttered, lost power and the plane began to lose height. Fortunately I was flying high and just managed to scramble into the field at Scrabster. I have often thought I must have received psychic warning the day before, because I could never have reached the shore with a full load.

My flight engineer was with me and we soon carried out repairs to the valve-operating gear which had come adrift on one cylinder. Within an hour we took off for Dalkeith but had to land at Huntly for petrol. My log book shows that we flew at 4,000 feet straight across the desolate moors to the coast. Approaching the mountains behind Helmsdale, we experienced terrific upward air-currents, which pushed us up to 6,000 feet within minutes. The plane was going up so quickly that I shut the motor off to check the ascent, but height was still maintained and so the plane was actually soaring.

Over Helmsdale, I decided again to risk the sea crossing of 40 miles across the Moray Firth to Banff to save time. The day was sunny and visibility the limit. We were flying at 6,000 feet and as we had just checked over the motor, I thought the chance a reasonable one. To make sure, I eased the load on the motor by throttling it down half-way over, and making the shore on a long glide. We landed at Huntly, on my joy-riding field of the previous year, a little after

54

noon. After lunch the aircraft was filled up with petrol, which was ordered over the phone, and we departed on the second leg of our journey around three o'clock in the afternoon. Eventually picking up the Firth of Forth, we crossed over and landed at Dalkeith after 2 hours and 50 minutes' flying time from Thurso.

There was a large crowd awaiting us and the following day, Sunday, we carried 110 passengers, two at a time. We stayed a week and the owner of the farm we were flying from, Archie Dodds, made life very pleasant for us. His house was just up the hill and a five-minute walk from the flying field. We spent much of our off-duty time there with Archie's charming mother and sister seeing to our needs. The time passed all too quickly. We moved on to Haddington, where we were booked to fly in the early part of October. Archie became a friend whom I used to see a lot up to the outbreak of World War II. His mother subsequently bought a house at Longniddry on the Firth of Forth. We used to call in when passing on our way south by car and always received a welcome to lunch or tea.

Our season was drawing to a close. We worked our way back to Hooton headquarters via Denny, Alloa and Kirkintilloch which terminated the 1931 tour. The Kirkintilloch field was flooded by heavy and continuous rain and operations on the Sunday after-noon resembled a seaplane taking off and landing. The middle of the field was quite deep in flood water, and landings and take-offs had to be made in a semi-circle so as to keep clear of the water. After carrying 75 passengers under such difficult conditions, I called it a day and made off next day for Hooton Park via Carlisle, Shap, Kendal and Preston, skirting Liverpool to the East and across the Mersey into Hooton on the South bank.

I had clocked 280 hours flying for the season and most of that in up and down flights lasting three minutes. That represented approxi-mately 4,000 take-offs and landings, which was very strenuous work. In addition to that, I had flown to the top end of the British Isles and back and put in quite a lot of night flying without proper lighting equipment at flying fields and no cockpit lights. Quite a bit of open sea had been flown over. Motor failure during such periods would have been disastrous and always represented an extra strain.

After a few days' rest at Hooton at my hotel quarters adjacent to the Eastham Ferry, I started to plan the ideas I had formulated dur-ing my Orkney tour. I felt certain I had something of great promise but to organise such a project appeared insuperable. It was going to cost a lot of money and capital was not easy to raise in those days.

"How am I to begin?" I repeatedly asked myself.

I discussed the matter with my partner Lance Rimmer; he did not appear very interested, but he changed his ideas later, when success was within my grasp.

I went to bed and slept on it. I decided next morning I would pay a visit to London as soon as our winter overhaul programme was under way. That was a major operation as aircraft and engines had to be completely stripped, and an inspection made by the Aircraft Inspection Directorate of the Air Ministry. On completion, the planes had to be flight tested and were then ready for the next season's tour.

In the first week of November 1931, I flew Moth 'Ah-WO' to Cramlington, Northumberland, for the annual renewal of the Certificate of Airworthiness. Cramlington was an old World War I airship base which boasted of a huge hangar which used to house the blimps, used in those days for coastal patrol. The Certificate of Airworthiness overhaul was to be carried out by the Cramlington Aircraft Company, managed by Miss Connie Leathart, a well-known lady pilot. I stayed for a day while the survey was made to find out how much work was required. I was then told I could collect the Moth the day before Christmas, 24th December 1931. I had arranged for the sister-in-law of Mr. Pobjoy, the designer of the aero-engine bearing his name, to bring my car north and we returned to Hooton by road. I knew Mr. Pobjoy well and his house was always open to me. It was there that I met his sister-in-law, Mrs. Gwen Simons.

On 22nd December, I went north by car to collect the Gipsy Moth from Cramlington. The same lady, Mrs. Gwen Simons, who drove my car up to take me back to Hooton when I put the Moth in for overhaul at the beginning of the month, accompanied me so that she might fly back in the Moth, and one of my engineers came with us to drive the car back. I little knew it at the time, but that lady was ultimately to become my second wife some three years later.

The Moth was almost ready and looked very smart. I tested it on 24th December and at ten o'clock that morning, we took off from Cramlington and steered a direct course for Hooton across the Pennines, 150 miles away. After passing Consett in Durham, we were forced to climb above a layer of thick cloud as the ground was rising and the ceiling was only some 1,500 feet. For half an hour or more we flew on without seeing any break in the cloud and the opaque mass beneath us was getting higher the further south we flew. As I had no means or aids to check my course and whether I could safely descend below the cloud when the estimated time of one hour and three-quarters had been completed, I reluctantly turned back and retraced my steps. When eventually we came to the edge of the clouds, I ducked down beneath them and steered south-east for Harrogate, intending to make for the Pennington Pass and over the mountains by Holmfirth. The cloud base got lower and lower and I nearly knocked the steeple off Ripon Church. I was relieved to pick up Harrogate and land on the Stray. I phoned through to Hooton, to be told that the weather was not too bad there. After an hour or so the cloud base improved and we set off for the Pass. As we got near the top the cloud began to merge with the ground again and as it was getting late, I deemed it wise to land in a field at Holmfirth, where we spent the night. My passenger was concerned that her sister would be worried at our non-arrival, so we phoned through to explain the position. I said we would start first thing next morning, Christmas Day, weather permitting.

Next morning, the weather looked a bit better and so I did not bother to phone Hooton. Therein lay the biggest mistake I had ever made in flying. I did not know it, but a large bad weather front was rapidly descending on us which meant low cloud and poor visibility with rain, and it nearly resulted in the death of my lady passenger and myself.

It was a difficult up-hill take-off with two up in the Moth but the wind was strong which helped a lot, and we cleared the four-foot stone dyke with a good 20 feet to spare. I headed for the main road and after picking it up, set a compass course for Hooton Park in case I had to go up into the clouds. I followed the road for a few miles, as it wound its way up the Penniston Pass and as I neared the top I was only a few feet above the road and then the clouds merged with the ground and I had to pull up into them. My last impression was of a man on a motorbike looking up in astonishment as we roared over his head and disappeared in the overcast above. We came out on top at 3,000 feet which meant I had climbed through nearly 2,000 feet of cloud and the weather was not too bad with distant visibility. I settled down on to a compass course, wondering what the cloud base would be at Hooton.

The distance to Hooton was only 50 miles and at 85 m.p.h. and without any headwind we should have reached there in 35 minutes. But I did not know what the wind was doing at that altitude. It was evident to me, as the cloud height was increasing, that the front was upon us and whereas the wind was strong S.W. when I took off, it could be quite different at 4,000 feet, the altitude at which I was flying. I decided to hold the course and allow for a wind from the S.W. After ten minutes or so I saw the top of a mountain sticking through a hole some way down, which meant that I was still over the Pennines; and then to the south I thought I saw the canal running from Chester to Nantwich and I then made grave error No. 2. I turned off course and made for the canal, only to find it was not there, after flying for some 15 minutes and that I was still above complete cloud coverage. I studied my map and came to the conclusion that I should be over Crewe, so decided to go down through the clouds. Down I dropped and at 2,000 feet on the altimeter I suddenly saw the corner of a stone dyke with several sheep in the corner only some 50 feet below me. Evidently I was still over the mountains and a long way off my estimated position. I immediately started to climb at full throttle waiting every moment for a shattering bang as I hit a mountain. Luck, however, was with me and I got on top again. I was severely shaken, more especially as the Moth did not carry cloud flying instruments and I had to rely on my compass for direction, a horizontal spirit level for lateral control and the air-speed indicator for fore and aft position. I had been in cloud for nearly a quarter of an hour and was a bit fuzzy.

"What's to be done?" I asked myself.

I turned the facts over in my mind and decided to fly west for 10 minutes. By this time the cloud top was 5,000 feet and I was then certain that I was caught up in dangerous weather underneath with probably little cloud base over flat ground and poor visibility. I looked to see how my passenger was faring. The only thing I could see was just the top of her flying helmet. Later I learned she was thoroughly frightened, and no wonder. I was feeling near that way myself. There was nothing for it but to go down again, but I hesitated. I remembered a well-known book I had read on weather written by an American expert. It was called *Through the Overcast* and mention was made of the happy-go-lucky pilot who said,

"Let's go down and have a look."

Then it read on "That's the last time he ever took a look."

So I flew on a bit longer. Had I known it, I was then flying into the teeth of a westerly gale blowing at 50–60 m.p.h., so that meant I was only doing about 25 m.p.h. over the ground.

Down I started to go. At 2,000 feet I could see nothing, at 1,000 feet I could see nothing and I was being bumped all over the sky which made cloud flying almost impossible, without proper instruments. I had to concentrate on keeping the plane level and on a correct descent angle. Suddenly I caught a glimpse of a field at 800 feet; at 700 feet I could see fields slipping directly by underneath and I passed over a field bordered by high trees. I had to make an instant decision. I did not think I could successfully keep control of the plane if I tried to go up again, my senses had suffered savagely on that last bumpy descent. I instantly made up my mind to take a most drastic step. If I tried a blind landing in a field I would almost certainly run into something at 45 m.p.h. and that would most certainly be fatal for my passenger, even though I might have got away with it in the back seat. So the next hedge which I passed over, I shut the motor off, pulled the nose up and sideslipped the plane down on to one wing.

There was a crunching roar, the poor Moth folded up and we were on the ground. I was all right except for a cut over my right eye. I jumped out of the wreckage and looked for my passenger. Poor soul, she was not to be seen except for a part of her fur coat which was sticking out from under the top-wing petrol tank, which had collapsed and was spurting petrol all over her. What a lucky thing the engine was off. Even so, the hot exhaust pipe might have ignited the cloud of petrol vapour which was pouring out. I tugged at the wreckage but could not lift it by myself. I was in despair when suddenly I noticed two farm hands gawping at me. I shrieked at them,

"Don't stand there like two idiots – come and give me a hand, there is a lady underneath that tank."

They hadn't realised it apparently as she was not to be seen. The reaction was swift. I said

"Lift this edge you," and the other, "That edge you," and I took another corner and between us we managed to lift the wreckage and clear Mrs. Simons who was lying ominously still and soaked with petrol. With the assistance of the farm hands, we got her out and laid her on the ground. She was breathing, thank goodness. I tore her fur coat off and gave her my leather flying jacket, or rather put it over her. After a while she began to come round. In five minutes she was sitting up but evidently badly concussed as she was mumbling sense-lessly. By that time the farmer had arrived, and I asked him where we were.

"You are seven miles away from Leek and to the east," he replied.

"Have you got a car?" I asked.

He said, "Yes, I will phone for an ambulance from Leek Hospital, she looks badly hurt."

He acted quickly, away he went and in no time an ambulance appeared. I accompanied my passenger into Leek, leaving the two farm hands to guard the wreckage, until I could get back.

The clouds were on the ground at 700 feet and as we drove down-hill into Leek losing height, the going became clear at about 500 feet, which meant that had I flown west for another five minutes I would have found clear ground and could have made a normal landing. Shocking bad luck I thought. I got Mrs. Simons into the hospital which was all agog. They had never had an air casualty before. The doctor after a somewhat lengthy examination came and told me that she had no broken limbs or other injury as far as he could ascertain, but was, as I had surmised, suffering from concussion. She was put to bed and spent Christmas Day and a few days after that in the hospital before being allowed to return by road to Hooton.

I made my way back to the crashed plane and arranged for a guard to prevent pilfering. The farmer was very helpful and interested to know the details of the flight which led to the crash and he under-took to see that the Moth wreckage came to no harm. On arrival back at the hospital, the doctor stitched my cut eyebrow which was bleeding profusely. I booked myself in at the local hotel and returned to the hospital to spend Christmas afternoon with my victim. To my surprise, I found her sitting up in bed in the midst of a Christmas party. She was surrounded by many of the visitors, who were obviously intrigued with a patient who had arrived by air in such an unorthodox manner.

That night, before going to sleep, I went over the happenings of the day. Two incidents stood out glaringly. Firstly, I should not have taken-off from Holmfirth without a weather report. Secondly, having obtained it and ascertained that the cloud height at Hooton was reasonable, I should have kept to my compass course above the clouds and not gone off course looking for canals or cloud breaks, which had turned out to be nothing more than a mirage, and a very realistic one at that. Thirdly, I thought how lucky we were to have got away with our lives. It was really a miracle that we were not killed. There would be a heavy bill in rail charges and rebuilding of the Moth. Actually it came to close on £100. A costly error but one that taught me a salutary lesson in subsequent years when flying over the North of Scotland air-routes in all weather.

CHAPTER THREE

I collected the Moth from Brooklands in the early part of February 1932 and flew north with Miss Pauer as passenger to Kirkwall, in order to raise support. As on the first trip, ten months before, we ran into a strong northerly wind in the Orkneys. We landed after a rough and tiring trip at around five in the afternoon, in a field adjacent to Virkie Pool on the outskirts of the town. The gusts were so strong that I decided I had to find shelter for the Moth somehow or other. To have left it pegged down in the field overnight would most likely have resulted in finding the machine on its back the next morning. So leaving Miss Pauer to hold the Moth down, with the help of some sturdy-looking men who had arrived to look at the plane, I walked the half mile into town to look for accommodation.

I found it with the leading firm of coal merchants in Kirkwall, J. G. Shearer in Albert Street. It was a corrugated shed with just sufficient span to allow the Moth to enter with the wings folded. Mr. Shearer found a boatman who had a small trolley which would be necessary to place under the tail skid so that the plane could be wheeled along the road. In addition, he found a couple of stone-masons, who would pull down the stone dyke which separated the field from the road to allow the Moth to pass through. They would likewise rebuild it after we had left. Then there was the farmer to visit, to obtain permission for the onslaught on his dyke. Within an hour we had the Moth trundling along the road into Kirkwall and pushed into the coal merchant's shed.

That night my weather forecast came true, for a gale of over 60 m.p.h. sprang up with heavy gusting. Listening to it in bed, I was thankful our trusty steed was safely tucked away in that shed. We stayed two days and I quickly got down to business, for that night I met my friends again and we discussed the best method of raising finance. They suggested that I should start on one of the two directors of the local distillery. From then on I spent many days being passed from person to person telling my story, stressing the advantages of a mail service and early delivery of newspapers, and explaining how advantageous a regular air service would be to the business popula-tion. Most people looked at me as though I were a creature from another world. They spoke of the difficulties of flying in Orkney

because of the weather and they explained that they could only put money up if their partners and colleagues would also contribute; their partners and colleagues said the same thing. I told them the capital sum I required, about £3,000 to start with and probably another £7,000 should the first year turn out successful with a mail and newspaper contract secured. Eventually, I called on Mr. Donald, Managing Director of the well-known Inverness motor engineers, Macrae & Dick Ltd. I had first met him when I was joy-riding the year before at Nairn, and had been up to his house on several occasions. I found him in and confided my hopes and plans for an Inverness-Orkney air service and the blank I had drawn in obtaining financial backing in Orkney. I mentioned that I had been given an introduction to Mr. George Law, a senior partner in *The Scotsman* of Edinburgh, and he encouraged me to visit him. At the mention of an air mail contract, I noted a stir of businesslike interest.

I had been given an introduction to Mr. Law by Walter Grant, a director of the Highland Park Distillery, to whom I had first gone on the advice of my friends as being somebody who might be pre-pared to give me a contract for carrying newspapers. When he told me about Mr. Law, Mr. Grant had said

"You know, George Law is very keen on the pipes and it is very likely that you will be taken to a practice centre, so try to take an interest and you will make a friend for life."

When I telephoned Mr. Law and he asked me if I liked bagpipes, I thought Good Lord, it has come already. I controlled myself, remembering Mr. Grant's advice, and said I loved them and was most interested.

"Good," said Mr. Law, "meet me at the Highland Rooms at seven o'clock."

I had an early meal and got to the rooms on time. I was taken to Mr. Law who was sitting in the main room with other onlookers surrounding the pipers; and then the fun started. I had to sit through the pipers' practice for two hours. In between times Mr. Law asked me about my plans. I found it very difficult to put on good sales talk in such a discordant and interrupted atmosphere, or so it appeared to my untrained ear. Between the skirls of the pipes I unfolded my proposition. Mr. Law didn't seem very impressed. He appeared more interested in Walter Grant and asked me if I knew him very well.

"No," I said, "I only met him for the first time during my recent visit to Kirkwall."

"How much did you get from him?"

"Only a letter to you, Mr. Law," I replied.

He appeared surprised but suddenly went off into raptures over a lament on the pipes played by some special exponent of the art. By that time my head was in a whirl when to my relief, Mr. Law said

"Time we were going, come to my house and have some supper."

He bade his farewells to his piping friends and took me to his car.

On arrival at some massive gates, which automatically opened as he rang the bell, I was led into a very fine house and before we sat down to supper, Mr. Law took me into his study; when we were seated he said to me,

"I'm interested in the proposal you have made. If you like to give me the sole rights for *The Scotsman* to be carried on your air service for a period of one year, I will back you. How much do you want?" I said,

"£500, plus 3d. a pound for the carriage of *The Scotsman*."

"How much can your plane carry?"

I was determined to carry all *The Scotsman* newspapers Mr. Law might ask me to, even if I had to make two trips a day, so I countered,

"What load do you want?"

"I'll let you know in the morning," he replied.

Before I left Edinburgh to fly back and report to Mr. Donald, I called at Mr. Law's office at North Bridge and was introduced to the circulation manager, Mr. Chisholm.

"Now Mr. Chisholm, Captain Fresson is organising a daily air service from Inverness to the Orkneys and is going to carry *The Scotsman* by air to Kirkwall as soon as he can get his air service organised. How much weight will you be wishing to despatch?"

Mr. Chisholm's eyebrows went up, and he went off to make enquiries. On his return he said,

"Sixty pounds to begin with."

"Good God," I thought, "is that all?" – aloud I said I was sure we could manage that.

"Well done," said Mr. Law, "we will pay your company 3d. per lb. freightage and a subsidy of £500 for the first year's sole rights for the carriage of the *Scotsman* by air to Kirkwall. When you get back, write and let me know when you hope to form your company and also let me have the date you expect to commence operations."

I was overjoyed at the generous terms offered.

"I promise to do that," I assured him and said that if we could obtain delivery of the Monospar monoplane in time, I would make every effort to start the following September – 1932.

"Anyhow, I will keep you constantly informed."

It was not until later that I was to realise what a good friend I had made and the immense support he would give when I got under way.

I was back in Inverness by lunch time. 'Ah-WO' had not been pulled to pieces by the crowd that was gathered around when I got back to the field preparatory to take-off, thanks to a policeman who was standing by. He asked me for my licence and aircraft registration which I produced and I was then free to take off.

Mr. Donald was very pleased at my good news and we confirmed by letter to Mr. Law what I had arranged. Mr. Donald told me I had better place a firm order for the Monospar as quickly as possible and, when we knew the date for collection I was to come north again and make the final arrangements for licensing the fields. Steps would then be taken to float the company which was to be known as Highland Airways Limited.

That afternoon, I visited the town clerk at Inverness, Mr. Smith-Laing; he was most surprised but charming and very helpful when I asked him if his council would consider making the Longman fields into the Municipal Airport. I explained to him about the proposed air service and the progress we had made. He told me he would take the matter up with his council as quickly as possible and he felt sure they would be highly interested. He sent for the Borough

Surveyor, Mr. Mackenzie, maps were speedily produced and I marked off the area I would require. Then there was the question of a long line of telephone wires which would have to be removed and re-sited.

"Right," said Mr. Smith-Laing, "we will see the Post Office and ask them if they can get them moved."

I had a long talk with the Borough Surveyor and gave him the details of Air Ministry requirements for surface and length of runway at four points of the compass. He thought there might be some difficulty about the south-west corner as the ground in that quarter was incorporated in a farm which was let. I left it to him to use the necessary persuasion, which he successfully did. We flew south to our base at Hooton Park and spent a week there putting the final touch to our 1932 joy-riding tour.

Within the week I was ready to leave for London. I phoned my parents at Northwood to expect me and set off in the Gipsy Moth after breakfast. I had with me a lady passenger, the wife of Mr. Pobjoy. I was to land her at Aylesbury, in a field near her mother's house. She sat in front of me. From the first, the going was rough and bumpy and thoroughly unpleasant. As we passed over the lower Pennines it got worse, and my passenger's head disappeared inside

the cockpit. A short while after a handkerchief went overboard, a few minutes later a scarf and then my passenger's felt hat disappeared.

The journey got rougher and the Moth was bucking like a steer, when the climax of the jettisoning ended with a salmon-coloured piece of apparel fluttering past me, which looked uncommonly like an under garment. I wondered whatever was happening and it was not until we landed at Aylesbury 40 minutes later that I discovered my poor passenger had been frightfully airsick and sooner than be sick on the floor of the aeroplane, had nobly discarded various garments, at some cost to her husband, as a means of overcoming her dilemma. Poor woman, she looked very pale, and pleased to get on terra firma again.

Next day I flew over to Croydon to see the General Aircraft Company who, I had been told, were producing a twin-engined monoplane which had very interesting possibilities. I had a friend there who used to be with the Aircraft Disposal Company Limited from whom North British Aviation bought their Le Rhône engine spares. They had their offices and factory at Croydon Airport. My friend introduced me to Captain Schofield, manager and test pilot for the company, who took us over to the hangar to inspect the prototype aeroplane. It looked a trim little aircraft, capable of carrying five passengers, excluding the pilot; a specially designed locker which could be attached under the fuselage would carry at least 60 lb. of mail and newspapers. In addition there was a locker at the back of the cabin which took care of a limited amount of passengers' luggage.

The production type was to be powered with two Pobjoy 80 h.p. R type radial motors, thus giving 160 h.p. for take-off. The price of the plane was attractive at £1,500 for an all-metal aircraft. Captain Schofield said he was flying down to Cowes that morning on the prototype and enquired whether I would like to accompany him.

"I'd be delighted," I answered.

We landed at the Saunders-Roe private airfield up on the hill behind Cowes. On the return flight, I piloted the plane and was impressed with the performance although it was only powered by two 50 h.p. (British) Salmson radial engines. There and then I asked him to put my name down for one of the first machines off the production line, which they hoped would be ready during the middle of 1932.

The prototype monoplane was made of three-ply and spruce but the production model was to be made in duralumin alloy and would be called the General Aircraft S.T.4 Monospar. The main wings had only one main spar which was specially stressed with kingposts and swage rods. This system also applied to the fuselage, the idea being to save weight and give the plane a better payload. This was of major importance to my project. The engines were manufactured at our headquarters Hooton Park Airfield by Pobjoy Air Motors Company Limited and already they had proved to be a reliable engine. They were exceedingly light for the power they produced.

Now that I had a plane available, my next move was to contact the Postmaster General's Department, but I waited for a few days to get the proposition properly presented. That accomplished, I wrote and asked for an appointment, and briefly explained my business. A reply came back very quickly, saying Sir Frederick Williamson would be pleased to see me if I called at a stated time. I was feeling a bit apprehensive but Sir Frederick immediately put me at my ease and introduced me to another official sitting by him, who was from the Air Ministry.

"Now what is your proposal, Captain Fresson?" Sir Frederick asked.

I described my recent visit to Orkney, and the time which could be saved if the mails could be flown from Inverness to Orkney and later joining up with Wick, thus serving the extreme North of Scotland. Sir Frederick asked

"Have you an established company to operate this service?"

"Not yet," I said, "this meeting you have so kindly arranged for me is for exploratory purposes and to find out whether the Post Office would approve in principle the carriage of air mail between Inverness and Orkney, should an air service be available. Naturally, it would make matters very much easier for me to establish an operating company if I could say that the Post Office would be interested in such a project. Besides offering a static daily load, it would attract passengers and newspaper freightage."

Sir Frederick looked at me seriously for a moment before replying,

"We have had many propositions like this put to us before, but they have all turned out to be without substance. What assurance can you give us that you are capable of maintaining a safe and regular air service that would justify us in entrusting His Majesty's Mail in your care?"

"Sir," I answered, "I am willing to run a service for a trial period, to be named by you, which will enable you to judge for yourself, and as long as I know the Post Office is behind me in the event of the desired regularity being achieved, I would be in the position to raise the capital to form an operating company."

Sir Frederick appeared satisfied with my answer and then referred to the Air Ministry official sitting by his side. He only asked me one question.

"You are aware, Captain Fresson, that the route you are talking about is a very stormy one and subject to rapid weather changes. As there are no weather stations along that route, how do you propose to provide yourself with meteorological information each day before commencing the flight?"

Sir Frederick was looking at me quizzically.

"That's easy," I countered without hesitation, "I will obtain telephone reports from my own observers, whom we shall train for the job. All we shall need is, cloud height, visibility, and approximate strength of the wind."

The Air Ministry man appeared nonplussed over such unorthodox methods, but Sir Frederick smiled, and I felt I had gained a point with him.

The outcome of the meeting left it open to me to approach the Post Office again at a later date, when I was further on with my plans. Sir Frederick Williamson's last words to me were

"Send us regularity figures for a year's operations and we will consider a contract if it is good enough."

With that, I considered we had enough ammunition to complete the financial arrangements. I had a plane available, together with a possible newspaper contract, plus the mail at a later date, an airminded public, and that seemed to me a good foundation with which to start trying to float the air company.

CHAPTER FOUR

B^Y the time April arrived, the Hatston airfield negotiations were
still dragging on and so I returned to Orkney for a final all-out
effort to get this thorny question disposed of.

First I contacted Mr. Ritchie who farmed the Hatston land which
I had used the previous summer for our joy-riding visit. However,
although he was most willing to help me, being one of the few to
perceive the advantages of air transport to Orkney, he was at the
mercy of the agents of the estate and of the solicitor who looked after
it. I spent a lot of time discussing my plans with Mr. Ritchie and Mr.
Bell, the owner of the estate and with the solicitor, Mr. Robertson.
But in the end I was unable to come to any arrangement over Hatston,
and I believe that this was due to the number of people in the town
who held shares in the shipping company and who were out to do
anything that would block air facilities to Orkney which would, in
their view, be injurious to the shipping interests.

I surveyed the island several times in the Moth, but it wasn't
until I was invited to Mr. Hayden's house for tea that any solution
to the problem appeared. Mr. Hayden had two good-looking
daughters, Patty and Jean. While at tea I told them of my fruitless
search and they asked me if I had looked at Wideford Farm. On
hearing that I had not, they took me after tea to the top of the hill.
It was a steep climb and there were many stone dykes to be scaled
but Patty and her sister Jean romped over them like goats and I did
my best to keep up. On arrival at the top, the girls said

"That's Wideford Farm," pointing down in front of a slight slope.

I gave a casual look and then stiffened. I could not believe my eyes.
There in front of me was a site even better than Hatston. It gave
me a south-east run, whereas Hatston did not, unless the main road
was diverted.

"My God," I said, "you have surely saved the situation. This is
the place without any doubt, let's get down and pace the field out."

Sure enough, I obtained two runs of 500 yards and two of around
450 yards. If the wind was strong enough to warrant using the two
shorter directions, then the length was sufficient. The surface, mostly
good, could be put in order at low cost, there were no obstructions
on the perimeter, and best of all the N.W.-S.E. runway was down-

hill for 100 yards, which on calm days and when the field was soggy in the winter, offered a catapulting effect to the take-off with full load. The really big job that required attention was the bridging of the four-feet-wide ditch which ran through the middle, North-West to South-East. The field turned out to be only one and a half miles from the town.

The farmer was Mr. Anderson who lived nearby. We lost no time in meeting him and I introduced myself to him and explained my problem. I told him that we were ready to form a company to operate an air service to Orkney from Inverness and serving Wick and Thurso but I could not find any suitable place to make an air-field in or around Kirkwall. Hatston was barred to us as there appeared to be a clash of interests in the town and the only other suitable place I could find after days of hunting were his fields. He asked me many questions as to how much ground I wanted and how many services we would run daily; also what would be the time of the last service, because he would require the ground for sheep grazing after five in the afternoon. I realised from his conditions that he was willing to help, if we could work our respective interests into a pattern. I explained what I should require to do to the ground to make it suitable, and that I might even have to lay drainage if the ground became soggy in winter. He agreed to the ditch being bridged and said that I could have the ground on a five-year lease at a very reasonable annual rental. I felt faint with relief. The last obstacle had been overcome and the 'Hatstonites' could go to the nethermost regions. I was all set now to return to Inverness and to form the company as soon as I knew when we could obtain delivery of our monoplane.

I went back to the hotel that night and as usual the old friends were collected in the private room. They were delighted at my news and the makings of a big night developed to celebrate the important event. One of them, a building contractor named Baikie, known to his friends as 'The Baron', said he would get the ditch covered at cost price and another said he could arrange for the ground to be levelled off. 'The Baron' also said that he would build us a reception hut at low cost and I then knew that I had valuable aid behind me; this subsequently proved well founded.

We broke up around midnight and were invited round to Mr. Baikie's building yard with John Shearer and the Town Clerk. He took us into the office and produced a bottle of good Scotch. By that time I was wondering how I was going to fly south next day, so I hurriedly excused myself. Having bid my friends au revoir, I eventually got back in the early hours to the hotel and slept soundly until I was called next morning. I had told Mr. Anderson at Wideford that our Inverness solicitors would draw up an agreement and a rough copy would be sent him for his approval. What a kindly man and valuable ally he turned out to be in our early struggle.

I arrived back in Inverness in time for lunch and at once went to see Mr. Donald. He was delighted with my news and agreed that as soon as we could ascertain the delivery date of the aircraft which would enable us to commence operations in 1932, immediate steps would be taken to form the company. He took me along to see his solicitor, Mr. Robert Wotherspoon, who was also interested in the project and who would join the Board as a director. Mr. Wotherspoon was to act as the company's legal adviser and Mr. Donald's firm, Macrae & Dick Limited, would provide office space and their secretary, Mr. William Hamilton, known to his friends as 'Willie', would be responsible for the books and statistics. Both of these gentlemen would also join the Board along with myself as managing director and chief pilot.

To complete the preliminaries, there now only remained the confirmation regarding the Inverness Airfield at Longman, so I called on Mr. Smith-Laing the Town Clerk before setting off in the Moth for Hooton Park.

"Hello, Captain Fresson," he said, "how did you get on in Orkney?"

I told him I had at last found and obtained the use of a good airfield and now I only wanted to be assured about the Inverness landing ground at Longman. I would attend to Thurso later. Mr. Smith-Laing told me that it was agreed in principle that there would be facilities given by the Town Council and if I would acquaint him with the date we proposed to start the air service, as quickly as possible, the ground would be prepared by the Council in time. At last the operating requirements were completed, so I now only required the aeroplane and an engineer to maintain it.

The day after my arrival at Hooton, I flew to Croydon to see the General Aircraft Company and urged them to hurry up the delivery of my plane and also asked them to look around and find me a competent engineer to maintain the monoplane and its two Pobjoy engines. If they could do that, I would arrange for the engineer to take a course on the engines at the Pobjoy factory at Hooton.

I still had a lot to do if we were to begin operations that year. There was the administration to look to – advertising, road transport at terminals – ground and office staff and a host of smaller matters.

I was speaking with the company's general manager and chief test pilot, Captain Schofield. The production manager was also present. He told me that the production line was obscure at that moment as they were in the midst of carrying out certain tests with the prototype and until those tests were completed they were unable to make any promises. The works manager, however, said he hoped to have news for me within a few weeks. Captain Schofield then sent for the engineer he had recommended to me. His name was Pugh and he appeared keen at the idea of joining me in Inverness. We discussed terms and I promised to send him a contract to sign when I arrived back in Hooton. I mentioned the training at the Pobjoy works at Hooton; he said he had been working on the Pobjoy engines for a month or so and had a fair knowledge of the engine. At the same time he was anxious to make use of a course at the Pobjoy factory. I was very pleased with this turn of events, more especially as he had the Gipsy I engine on his licence and so could service the Gipsy Moth.

After spending two days with my parents in Northwood, I took off from Brooklands Airfield with Miss Pauer as passenger. We were making for Ratcliffe Hall in Leicestershire, which was the home of Sir Lindsay Everard. On the way we stopped for the night at the Crown Hotel, Framlingham, and I visited my old college for tea.

On Sunday, we arrived at Ratcliffe Hall where Sir Lindsay kept a private airfield and where Miss Winifred Spooner, who was one of the early women pilots, acted as his private pilot. She had invited me to drop in if I was ever passing, so here was a good opportunity. We were made very welcome and Sir Lindsay came down and had a chat with me in Miss Spooner's charming cottage. Sir Lindsay was chairman of the Royal Aero Club and he was genuinely pleased to see me.

"I have read about your air service plans to the Orkney Islands," he said. "I'm most interested and admire your pioneering spirit. You will be the only operator outside the Imperial Airways Group you know. When do you expect to start operations?"

"That is difficult to answer," I replied. "It all depends when the General Aircraft Company can deliver the monoplane I have on order. I am, however, hoping to get under way by the beginning of September."

He went on chatting and asked many questions about the meteorological conditions in the North.

"I have always heard," he said, "that it's pretty stormy."

"You are not far wrong," I replied. "However I feel confident we shall be able to overcome any hazards which may exist."

"Let me fill your glass," he said, "then I must be getting along. Miss Spooner tells me she has invited you to lunch and I'm sure you will be well looked after."

He got up, and bade us good-bye.

"Call in again whenever you are passing – I shall watch your progress with great interest."

Unfortunately I never saw him again, for Scotland kept me tied to the northern latitudes and Ratcliffe Hall was off the beaten track for the flight down the east coast to London.

Back at Hooton I got dug into the North British Aviation programme for the coming season. If I could not take part, then my partner Lance Rimmer would work on his own. Alternatively, if the aircraft for the air service would not be available in time, I would take my share in the operations.

A week or so later, a letter arrived from the General Aircraft Company, which caused us much concern. It informed me with regret that their experimental aircraft had been severely damaged after a test flight. That meant at least a year's delay in commencing production. It finished by expressing their great regrets and assuring me that every effort would be made to deliver my aircraft in early April 1933.

At once, I advised the three Municipal Councils in Kirkwall, Wick and Inverness of the contents of this letter and said that this delay would mean putting back the air service opening date until spring 1933. I also wrote a letter to the newspapers in each town explaining the situation and asking them to make an announcement in their next issue. Inverness and Wick accepted the events for which we could not be held responsible, but in Kirkwall, the hard core, to which I have referred previously, immediately rubbed their hands and were vociferous in their 'I told you so' attitude that no aeroplane could operate across the stormy Pentland Firth. They failed to say that their steamer also had the greatest difficulty at times.

Now that the position was known, it was clear that I had to finalise preparations for a joy-riding tour for the 1932 season, so I first tackled my engineer, Bert Farminer, regarding the overhaul of my Avro aeroplane, which had been left, pending the decision to commence the air service. The motor had done really hard work during the past season and required a complete overhaul. That meant taking it out. As I have said, Bert was an old hand from the pre-war days of flying. He had joined the Sopwith company as a boy-apprentice and so grew up with rotary engines and with the experience he had gained with years of joy-riding behind him, what he didn't know about the 110 h.p. Le Rhône rotary motor could be written on an old-time threepenny piece.

I got busy planning the tour. Some towns were already signed up to the end of May, and so that left the summer and autumn to button up. Before I had the Moth, I used to do this job by car and it took a long time. Now, with the Moth, it was a far quicker process.

Firstly, having decided on the town, one could spot likely fields from the air more quickly and easily, come down low, test them for approach, and if the surface looked good, effect a landing, walk the field over and measure the runs by pacing, as this information would be required when applying to the Air Ministry for a licence to operate a temporary aerodrome. Lastly, if the conditions appeared in good order, search out the farmer and endeavour to sign him up for as reasonable a fee as possible.

One has no conception of the host of objections that had to be overcome with farmers in many instances, especially when one particular field was the only suitable place for flying in the neighbourhood. However, on the whole, we found the farmers very helpful and co-operative, and in many instances they became our very good friends.

In a month, I had completed the second tour which was to take me to Ashbourne in Derbyshire, Wrexham in Denbighshire and then up to Kirkby Stephen, Keswick, Penrith, Kirkby Lonsdale, Bedale, Richmond, Barnard's Castle, Easingwold, Northallerton, Thirsk, Morpeth, Whitley Bay, Dunbar, Cramlington, Blyth, Wooler, Rothbury, Coldstream, Musselburgh, Portabello, Pitlochry, Banchory, Aboyne, Ballater, Eyemouth, North Shields and the tour finished the first week in November at Durham.

I have gone to some length in quoting the towns visited in a season to show the area covered in a normal season's barnstorming. As may be imagined, it was hard work, as literally thousands of take-offs and landings were accomplished in a season, and of course each week-end there was an aerobatic display to be given to the crowd who had paid gate money for admittance to the heavily screened flying field. For, not only did we charge for the flying, but there was a gate admittance of sixpence. Many people in those days had not seen an aeroplane at close quarters and provided they could not watch free of charge from the roadside, they would come in and pay their tanner. It was not uncommon for a one-man show to take £50 to £60 gate money of a Sunday afternoon; that meant an attendance of upwards of 2,000 people. Thus to ensure privacy of operations when there was no high hedge to shield us from the outside onlooker, we carried several hundred yards of sackcloth and poles with ropes and pegs and a screen would rapidly be thrown up.

That was my last season joy-riding, for next year was to be the year I planned to leave Hooton Park and settle down to live in Inverness. Early in December 1932, I received a letter from the General Aircraft Company, saying they could guarantee delivery of my monoplane in the early part of April 1933, so I severed my working connection with the North British Aviation Company and flew back to Inverness intending to stay there until the three airfields were well on their way to completion to my satisfaction.

I returned from the North of Scotland in the middle of December and left the Moth at Cramlington for its annual overhaul and renewal of Certificate of Airworthiness. I had found a site at Thurso and at Wick, arranged booking agents at Robertson's Garage in the High Street next door to the Station Hotel, which would act as a 'waiting-room'. At Inverness, Macrae & Dick Ltd. were attending to the registration of the operating company which was to be known as Highland Airways Ltd. Work was proceeding in preparing the Kirkwall airfield and the ditch was well on the way to being covered over.

The middle of January 1933 saw me at Croydon inspecting my S.T.4 aircraft which was beginning to take shape. Captain Schofield, the test pilot, was flying down to Cowes again, this time in the company's production metal monoplane and for the second time I accompanied him and got some dual flying practice in. The plane handled very nicely. The Saunders-Roe officials asked us to lunch and were very interested when they were told of my plans to open an air service in the North of Scotland. We returned to Croydon in the afternoon.

Next day I returned by road to Newcastle and went out to Cramlington airfield to collect the Moth after its overhaul. The test flight proved that everything was in good order and I took off for Inverness, via Edinburgh. Heavy snowstorms were encountered and I had to fly around in circles for half an hour waiting for a particularly black storm to pass over the Cheviot Hills. The weather report was not good – heavy continuous snow – so I bedded down in Edinburgh and managed to get through to Inverness next day above the clouds in blue sky and sunshine. My presence was needed to take part in the final arrangements for floating the company.

With that essential business completed I inspected the work of constructing the airfield which was in progress, and then went along to see the Town Clerk, Mr. Smith-Laing, to congratulate him on the

speed with which the airfield was being built. I told him we were planning to open the Orkney service on 8th May 1933. That afternoon I left for Hooton Park to settle my affairs finally with the North British Aviation Company.

The beginning of March found me back in Inverness with Miss Pauer as passenger. I gave a number of short flights in the Moth at Inverness and nearby towns to advertise the coming air service. Inverness airfield was almost finished and it only remained to drop the telephone wires. I found it a very nice airfield to operate out of and Mr. Mackenzie the Borough Surveyor had made a good job of it. The terms of use were discussed and the Inverness Council were very generous in granting us free use of the airfield for the first year, a low rent for the second year and a final and very nominal rent thereafter. Wick also did the same for us, but in Kirkwall the same stonewalling influences were at work and we got no financial help from the Council there. However, farmer Anderson, the owner of the airfield, was extremely generous to us and made up for the Council's omissions.

I have often thought about the official Orkney attitude at that crucial time, inasmuch as Orkney had so much to gain from an air service. After all, only a limited number of the population could have shares in the steamer company whose interest they were evidently trying to protect. They little suspected at that time that the North of Scotland Steam Navigation Company Ltd., which operated the steamer service, would very soon join the board of Highland Airways Ltd. Their managing director, Mr. McCallum, became a great supporter of the Highland Airways and subsequently gave valuable assistance to the development of the air service.

I returned south at the end of March. Information was awaiting me that our monoplane would be ready at the beginning of April, right up to time. I spent three days at Croydon watching the finishing touches being put to the aircraft, which was registered G-ACEW. It was subsequently christened *Inverness* and on 7th April 1933 I flew on the test flight with Captain Schofield. After half a dozen take-offs and landings with him, he got out and I made another three landings on my own. Next day I took off for Hooton Park with Mrs. Simons who had come down specially for the flight.

On Wednesday, 12th April, engineer Pugh, who was seconded to me by General Aircraft Limited, arrived from Croydon and we left immediately after lunch for Inverness. First stop Cramlington, Newcastle, and then on to Edinburgh, where we stayed the night, for by now there was a strong head-wind of some 40 m.p.h. blowing, and it appeared that we would not make Inverness before dark. Next afternoon we set off with a bad weather report. On reaching Blair Atholl there was a black snowstorm ahead and it extended as far as the eye could see east and west. Consequently, I altered course and flew east alongside the blizzard and worked my way up to the Dee Valley only to find the black wall of snow still blocking our way to the north. I said to engineer Pugh

"It doesn't look as if we can get through to Inverness unless we take the long route round the coast. I think we will land in the field I used last year for joy-riding at Banchory and stay the night."

"Good idea, Captain Fresson," he said.

So I altered course to west and came to our field which was well in the fringe of the blizzard.

It was snowing hard, making visibility difficult. I was not sure whether the field was long enough for a plane which stalled at 55 m.p.h., so I had to make a dummy run. The snow beat on the windscreen and the turbulence was terrific. It was with great difficulty that I managed to turn in the valley, in order to get into the wind for landing. The strong wind helped a lot and we settled down in a matter of 200 yards leaving as much again to spare. We picketed

78

the plane down, and hailed a passing motorist who took us into town
to the local hotel, where mine host of the year before gave us a warm
welcome. He produced some extra special Scotch to thaw us out. We
were certainly very cold.

The next day I phoned Inverness and was given a good weather
report. I told them that we expected to arrive at Longman airfield
at eleven o'clock that morning, and asked them to send a car to meet
us. I explained about the hold-up the night before. Mr. Donald said
he was worried about our non-arrival, but guessed that the weather
was the cause. On arrival at the field, we found that the monoplane
was surrounded by a number of locals. The wind had died down and
in place of the strong westerly blow of the night before, now blew
gently from the east. Would the Monospar clear the four-foot stone
dyke at the end of the available run in time, I worried. I had not as
yet determined exact unstick performances in the short time that I
had been flying the plane, as all my landings and take-offs had been
at proper airfields with plenty of room to spare.

I first paced the field out. Just 400 yards, petrol tanks were not full
and only one passenger. I thought about my previous take-offs at
Croydon, Hooton and Meir and guessed that the plane was taking
about 350 yards to get unstuck.

"Come on Pugh," I said, "I think she will just do it."

We got the tail right up against the west dyke, opened the engines up after a good warming with the brakes full on, and then let go. The tail came up quickly and we were off the ground a little over half-way down the field. I climbed the plane hard to 5,000 feet and made off on a direct course for Inverness. Passing over some high mountains, we picked up the Spey Valley by Grantown-on-Spey and in 40 minutes from leaving Banchory we were circling Inverness in brilliant sunshine at twenty minutes to eleven, ahead of our schedule.

I hung around over Macrae & Dick's garage for a while to let them know we had arrived, and then passed over the airfield preparatory to effecting a landing, when I espied a car and two or three people standing on the edge of the airfield.

On landing, Donald and Willie Hamilton came forward to welcome us and they looked pleased with the trim monoplane I had brought up.

"So you ran into bad weather," Donald said to me. "It was not looking at all good here yesterday afternoon and there was a big storm raging just over the hills. I think you did the wise thing putting down at Banchory."

The day was perfect that morning and Inverness looked a fairy town from the air, glittering in the sun, with the Moray Firth blue as blue could be, lapping almost up to its back door and along the edge of Longman airfield.

"Let's get the plane into the shed, Pugh," I said.

To do this we had to fold the wings. To save initial cost, I had the smallest hangar possible made to house our first aircraft. The wings folded very easily and quickly and in no time we had the plane inside. It was arranged that I would give Donald a flight that afternoon.

Next day we had our first Board meeting. The company was registered and the directors were Dr. Alexander of Elgin, chairman; myself as managing director; Mr. Donald, director; Mr. R. Wotherspoon, director and legal adviser and Mr. Hamilton, secretary. Offices were provided at Macrae & Dick's Ltd., Academy Street. It was agreed that we should open the service on Monday, 8th May 1933, a little over three weeks ahead. In the meantime, I was to give local flights to show and advertise the aircraft, and get the people of Inverness interested in flying. The local newspapers co-operated loyally and their reports were quoted in the national press in the south, which spread the publicity that we required.

On 22nd April, a Saturday afternoon, I visited Tain and during the afternoon I initiated 161 passengers to become potential air travellers. During the ten days' operations at Inverness Airport, we carried 358 passengers in 94 flights.

We next visited Elgin for two days and 151 of its inhabitants took to the air. Kirkwall became the next port of call for one afternoon, when only 40 passengers booked flights. The following day we returned to Golspie via Thurso and Wick. On that trip I had my first real taste of coastal fog and was obliged to fly above it at 2,000 feet. Fortunately it cleared south of Helmsdale and the weather was clear for the Golspie operations. There was great interest and keenness for such a small place. I was kept going hard for the whole afternoon, carrying no less than 161 passengers in three and a quarter hours' continuous flying.

Comparing the 40 passengers at Kirkwall with the other towns visited, it was easy to see how little interest Kirkwall took in this tour, and yet, when I had given short flights there last year, the support was excellent. It seemed only too apparent that the same influential interest was still acting against the proposed air service. However, after we had been operating a short while and the mail contract was granted, Kirkwall redeemed itself, and they took to the air like ducks to water. Also they turned out to be very loyal to Highland Airways in the competition we had to combat later on.

These happenings were the last of the lengthy preparations I have recorded, for two days later, on 8th May 1933, the air service became an established fact.

CHAPTER FIVE

T HE day, 8th May, dawned fine and sunny. My thoughts on that morning as I was dressing in the Queensgate Hotel were apprehensive, to say the least. My journeyings backwards and forwards in the Moth left me in little doubt that I was up against a really tough proposition and some of the worst weather to be found in the British Isles, which I would have to combat on my own. I had no radio facilities to assist me when the visibility was down to almost zero, which would have enabled me to climb into or above the clouds to a safe altitude, and 'home' on the station I was heading for. Neither did I possess the Sperry artificial horizon and directional gyro, which are essential for accurate control of the aircraft in cloud. Under such circumstances, one was confined to crawling along low down under the overcast and on misty or foggy days, when visibility was down to a few hundred yards, piloting became very difficult and was a severe strain on me.

I was to have more than my share of that type of flying in order to maintain a high enough degree of regularity to enable me to claim the coveted mail contract at the end of the first year's operations.

By the time we got down to Longman airfield, there was a sizeable crowd gathered to witness the opening ceremony.

The most urgent matter I had to attend to was the loading of *The Scotsman* newspapers. We had a load of some 70 lb. especially done up in bundles not exceeding six inches thick. This was essential, because we had to load the bundles into the special tray which was designed and attached underneath the seating compartment of the aircraft and it was only some eight inches deep so that it would not interrupt the airflow over the fuselage. This special tray was essential as there was no room inside the plane when carrying a full load of four passengers and luggage. Mr. Chisholm, *The Scotsman's* despatch manager, was present to see that his company's interests were properly looked after. Mr. George Law had seen to that. He also brought a letter from Mr. Law wishing me the best of good luck on this first trip and for the future.

Provost Macdonald and his wife officiated at the proceedings on behalf of the Town Council and Mrs. Macdonald christened the monoplane *Inverness*. The official opening of the airport was left over to the middle of June.

I quote the press report of the proceedings on that auspicious morning:

To the North by Air
Epoch Making Plane Service
Inverness Linked with Orkney

"9th May 1933. History was made yesterday by the opening of the air service between Inverness and Orkney, the double journey occupying somewhat under two and a half hours.

"On a perfect May morning, the beautiful twin-engined monoplane *Inverness* of Highland Airways Limited took the air from the Longman Municipal Aerodrome. Appropriately christened with 'Highland Dew' by Mrs. Macdonald, wife of Provost Macdonald, the plane set off promptly at ten o'clock with three passengers and the pilot, Captain E. E. Fresson, on board. The passengers were Sir Edmund Findlay, Bt., of *The Scotsman*, Mr. Douglas S. Gabriel of the Anglo-American Oil Company and Mr. D. Smith of the White Horse Whisky Company. A large and representative gathering was present at the christening ceremony and the Town Council was represented by Bailie A. A. Noble, Dean of Guild John Mackenzie; Councillors H. A. Braine, H. Munro and N. D. Mackintosh; Mr. G. Smith-Laing, Town Clerk; Mr. James Maxwell, Town Chamberlain; Mr. D. Mackenzie Reid, Town Clerk Deputy; Deputy Chief Constable Wm. Dalgleish, and Mr. Wm. Emm, County Assessor; Dr. Alexander Elgin, Chairman of Highland Airways Limited; Mr. R. Donald, director and Mr. Robert Wotherspoon, director and legal adviser to the company and Mr. Wm. Hamilton, secretary, were also present.

"With a bottle of whisky in place of the traditional champagne, Mrs. Macdonald christened the plane *Inverness*. 'This is a unique occasion in the history of transport in the Highlands,' she said. 'It will bring the remotest part of Scotland to our front door. I wish the service every success.' The bottle crashed on the propeller of one of the motors and liberally besprinkled it with the 'Dew of the Highlands'.

"Dr. Alexander, who returned thanks to the Council for the great interest they had shown in the venture and the facilities they had provided, foreshadowed an extension of the service to the Western Isles. Captain Fresson also spoke warmly thanking Mrs. Macdonald and Sir Edmund Findlay for their interest. Captain Fresson's time

83

from Inverness to Wick was 50 minutes. A stop of 15 minutes was made at Wick and the completed flying time to Orkney was one hour and fifteen minutes. Weather conditions were not good between Helmsdale and Latheron but cleared up by the time Wick was reached. The plane flew at 200 feet above the sea for 15 miles to keep under the overcast. On the return journey the weather south of Wick had improved, and the elapsed time for the Kirkwall-Inverness journey was one hour twelve minutes. The plane landed at Inverness at twenty minutes past five in the afternoon. This was not the regular time of returning, but was made so as to suit the convenience of the passengers. Both Mr. Gabriel and Mr. Smith conducted business in the town of Kirkwall before flying back to Inverness. The *Inverness* landed at Hillhead, Wick. The passengers were delighted with the trip and praised the scenery between Inverness and Wick which they described as unexpectedly beautiful.

"Beautiful weather prevailed at Kirkwall when Mr. J. Storer Clouston of Orphir, the novelist and Convener of the County, with Provost John M. Slater of Kirkwall extended a welcome at Wideford Airport to the passengers of the plane and the pilot."

Such was the version of the press which gave an accurate account of the first trip, with the exception of the last reference. Provost Slater cut me dead on arrival and I do not think Mr. Storer Clouston noticed me, he was so taken up with Sir Edmund Findlay. It was in line at that time with the hard core against air transport, already described during the early days. I suspect the Provost was interested in other means of transport. Whatever it was I got no support from him for some time to come.

The deterioration of weather mentioned between Helmsdale and Latheron was similar to that experienced on my first trip up north in the Avro 504K described in Chapter Two and I had noticed it on several occasions during my journeys in the D.H. Moth. I knew by then what I had to cope with and acted accordingly.

For the remaining 23 days of May I had my fair share of bad weather, for no less than 10 days were either foggy or else extremely heavy rain storms were encountered along the route. On several occasions, I climbed above the fog hoping for a hole to get down through on reaching Kirkwall. The foggy weather usually started at Helmsdale so on those occasions it was worth trying to fly above the murk, as the weather south was clear and one could always return safely. On the really bad days, when we had fog from Inverness all the way up the coast, I used to take my car up to Culloden Moor, to see if it was fine. I had a landing-field located there alongside the famous battlefield so that when Inverness was fogbound and Culloden Moor in the clear I would take off and climb through the fog which was seldom more than 1,000 feet high. On returning I would land in a field at Culloden Moor. A car would meet us and the journey to Inverness would be completed by road.

On 24th May, I had my first miss and the Kirkwall trip was not completed, the weather being clamped down at Kirkwall. In the early days and after service hours, we had organised short flights around the countryside in our continued effort to make the people air-travel conscious. That particular afternoon we were booked to fly at Kingussie. It was raining hard with low cloud over the mountains, but in spite of the weather I managed to reach the place. In spite of the rain, the locals turned up in their hundreds. With the windscreen of the plane blurred with water, which made taking off and landing very difficult, 112 passengers were carried in three hours' flying. We returned to Inverness at dusk and had great difficulty in scraping over the Slochd pass through the rain-swept clouds enveloping those hills.

By the end of May we had carried 143 passengers on the daily service and through a particularly bad spell of weather. I had thus proved that it was possible to maintain a regular service by flying in contact with the ground and sea in bad visibility. But, as I have said, it was a nerve-wearing form of flying that I disliked intensely.

The first half of June produced an improvement in the weather and on 17th June 1933 the Duke and Duchess of Sutherland officially opened the Inverness Longman airfield. For the past month after flying hours I worked long into the night with the help of a secretary organising the event. A big Air Display was planned and it was advertised from Cape Wrath to Wick in the North and from Dundee to Fort William in the South. Our chairman Mr. Donald was getting a bit anxious over the money I was spending on advertising and he asked me one day how many people I expected to draw at the gate for which a charge of admission was levied. My answer of 20,000 amazed him. I can see his look of incredulity as he shot back at me,

"If you get 2,000 in these parts you'll be lucky. Inverness is not like the south you know," he warned me.

It was left at that and I went ahead.

There was an air-pageant ball given at the Station Hotel the Friday night before. It was crowded at eight shillings per head, which I thought a good omen for the morrow's Air Display. I had arranged for many well-known fliers to come up as our guests from

England and John Tranum, the famous parachutist arrived to do a drop. The next day a luncheon party was given by the Town Council for the Duke and Duchess and local celebrities. Mr. Donald, Mr. Hamilton and myself were invited, although I felt I should have been at the airport to keep an eye on catering for the crowds I expected would attend. I left early for Longman Airfield only to find that a crowd of thousands of people had crashed through the gate and were enjoying a free view of the proceedings to come, along the road adjoining the airfield which had been closed by the police for the day. Quickly I gathered all the police I could and marched them across the aerodrome to the end of the road situated alongside the airport. We closed arms and marched forward, holding the barbed wire barrier in front of us, the police at the same time shouting to the crowd to get back. Gradually, they retreated and at last we got them behind the houses on the Longman Road. We then admitted them after payment of an admission fee. My early departure from an uneasy lunch had saved a substantial part of the gate money. It was estimated from the air, that there were at least 20,000 spectators present.

June was a mixed month for weather, but there were no missed flights. Passengers increased to 206 for the month and then the 3rd July brought disaster which rudely shook the confidence I was

Duxford, 1918: Fresson at centre.

Nanking, 1921.

Hangchow, 1921.

The Armstrong Whitworth F.K.8 after its forced landing near Shanghai. 'Runway' for take-off being levelled by coolies.

*Early stages during
the building of the
aeroplane in
Shansi.*

beginning to feel. On that day, I left Inverness for Kirkwall in fine weather with three passengers, and *Scotsman* newspapers plus luggage which constituted a full load. Telephone reports from Kirkwall gave fog at our Wideford airfield but about 70 feet ceiling at Kirkwall sea level. We ran into the fog at Wick and scuttled across the Firth under it, reaching Scapa Pier and then Kirkwall town. Instead of putting down in the field at Hatston which was at sea level, as I should have done, I chose to follow the road up the hill to Wideford. Soon the plane was completely enveloped in swirling mist and I turned at right angles to the North to slip down the hill towards the sea. We got under it again and had another try to reach Wideford. As I almost reached our airfield, I started to run into swirling mist again and as there was a nice flat field in front of me and uphill, I put the plane down just over the stone dyke. There was a terrific bump and the plane quickly came to rest. What a sight presented itself when we got out of the aircraft. The two motors were hanging down as if they were falling out of the wings, and the undercarriage was twisted and bent. We went back along the line of landing to find out what had happened, and discovered that there was a shallow pit which was completely overgrown with high grass. The landing wheels had struck it about six inches below the sharp edge and the force of impact must have been terrific at the speed we were travelling. No wonder the plane was bent, and what frightful luck, for there was r~.. another rough place in the whole field and had I been five yards right or left or three feet higher, I should have missed that lone hole.

As I stood feeling completely overcome with despair, and with the condolences of my passengers ringing in my ears, figures came running towards us from the road. They turned out to be my car driver and a couple of people who were sightseers on the aerodrome. I told Norn, my driver, that the plane was damaged and to get me into town as quickly as possible. The passengers scrambled in behind and we were soon at our booking office in the *Orcadian* newspaper premises. Mr. Mackintosh, the owner, was very kindly acting as our booking agent and he did this work free for a number of years until we had established ourselves sufficiently to open our own office. I told him what had happened and he was terribly upset as it meant the service might not be able to operate for weeks. The plane would have to be shipped south to Croydon for repairs, and that would give the Jonahs full rein to vent their spite. He was angry with me, but when he later saw the field and the trap it harboured he graciously withdrew what he had said earlier.

I at once phoned Mr. Donald at Macrae & Dick Limited, Inverness, and he suggested that we should endeavour to hire a plane to keep a skeleton service going, while our plane was being repaired.

"Why not try Mr. John Sword," he said, "at Renfrew?"

Mr. Sword had been at the opening of Inverness Airport and had a fleet of aircraft including some D.H. Dragon twin-engined eightseaters. So I rang John Sword and told him what had happened. Mr. Sword was unable to hire me one of his Dragon aircraft, as they were short of that type because two were undergoing annual overhaul. But he was able to offer me a four-seater Fox Moth with a pilot. I thought this over for a time. The Fox Moth certainly carried four passengers as was the case with our damaged plane but it had no extra accommodation for newspapers in the form of a newspaper tray as did our aircraft. That meant we would have to forgo one seat on the northbound journey, which would be used for loading *The Scotsman*. However, there was nowhere else where I could obtain a relief plane at a moment's notice so the Fox Moth had to do. Anything, I reasoned, would be better than closing the air service down while repairs were carried out to our S.T.4 monoplane, so soon after commencing it. I gratefully accepted the offer. I asked Mr. Sword on the phone,

"Can you send the Fox Moth up?"

"Right away," came the reply.

"And how much will you charge?" I enquired.

"Don't bother about that," he said, "wait and see how many hours the Fox Moth flies while in your service – you can trust me not to charge you too much."

With that we hung up. When my local agent asked if I had got a plane I said yes and told him he would only have three available seats for the northern run because of the *Scotsman* load.

"That doesn't matter," he replied, "as long as the newspapers get through. The people here look upon their early delivery of *The Scotsman* with great expectation."

That afternoon the Fox Moth arrived in Inverness piloted by Captain Cyril Coleman, and as the fog had lifted by that time in Kirkwall, he picked up engineer Pugh and his tool case and flew on to Orkney. He then made a quick turn around after taking a quick look at the damaged monoplane across the way, and returned to Inverness with the southbound passengers.

I felt as if my world had collapsed around me, when I again took a look at our wrecked plane. I did not think Cyril Coleman could ever tackle the Orkney weather in a Fox Moth and then there was the expense of sending our plane back to the makers in London and the cost of repairs. We had very little money in the kitty for such contingencies, in case the insurance company refused to pay up. They might say, I reasoned, that I should not have been flying in such weather. My ruminations were suddenly interrupted by a slap on the back and a "Hullo old chap".

I turned quickly and observed my previous benefactor, surgeon McClure. "Cheer up," he said, evidently seeing the look of despair in my face, "you'll get over the difficulty somehow. Come up to the house and have lunch with us. A good dram will do you the world of good."

"That's a good offer," I replied, glad of the interruption to my thoughts, so up we marched to his house 'Innistore' a little way up the hill to Wideford, and were warmly welcomed by Mrs. McClure who introduced me to another visitor, Mr. MacKenzie, chief of Metal Industries at Scapa Flow. He was engaged in raising the sunken German warships from the bottom of the Flow, where they were scuttled by the Germans after World War I. The lunch was a pleasant one and my spirits revived after so much hospitality. Meanwhile, a phone call had come in to say that Captain Coleman was on the way, so I hurried up to the airfield to meet him and engineer Pugh.

We all went along to see the *Inverness* which was lying in the next field over the road, so near and yet so far from safety.

"I'm afraid, Captain Fresson," Coleman said, "that you're not going to have the use of that aircraft again for some time."

I agreed with him.

"What bad luck," he said, "another yard at touch-down and you would have been in the clear."

We saw him off on the southbound trip and returned to the damaged plane. A thorough examination showed damage to the engine bearers and undercarriage struts, but we could not be sure of the main stub wing spars which the engine bearers were attached to. I left Pugh to get all the nuts and bolts freed and ready to take the wings off, then went down to town to obtain transport and some men to help lift the wings from the plane. I was back in an hour with a lorry and the men. Pugh had worked fast. Everything was ready for dismantling and we lifted the wings clear of the body and put them on the truck. We thought the undercarriage would stand up in its damaged condition and allow us to tow the fuselage behind the truck, so we pushed the fuselage through the gate and got the tail end roped on to the rear of the truck where Pugh sat. I sat behind the cab, ready to signal the driver if anything went wrong and we wished to stop quickly. All went well, however, until we came to the edge of the town when another vehicle appeared coming towards us. There was not enough room for him to get by as the stub wings stretched right across the road. So, I had to jump off and get the driver of the oncoming car to back on to the main road, a short way off, which allowed us to pass and then we were all set for a straight run to the edge of the town. I then had to go ahead to keep the narrow streets of Kirkwall clear to the wharf and quay.

We put the plane on the quay with the wings each side standing on their leading edges, and covered the wreckage with tarpaulins, roping them secure. The North of Scotland Shipping Company, our competitors, who would have to carry the damaged monoplane to Aberdeen, were extremely nice to me. Far from being in a gloating mood over my misadventure, they did all they could to help and made special arrangements for the plane to be loaded on the s.s. *St. Magnus* which would arrive from Shetland next day. They were wondering about the length of the fuselage, and where to stow it, but when the Captain arrived he soon figured that difficulty out.

We set off by sea next day to Aberdeen, I and the *Inverness*. I was an object of great interest to the passengers but I have always wondered what they really thought – 'So much damage in such a short while'. Well, the next time was a very, very long while, because in the next 15 years I did no further damage to my aircraft and I flew in far worse weather than that of the morning which had been the cause of the trouble.

On arrival in Aberdeen, we supervised the transfer from s.s. *St. Magnus* to the London steamer, and then joined my car, which had been brought over from Inverness where we returned by road. The General Aircraft Company Limited were informed over the phone and asked by letter to effect repairs as quickly as possible and there is little doubt that they must have dropped everything and given us first priority, for the repairs were finished early in August.

I saw Captain Coleman on my return to Inverness and he told me that he had managed to keep an unbroken schedule, although he had been bothered by a lot of fog. In fact he put up a splendid show as he was only flying a single-engined aircraft, and what would have happened if motor trouble had been experienced in that kind of weather I hate to think.

A search then commenced for another plane to take the *Inverness* monoplane's place. Through the firm of Brian Lewis Limited at Heston airfield, we located another Monospar G-ABVH and as we were negotiating to buy a D.H. Dragon eight-seater plane from them, they hired it to us for a very nominal sum. So on 15th July, 12 days after my misfortune in Orkney, I left Heston Airport in the replacement Monospar and flew it to the de Havilland factory at Stag Lane airfield, near Hendon. After inspecting our new aeroplane on the stocks, I went home to my parents at Northwood for the night. They greeted me. They were having tea. My young daughter Betty came running in. She was surprised to see me and greeted me shyly. My parents had been looking after her for me since she lost her mother in Shanghai in 1920, when she was three months old.

"Hello, Daddy," she said, "what a surprise seeing you, I've only just got back from school. How long are you staying?" she enquired.

"I'm afraid, Betty dear, I have to leave for Inverness early to-morrow morning. I am flying up a new aeroplane from Stag Lane." Then I had to tell her all about the accident to the monoplane *Inverness*. She said

"Can I fly up with you, Daddy?" I shook my head.

"No, I'm afraid you can't leave your lessons in the middle of term. You can come up later on with your Granny."

That seemed to satisfy her for she ran up and hugged me.

I bade them farewell in the morning and proceeded to Stag Lane airfield. The de Havilland factory told me they hoped to finish our new D.H.84 by the end of the month, and we arranged that one of Brian Lewis's pilots should fly it up to Turnhouse, Edinburgh, and I would go down and collect it there. This was quite a different plane to the Monospar *Inverness*. It was a biplane and had a large fuselage with eight comfortable seats and room for mail and luggage behind. It was powered by two 130 h.p. de Havilland Gipsy Major engines and would cruise at 100 m.p.h. It also enjoyed a good range of 400 miles and was fitted with Sperry cloud flying instruments ready for the day when we obtained radio facilities. The advent of this aeroplane with its comfortable seating and plenty of leg room immediately boosted our traffic and reduced our operating costs so it was not long before we were obliged to add another to our fleet.

I set off from Stag Lane airfield in the S.T.4 monoplane around eleven, arriving at Cramlington in time for a late lunch. I met Connie Leathart of the Cramlington Aircraft Company that used to carry out the Certificate of Airworthiness for the Moth 'Ah-WO'. She was most interested in our air service to the Orkneys and kept me chatting quite a while.

The weather to the north was reasonably good so I set off for Inverness, taking a direct course across the mountains. On arrival,

I was pleasantly surprised to see Brian Lewis's Dragon G-ACCE and their sales representative Mr. Gairdner who was piloting the plane. He had apparently arrived several days before to see me, but as I was away he stayed on and gave a helping hand to Captain Coleman in the Fox Moth as the traffic had completely swamped the carrying capacity of his small machine. Bill Gairdner remained over a few days extra, and that gave me an opportunity to fly the Dragon over the air route and put in some practice handling that plane, ready for the delivery of our own Dragon from the de Havilland Aircraft Company, the order for which incidentally had been placed through Brian Lewis as agents for our part of the country.

Captain Coleman said goodbye to us next morning and returned to Renfrew. He had done exceedingly well for us and I shall never forget his great service in maintaining an unbroken schedule during two weeks of continuous fog in that little single-engined plane, while I was in the south. His services undoubtedly saved Highland Airways, for public confidence was maintained. It would have been shattered for some considerable time had we broken the continuity owing to the unfortunate mishap with our monoplane in the fog. The maintenance of continuity also had impressed the postal officials who, we were told, were watching our operations very closely.

After several days operating the Dragon to Kirkwall, it was obvious that it was an ideal plane for the job. It was an easy and delightful plane to fly and had a remarkable take-off with full load which fitted in very well with our small airfields. Even in the few days Brian Lewis's plane had been on the run, there was a noticeable increase in our bookings and so I looked forward to the delivery of our new Dragon G-ACIT[1] at the end of the month with great hopes.

With the advent of the Dragon we should definitely require a new pilot, so I sent for a pilot I had interviewed at Meir, Stoke-on-Trent. He arrived on the morning train and I met him and took him to the hotel where I had booked him in. We got talking about the route and I suggested that as I had a spare seat on the service at ten o'clock next day, he might like to come along and I could give him some dual instruction on the Monospar and he could also take a look at the route. I did the flying on the northbound trip. It was a good day and we had no trouble in reaching Kirkwall. I was informed that we had a full load for the return trip and that I would not be able to carry the new pilot back. He had to stay behind, but he didn't seem to mind. I learned afterwards, he had made straight for the Kirkwall Hotel bar. When I returned in the afternoon, our car

[1] The Dragon G–ACIT was still airworthy in the summer of 1966.

driver told me later, he had difficulty in getting him away to take him up to the airfield.

I was back by half past five, and I had to wait a while for the car bringing the pilot from the town. On arrival I thought he looked a bit queer and when we got in the air I handed the controls over to him. We seemed to steer a very zig-zag course and he did not appear able to keep the plane in a horizontal position. First one wing would drop and then the other. I kept on telling him but it did not seem to make much difference. The limit was reached when we got to Inverness and he tried to land me in a large field some three miles to the West of Longman Airport. He kept on insisting that this field was the Airport and became angry when I took control and landed at our base. Out of the plane he complained of not feeling well. I was suspicious, and took him round to our doctor for attention. I left him there and Doctor Mitchell said he would see him back to his hotel. Next day, I saw Doctor Mitchell and asked him what was wrong with my new pilot.

"Drunk," he said, "drunk as a tick."

With that explanation our friend was hustled South on the afternoon express. He must have had a real innings at the Kirkwall Hotel while waiting for my return.

We had to look quickly for another pilot, but where? They did not grow on trees. Luck, however, favoured me. I was in Aberdeen a day or two later and was told there was a three-seat aeroplane giving joy-rides off Anderson Drive. So I took the car out to see who it was. I recognised the joy-ride firm's name but did not recognise the pilot. I watched him for a time and I thought to myself, that chap is no novice at the game, let's go and have a chat with him. So in between passenger loads I got into conversation. His engineer called him Captain Holmes but I could not recall having met him before.

"You appear to be busy, Captain Holmes," I said.

"Yes, we are not doing too badly," he replied, "would you like a trip?"

I excused myself and got him talking. He told me he was flying for Scottish Motor Traction at Edinburgh, and had several thousand hours' flying to his credit, most of which I gathered had been gained with the R.A.F. What interested me most was the fact that he had quite a few hours in his log book flying D.H.84 Dragons. I just had to have a pilot quickly, so I took the plunge.

"Would you like a job on the Inverness-Orkney service?" I asked him.

I could see he was interested. He thought a moment.

"Why, have you anything to do with Highland Airways?" he asked me.

I told him who I was.

"Glad to see you, Captain Fresson," he said, shaking me by the hand, "I have read and heard a lot about you and have for some time hoped to meet you. Yes, I would be very pleased to join you. When would you want me?"

I explained that we had a new Dragon arriving at the end of the month and I should require his services immediately.

"Well, I don't know about that. You see, I have undertaken to carry out this job for another month, but I don't want to lose your offer. What would the salary be?"

I told him a figure and made it clear we did not give flying pay as was the case with the joy-riding companies. I liked him for his frankness and loyalty to the job he had undertaken, so I said to him

"I suggest you get in touch with your employers, be frank with them and ask how quickly they can release you and then let me know. Here is my phone number."

"Right," he said, "I will do that."

Within a week of my return to Inverness, Captain Holmes phoned me to say that he had obtained his release from his employers and he would report at Inverness at the beginning of the week.

At the end of the month, I went by car to Turnhouse airfield with six friends, and as we arrived to collect our Dragon, it came in from the south piloted by Bill Gairdner. He told me that I had got a first-class plane in G-ACIT and that the engines were particularly sweet. Some years later, when the rail/air interests merged with Highland Airways, he joined the new company, Scottish Airways, of which Highland Airways became a member. After a chat he left me, having handed over the documents of the aircraft. He had to catch a train back to London. Having got my friends on board, we took off and flew up to Edzell in Angus, where we landed for tea, and arrived in Inverness in time for dinner. My passengers were delighted with the trip and they commented on the comfort of the Dragon.

Three days later G-ACIT went into service on the Orkney run flown by Captain Holmes and I continued for a while to fly the Monospar as an extra. The question now arose as to the best means of financing the D.H.84 Dragon; £2,500 had to be found. Inverness interests would go half of the way, so I suggested to Mr. Donald that we should fly over on Sunday in the Moth and land at Mr. Law's shooting lodge at Achintoul. I had already made one visit in the

Monospar and had managed lightly loaded to get down and off, on the heather moorland which was pretty rough. I phoned Mr. Law to say that we were going to pay him a visit and he asked us to lunch. We duly arrived over the lodge in the Moth 'Ah-WO' just after mid-day, Sunday, and landed up the hill on the moorland field by the side of the lodge. There were quite a few guests and the party developed into a good one, so much so that Mr. Donald did not see me sneak off into another room with Mr. Law for a talk. When we were seated Mr. Law asked me a few questions about our operations. Suddenly he turned from looking out of the window and said to me,

"Captain Fresson, Mr. Chisholm, our circulation manager, tells me you have carried *The Scotsman* regularly since the service started two months ago and I hear the people in Orkney are delighted; so much so that the demand for our paper has increased. I am very pleased with you. I think you are right about the larger aircraft: how much do you want?"

"One thousand pounds," I said quickly, holding my breath.

"You can have it," he said, and on the spot he wrote me a cheque. "You can tell your secretary Mr. Hamilton to send the share certificates to me at Edinburgh."

My relief knew no bounds. Two years later, when Highland Airways amalgamated with United Airways, Mr. Law received £1,500 back for his £1,000 investment. I was proud to have repaid his faith in me so well.

Having said good-bye to the guests and Mr. Law, we all walked out to the Moth. The motor started at first swing and after strapping ourselves in, we taxied the plane up the rough ground to the top of the hill and made ready for take-off. There was about 300 yards of rough heather ground to get off in. With the extra weight of a fairly heavy passenger and the rough going, I felt anxious as I opened the throttle. Would the Moth make it? There would be no second chance once we were well under way. The plane gathered speed slowly; half-way down the slope it had only attained 30 m.p.h., and 45 m.p.h. was needed for the Moth to become airborne. The fence rushed up to meet us and still the plane was glued to the ground. I took a quick glance at the airspeed indicator, it showed just over 40 m.p.h. – it was now or never – one good pull on the stick and at that moment we hit a bad hump, the plane catapulted into the air and then began to sag. Fortunately the ground sloped down over the road to Loch An Ruathair. Easing the control column forward, flying speed was attained with the wheels brushing the heather and we began to climb.

"Whoof," I exclaimed, "that was a close shave."

My passenger thought likewise from what he said to me on the completion of the flight at Inverness.

The Dragon was very well received in Orkney and the Press had this to say:

"Glittering silver and green – the new eight-seater cabin plane which Highland Airways have added to the Pentland Firth service arrived at Kirkwall Airport on Tuesday, 2nd August 1933, from Inverness. The machine made flights to Thurso and Wick with passengers, before returning to Inverness with other passengers for the 3.45 p.m. and 4.00 p.m. trains for the south. The pilot was Captain G. B. Holmes who recently joined Highland Airways Ltd., from the S.M.T. Airplane Service department, Edinburgh. Captain Fresson, the managing director, piloted the four-seater monoplane which accompanied the new airliner. The monoplane returned immediately to Inverness with passengers who wished to catch an earlier train."

During the middle of August I returned the borrowed Monospar to Heston, as our own plane had to be collected, repairs to it having been completed. It was a dirty trip the whole way with usual low cloud and heavy rain. The General Aircraft Company had made a good job of G-ACEW and Captain Schofield laughingly said

"Don't give it any more bumps like the last one, you may not be so lucky next time."

After a test flight, I bid them adieu and with Mr. Donald as passenger we commenced the return journey. We had lunch in Edinburgh and then set off from Turnhouse on the last leg. Approaching Perth the starboard engine packed up.

"We've got to find a field," I shouted to Donald, "she won't cross the Grampians on one motor."

Circling the town, I saw a possible field on top of the hill to the south and adjacent to the main road leading to the Forth Bridge. As we dropped off height, and neared the hedge, my passenger shouted

"Look out, the field is full of cattle."

We were too low to start climbing again on the remaining motor, so I shouted back

"Never mind the cows, I've got to land."

I caught a glimpse of him out of the corner of my eye; he looked a bit strained. I chose a run between the middle of the herd, hoping

96

they would break and run, which is precisely what they did.

"There you are," I said, "what obliging creatures," to which Donald heartily agreed.

In no time there was a crowd. Having press-ganged two sturdy-looking youths to guard the plane, we cadged a lift into town and telephoned Inverness. Engineer Pugh was soon on his way with a spare engine and arrived before dark. The job was completed next morning. Taking our engineer with us we were soon back in Inverness.

In September, I again met my old friend Peter Angus, who had hired the Avro 504K in 1931 to take him from Thurso to Kirkwall and back for a business call. He wanted to know if I could fly him to Brora for another commercial appointment. I didn't know of any landing place at Brora, but I knew the fields there were exceedingly small and undulating. Nevertheless, we set off in the Moth and found a somewhat tight field a mile out on the Helmsdale Road. I went into the village with my passenger and waited at the Grand Hotel. Within an hour he was back, having made good use of his time and no doubt helped by the publicity the flight had brought him. Encouraged by this and the Thurso business air trip Peter again pressed me into service on 3rd October to fly him to Shetland. I had not been to

Shetland before, but knew it was possible to land on the links at Sumburgh some 25 miles south of Lerwick. The plane was first to visit Kirkwall for business calls, and we left for Lerwick the next morning. Half-way across to Fair Isle we ran into low rain cloud, and without radio assistance, it was too chancy looking for the narrow landfall of Shetland under such conditions. From my early days in aviation, I always remember an advertisement in one of the aviation magazines on behalf of one of the insurance companies which announced: 'The wise pilot is always he who knows when to turn back.' I took the hint on that occasion and we returned and landed on the Island of Sanday, staying at the Kettletoft Hotel the night. The field we landed in was most convenient as it was adjacent to the hotel's front door. Ultimately, it became our landing field for the island service.

Next day the weather improved and we again set off and found good weather over the 58 miles of open sea. Peter said to me

"Let's go up to the Island of Bressay, just across the Sound from Lerwick and see if you can land there. I know of a number of flat fields."

Sure enough there was one possible; it was bounded on the south by a telephone wire some 15 feet high, but I thought I could make it. We landed after flying around Lerwick for ten minutes or so, to let the inhabitants know of our arrival. The s.s. *St. Magnus* was tied up to the wharf. That steamer belonged to the North of Scotland Shipping Company and was the very one that carried the damaged monoplane to Aberdeen last July. The Captain had evidently become conscious of the competition of the air, for on being told by the mate, the story goes, that the plane he had watched flying over his ship a quarter of an hour earlier had landed on the Island of Bressay, he was quoted as having put his hand to his brow and commented in a hoarse voice

"A plane landed in Bressay! A bad omen, man – a bad omen."

The poor Captain, however, had some respite, for it was not until three years later that we were able to extend our air service to compete with him on the Shetland run. And then it took a long, long time to woo the Shetlanders away from sea travel. That was quite the opposite of Orkney, which after the first six months used air travel in preference to surface transport.

We spent three days in Lerwick, staying with Peter Angus's firm's agent, Mr. Mowatt. During that time I took Mr. Mowatt and his family over to look at the plane and I gave three joy-rides to our good friends, having got the Post Office to drop the telephone wire. Again my friend Peter did exceptionally well with his business. He

98

told me he had obtained orders that had never come his way before. Everyone wanted to talk to him about his flight to Shetland.

We left on 7th October, arriving in Kirkwall in time for lunch. It was decided that further business calls should be made, and we arrived back in Inverness flying through low cloud and heavy rain. The exact opposite of the sunshine the day before, which shows how unpredictable the weather is in latitudes 58/60.

The business value of this trip rapidly spread, for a week later we received an urgent call from a business man in Aberdeen who wanted to charter G-ACEW with two business friends for a similar flight direct to Shetland, starting from Aberdeen. The problem in this case was, we had no known landing or take-off field at Aberdeen. Mr. J. L. Swanney, who was apparently the leader of the expedition, suggested Dyce. He said there was talk of an airfield being built there. I went over by car to look at the ground and found a number of small fields, bordered by heavy stone dykes. I chose two of the largest and after obtaining the farmer's permission, arranged for the middle dyke to be taken down leaving a gap of around 100 feet. There was also a very large rock sticking out in the middle of the run. The contractor, Reggie Bissett, who subsequently became a very close friend of mine, soon blew the rock up and we then had a strip 400 yards long. Within two years Dyce airfield was constructed around that site and so we were the first to use the centre of the airport.

Departure for Shetland was arranged for Monday, 16th October and I picked up my three passengers at two-thirty in the afternoon, at the prepared air strip. It was a blustery day, and was rapidly getting worse. I had a very rough trip over from Inverness, so I warned my passengers, J. L. Swanney, E. G. Macrae and a Mr. Williamson that we would have a strong headwind which would slow us down considerably, and that the journey would likely be very rough. Mr. Swanney sat in the front beside me and the other two sat behind with the luggage.

We left the Buchan coast at MacDuff with 56 miles of foam-tossed sea ahead, between us and Wick. Our progress was very slow with a 50 m.p.h. headwind so I flew fairly low at 1,600 feet across the sea, to avoid the stronger winds higher up. We arrived in Kirkwall at five in the afternoon having taken two and a half hours for a normal one hour and a quarter's flight, just double the time. It would have taken close on two hours to reach Sumburgh in that gale, so the passengers decided they had had enough and asked me to stay over in Kirkwall for the night. I was glad, as we should have been hard put to it to reach Shetland before dark. We spent a comfortable night in the Kirkwall Hotel with plenty of 'good cheer' flowing and early next morning we departed for Shetland.

Like the last trip, two weeks earlier, the weather improved with the morning, and we diverted off course a bit to have a good look at Fair Isle. I spotted a possible landing-ground on the south side of the Island near the lighthouse, and dropped down low and made a dummy run in. It looked perhaps a bit rough, and I decided to return one day by steamer and look it over. We overflew Sumburgh and landed for the second time on the same field at Bressay, and again the phone wires had to come down. They had only been put back the day before. However, the Post Office engineers took it in good part.

My passengers decided to stay two days, and by the time they were ready to go back, they also were apparently very pleased with the results of their air visits. The third member of the party decided to remain another day and would return by ship. Again Mr. and Mrs. Mowatt made us very welcome and I was introduced to Mr. R. G. Ganson who operated a garage and bus service. I had no illusions about Shetland, an air service to Aberdeen was a must at some time in the not too distant future, but radio directional service was absolutely essential for safety. I opened my mind to Mr. Ganson and he undertook to be my agent in Shetland and to put on a bus service to Sumburgh to meet the plane when the service arrived. He took me to the west coast by car and showed me the centre of the Island very thoroughly. I could not find another flat place that could have been made into an airfield anywhere near Lerwick. The country was nothing but mountains and valleys.

The weather was not very good when we took off for Kirkwall and having left Sumburgh behind the visibility dropped down to a couple of miles or so. There was a fair cross-wind blowing and it was essential for me to pick up Fair Isle to check my drift before turning off for Orkney. I had in mind two American flyers who, a year or so before, had left Shetland in a seaplane and had never been heard of again. So I decided to play safe. Swanney and friend were relieved to see me turn back – I told them I was going to wait at Sumburgh for the visibility to improve. We waited till next morning, and even then it was not as good as I would have liked it, however, I decided to have a go at it and we departed with our third passenger on board. He had arrived by car the previous night, having heard that we had not as yet left the Island. After 15 minutes I looked for Fair Isle but saw no sign of it on the port side. We flew on; I would give it another five minutes. Swanney who was sitting behind me casually remarked

"That must be Fair Isle over there."

I looked up and there it was at least four miles away on my starboard side. The drift was considerably more than I had expected,
for we were on the wrong side of the Island, and that just showed the
wisdom of not taking chances over that sea in bad visibility without
radio control. We pulled up to the south end of the Island and I reset
course, and then steered a deliberate five degree error to the south to
make sure we did not pass North Ronaldsay to the north and thus
get ourselves hopelessly lost out at sea. In any event, I was getting a
bit short on petrol and had not enough to go looking for land for too
long. We should have seen North Ronaldsay in 25 minutes, but it

did not appear on the horizon. Just a yellow circle of mist about three
miles' radius around us persisted. Thirty minutes went by, then thirty-
five; we were well over the time now. I was beginning to get worried
when a mournful voice from behind bleated

"Say you chaps, do you remember those Yankees who left Shetland
not so long ago and were never seen again."

"Shut up," said Swanney, who was versed in sea navigation, and
was beginning to wonder just where we were. He knew we should
have seen land before now, and conveyed his thoughts to me. I
explained to him that I was steering an error course to the left so as
to be sure we would not pass to the north of Ronaldsay.

"If we don't see land in 40 minutes, I will turn west." There was no land to be seen within 40 minutes, and we altered course to the west. Shortly, a coastline showed up, and soon we were over an island which I recognised as Stronsay. We had flown well south of our course and were that much nearer Kirkwall. After a short while, we suddenly ran out of the mist into bright sunshine and the rest of the trip was easy.

As my passengers had completed their business in Kirkwall on the trip north, we only stayed for lunch and flew back to Inverness where a car was waiting to take them back to Aberdeen.

Our first tussle with the famous Orkney gales was successful and I was relieved to know that we need not fear them as much as we thought we should do. The main difficulty was to avoid being blown over on the ground after landing. To overcome this we organised landing parties who would grab the plane as the tail dropped and we would then tie it down to a car or sometimes a lorry if available. I shall have more to say about gale-flying much later on in my story, for during World War II I subsequently flew to Sumburgh and landed in a gale blowing at 80 m.p.h.

On 1st November, we commenced our trans-Pentland operations from Kirkwall. A hangar had been built at Wideford and engineer Pugh moved North to maintain the aircraft. Captain Holmes and myself shared the flying on alternate weeks, and we ran a once weekly trip to Inverness return so that we could switch pilots. There was not so much flying to be done on this restricted service, although sometimes we flew the Firth several times a day.

Now that we had definite and known fields on which it was possible to land on the North Isles group, we were soon called in by the County Council to attend to ambulance flights by the Balfour Hospital, Kirkwall, surgeon McClure being the prime mover, and charter flights grew apace.

December soon came and passed and we saw the New Year in with important developments pending. For an airmail contract was to be entrusted to us, and a year exactly to the day, Aberdeen was connected by air to the Orkneys direct via Wick. The accomplishments gained during the year 1933 had firmly established the company and we made ourselves ready for greater conquests to come.

CHAPTER SIX

THE New Year brought with it a new chairman. Doctor Alexander went out after a hectic Board meeting of disagreement and Mr. R. Donald took his place. As a result, my work became easier and more agreeable. It was decided that no time should be lost in establishing an Aberdeen-Orkney air connection in view of possible competition in the offing. We planned to do this on the anniversary of the opening of the Inverness-Orkney airline, namely, Monday, 7th May 1934.

To carry out these plans we needed more capital. It was generally agreed that operating out of Aberdeen would involve hotting up competition with the North of Scotland Steam Navigation Company, so it would be mutually advantageous if they could be persuaded to join the Highland Airways Board. Mr. Donald and myself were charged with the task of making contact. In consequence, we called on the managing director of the shipping company, Mr. McCallum, by appointment, and laid our proposition before him. Mr. McCallum appeared to us to be a very hard business man and from the conversation which developed it was clear that he had been watching our operations very closely. From the early days of disbelief in air transport operating in the stormy north, they now appeared to have accepted the fact that air transport had come to stay and, what was more important, was making a hole in the shipping company's receipts. Further, my two air trips and landings in Shetland had not gone unnoticed and they realised that it would not be long before air transport was extended to Shetland. So we were well received. After inspection and consideration of our traffic returns and accounts for the first nine months of operation, the matter was placed before their Board of Directors.

Within a few days, we received a letter accepting our proposals and the North of Scotland Shipping Company became shareholders in Highland Airways Ltd., and Mr. McCallum was nominated to our board. Mr. Adams, another director of the shipping company, was intensely interested in the link-up and I found him very helpful in guiding his fellow directors to see eye to eye with us until they got accustomed to the difference between air and sea operations. As a result of this marriage, our position was considerably strengthened.

We were now in a position to put into operation our plans for the commencement of the Aberdeen-Orkney service on Monday, 7th May 1934 and a further Dragon was ordered. I collected this aeroplane from de Havillands at Stag Lane and flew it north on 25th April.

About this time we learned that Mr. Eric Gandar Dower had purchased the property at Dyce, Aberdeen, from which I had taken off for Shetland the previous autumn, and intended constructing an airfield. In addition, rumour had it, competition might be in the offing from him *vis-à-vis* Aberdeen-Orkney and later to the Shetland Isles, which we were now committed to. This was disturbing news as it was clear to us that there was no room for competition; the density of traffic simply didn't exist for two companies. Accordingly, I slipped over by road to Aberdeen one Sunday morning having heard that Mr. Dower was visiting Aberdeen and staying at the Caledonian Hotel.

I arrived early to be sure of catching him in, and my name was sent up to his apartment. A secretary appeared to enquire my business. I explained who I was and told her I would like to see Mr. Gandar Dower in connection with aviation interests in the North of Scotland. I gave the secretary my card and she departed upstairs in the lift. When she returned, she said apologetically that Mr. Gandar Dower was unable to see me. I was nonplussed, having motored all the way from Inverness for an interview. I explained that I had come from Inverness that morning especially to see him. She returned upstairs for the second time, and came back with a message that he would see me at 4.30 that afternoon.

"But that's five hours ahead and I've got to get back to Inverness," I exclaimed.

The secretary looked embarrassed; she appeared to be a very nice person, and I learned later that her name was Miss Hopkinson. I got the impression she was a bit subjugated under the influence of a strong personality. However, very reluctantly she went upstairs again and succeeded in getting the time changed to 12.30 midday. I blessed her for her perseverance on my behalf. At 12.45 p.m. or thereabouts, my 'quarry' turned up a quarter of an hour late.

The secretary introduced us. I did not beat about the bush and came straight to the point.

"I hear, Mr. Gandar Dower, that you intend to construct an aerodrome at Dyce and will then commence air operations to Orkney and Edinburgh."

"That's materially correct, Captain Fresson," he answered.

"I wish to suggest to you that there is no room for two services in competition on the Orkney route. Those Islands are very sparsely populated and there just isn't the business for two companies. We would both lose money and in any event Highland Airways are in the field first. You are aware, of course, that the North of Scotland Shipping Company are now interested in Highland Airways which means we have strong backing."

He looked surprised.

"I had not heard that," he said.

Coming directly to the point, he enquired,

"What's your proposition, Captain Fresson?"

"It's this," I answered, "we also are planning to run a service south from Aberdeen to Dundee, Perth, Edinburgh and Glasgow. That should be a very remunerative route, serving such large cities. I will recommend my board to let that one go, if you will reciprocate by keeping off the northern routes which we have pioneered and are now running from Inverness. It may also interest you to know that we are commencing to operate an air service from Aberdeen to Orkney next month."

He appeared a bit taken aback.

"Where will you operate from in Aberdeen?" he enquired.

"From Seaton alongside the promenade," I said. "We have a lease on the ground and it is licensed and levelled."

He gave me a penetrating look.

"You move quickly, Captain Fresson," he said. "I am inclined to accept your proposition. Send me your proposals in writing regarding the Aberdeen-Edinburgh and Glasgow routes and your willingness to abstain from operating south and I will consider your proposition regarding the northern routes."

My board duly approved the proposed letter but I do not recollect receiving any acceptance.

In a little over a year, Aberdeen Airways had been promoted by Mr. Gandar Dower and, contrary to what had been discussed, commenced operating along our routes. From that date a war of attrition began and was to last until 1939 when a Licensing Court which sat under the Maybury recommendations and the chairmanship of Mr. Trustram Eve, robbed us of our Aberdeen services and gave all operations out of Aberdeen to the 'cuckoo in the nest'. It will be explained later how it all worked out.

Next day, Monday, fog blotted out everything along the Wick-Orkney route. The ten o'clock service had to be delayed until the weather improved. We still had no ground radio direction stations. There was only one passenger booked so I was using the monoplane *Inverness*, the load being light for that day. The passenger was a young business man travelling to Wick. After an hour's delay, he began to get impatient. I learned that he was the son of Mr. D. W. Georgeson who, along with Colonel Robertson was a shareholder in Highland Airways. I thereupon gave him V.I.P. treatment.

"When do you think you will start, Captain Fresson?" he enquired.

"Just as soon as the fog lifts 100 feet. It usually lifts around lunch time."

He must have been down to Longman Airport four times before lunch. At two o'clock, back at Longman Airfield the fog began to lift slightly. I was looking over at the Black Isle trying to gauge the height of the fog against the cliffs, when suddenly a voice behind me said

"Captain, it looks fine now, are we going?"

I turned, and there was my passenger again.

"I think we should wait a little longer," I replied.

"I don't know what you're bothering about Captain," he said, "it's quite easy, all you have to do is to climb above the fog until you get to Wick, come down through it and we're there."

"Really," I said, "it sounds most simple and interesting, but I'm afraid it is not so easy as all that. How do you propose I should find my way above fog and drop down over Wick airfield, without radio assistance?"

"Navigation my dear sir – simple navigation."

"And how do we navigate?" I enquired.

"Easy," he said, "If you can't do it, I will be your navigator."

"Good God," I thought, "what an optimist – how can anyone navigate accurately without seeing the ground unless there is a radio station to work on."

Trying to be as polite as possible, I ventured to say

"That method might be a bit risky, and we should end up by getting our necks broken."

"Ha! Ha! Ha!" he laughed, "don't worry about that, Captain, I'd just as soon die with you as any other man."

I gave up. If he was so keen on getting killed, he could do it without me. Half an hour later, the fog rose to about 60 feet and much against my better judgement, but under intense pressure, I decided to have a go at it. We took off and crawled along the edge of the Black Isles cliffs to Cromarty opening. Never seeing much more than half a mile ahead, we picked up one of the Cromarty World War I 'look-out' pillboxes perched half-way up a cliff, and followed the cliffs round to Cromarty village. We then cut across the low ground on a compass course to Dornoch, skimming over trees and a small loch, which I recognised.

The fog cleared a little but clamped down again as soon as we picked up Dornoch and the sea. Crawling up the coast at 50 feet, perspiration dripping off my brow, we passed Brora which was barely visible. Soon we were approaching the high cliffs of Helmsdale. Visibility was then almost nil ahead. I could just pick out the cliffs about 100 feet away on my left. I was scared of running into them if

they jutted out ever so little. All of a sudden, something black loomed ahead. I had not time to think. Automatically I slammed on full power and pulled the stick back and put on rudder out to sea. The next moment, we were roaring over a large vessel moored close into the cliffs. My passenger said it was a cruiser belonging to the Navy. Apparently they frequently exercised close inshore. In a moment, we were swallowed up in thick fog and I was committed to a most dangerous form of flying, that I had been trying all the morning to dodge.

I hoped the west coast would be clear, so I decided to turn west immediately we had reached 2,000 feet altitude, and seek refuge on

Achnahaird beach, west of Ullapool. At 1,000 feet the fog began to get lighter and at 1,200 feet we climbed into bright sunshine. That was a relief. I turned West and to my astonishment, a couple of miles inland the land was in the clear. Turning on course, and following the edge of the fog on the landward side, we reached the main Thurso-Wick highway, when all I had to do was to follow it low down to our landing field at Hillhead. The fog thickened as we approached the outskirts of the town but the field was safely reached and cutting both motors, we slid in over the fence, and landed in one piece.

"Jolly good," said my passenger, "Jolly good old chap – I knew we could do it. Whatever did you wait so long for?"

By that time I felt quite limp. We had escaped with our lives by a miracle. We hadn't cleared that cruiser's masts by more than a few feet, and here was I being chided for not leaving earlier.

North of Wick the fog was better and a phone call from Kirkwall reported that there were many clear patches in the overcast. Thereupon, I phoned Inverness to ascertain whether the emergency field at Culloden Moor was clear and if in the affirmative, to phone the information through to Kirkwall.

That done, we loaded four passengers aboard, and took off for Kirkwall which was reached without difficulty, flying in sunshine above the fog. Slipping down through one of the holes in the fog, the landing was made at Wideford airfield without difficulty. A message was handed to me by our traffic manager saying that a phone call had been received from Inverness reporting Culloden Moor to be clear.

Unloading my Wick passengers and *The Scotsman* I took aboard the passengers for Inverness and overflew Wick. A car was out to meet us at Culloden Moor, and after picketing the plane down, we were soon in Inverness. How easy the journey back had been in sunshine with the white fog floor beneath us, compared with that nightmare journey north.

With the near approach of the opening of the Aberdeen-Orkney service, another pilot by the name of Greenshields was taken on to operate it. He arrived during April which gave me time to put him through route familiarisation training on the Inverness-Orkney run. He was an ex-R.A.F. officer and so had some years' flying experience at home and abroad. He turned out to be an excellent pilot and was able to fly through any weather without turning a hair.

On 5th April 1934, I was married to my unfortunate passenger, Mrs. Simons, who crashed with me in the Moth at Leek in 1931.

After the ceremony, I took the air service to Orkney and she accompanied me, as I was to relieve the pilot for a few days on the Pentland crossing. We were pelted with confetti and some must have stuck to our clothes as one of the passengers said to me on arrival at Kirkwall,

"Has there been a wedding, Captain Fresson?"

"Why do you ask?"

"Oh, there is confetti all over the floor of the plane."

I knew the passenger by sight, he was a business man who travelled frequently with us.

"Do you know who it was?" he enquired.

"One of the members of our staff," I answered.

He got out of the plane and we left it at that. Some weeks later, he caught up with me.

"I've a bone to pick with you, Captain. Just to think I flew with you and your wife on the day you were married and you did not tell me. I would liked to have wished you both all good happiness and good health over a dram, and you denied me that pleasure."

However, he made up for it on the spot, that evening at the Kirkwall Hotel.

The 7th May 1934 was close on us, when the service was due to commence from Aberdeen to Orkney. We left Inverness on a Sunday afternoon to ferry over to Aberdeen the aircraft which was to operate the new schedule. On board, were my wife, Mr. Donald, Pugh our engineer, and Greenshields our new pilot. I was piloting the Dragon, G-ACIT. It was a nice sunny afternoon when we left Longman Airport with scarcely any wind. After passing Elgin, the weather began to change, and a strong wind developed from the south-east which was roughly the course we were steering. By the time we had reached Huntly, the plane did not appear to be making any headway over the ground, and the bumps were colossal. One of the passengers was laid out on the floor violently sick and Greenshields, who was sitting immediately behind me, said that my wife wanted me to return; she was very frightened. I wanted to reach my target that afternoon, if at all possible, and stayed on course for another ten minutes in which time we had only covered five miles over the ground. That represented a gale of 80 m.p.h. and a ground speed of only 30 m.p.h. and as we had nearly 40 miles to go, that was over an hour's flying. By now the passengers were in a bad way and I didn't think they could very well stand such a hammering for that length of time, so reluctantly I turned about and made for Lossiemouth field where Mr. Ramsay MacDonald the Prime Minister's R.A.F. plane used to land when he flew home to that town. We arrived there in a few minutes with a ground speed of around 170 m.p.h. The wind was not blowing so hard at Lossie, but I figured from the chimney smoke that it was at least 50 m.p.h.

Before landing, I got engineer Pugh and pilot Greenshields to get ready by the door. I was frightened that the plane might be blown over after it had landed, without a landing party to hold it down.

Immediately the plane came to a halt with the tail high in the air, those two were to jump out, dodge under the wing each side and grab one of the outer wing struts each and hold on while I let the tail drop. That worked fine. I then hurried out and screwed pickets into the ground and roped the aircraft down. We also lashed the tail, and the plane rode the storm out safely through the night. Very soon the usual crowd of sightseers gathered and there was no trouble getting a lift into Lossie where we put up at the Marine Hotel. Our first call was for a stiff dram to calm the passengers and also the crew.

Next morning dawned sunny and the wind had abated. We left early for Aberdeen, arriving at half past eight, where the christening ceremony took place at half past nine. The plane was christened *Aberdeen* by Lady Provost Alexander and after speeches and good wishes it left for Wick and Kirkwall with a full load of return passengers.

This time, on arrival at Kirkwall, I received a hearty welcome and handshake from Provost Slater and from that day he did all in his power to help me. I suspect the North of Scotland Shipping Company's interest in our company at that date had a lot to do with the transformation.

Next day, pilot Greenshields took over the service. He was a remarkable pilot, I used to watch him arrive at Kirkwall airfield quite unruffled, having flown across 60 miles of open storm-ridden sea and atrocious weather without any navigational aids, and he kept 100 per cent regularity. Even the steamer skippers complimented him and said they would not have believed it possible.

With the Aberdeen service under way, my next project was to survey the Stornoway route. I was anxious to get the whole of the North of Scotland tied up before outsiders started to poke their noses in. Already I had heard rumours of a southern aviation company having designing eyes on Stornoway, and I wanted to be in first. A long conversation on the phone with my friend Kenny Ross at the Caledonian Hotel, Stornoway, ensued. He would mark a 300-yard strip off for me on the Melbost Golf Links in the direction of the prevailing wind. He said there would be two bunkers in the middle with only a 30-feet gap between – would that be all right?

"A bit close," I said, "the Dragon's wheels are around 13 feet apart. That doesn't leave much room does it, Kenny?"

"Well, Captain, I don't see what we can do as there isn't another strip that long with suitable surface."

"All right, Kenny," I said, "we'll have to make it do. Can you mark the top inside edge of the bunkers with a linen sheet and place one in the middle of the run, in between?"

"Certainly, Captain. We have plenty of old sheets in the hotel, I'll get that done."

"Also," I said, "light a smoke fire as soon as I circle the golf links."

"Yes, we'll do just that."

A few days later, on a brilliant Thursday morning, we took off from Inverness in Dragon G-ACIT with Willie Hamilton our secretary, engineer Pugh and two other passengers, arriving over the Stornoway golf course at midday. The markings were clear as I dropped off height and took a dummy approach and low run over the strip. The smoke wind director was going strong and the bunker gap, although very narrow, was well marked and looked possible.

There were quite a number of onlookers to witness the first landing on Melbost Golf Course, Lewis.

After another circuit we dropped down low over the golf course, motoring in at minimum speed and touched down almost on top of the first marker. By keeping the tail up I had no difficulty in steering for the middle-bunker marker, and we ran through the 'bunker straits' without any difficulty, pulling up with 50 yards to spare. We had a good look round the golf course before going into town and I found it had great possibilities for an airfield. I estimated it would cost a few thousand pounds to remove bunkers, and level and grade four strips of 600 yards each.

I decided to make a report on the Melbost Golf Course survey, and submit it to our next Board meeting. Obviously we should need help from the Town Council to build an airfield in Stornoway in view of the magnitude of the work required. Then there would need to be a good measure of public pressure to obtain the use of the golf course for our purpose. It would mean extensive alterations to the golf course layout but I figured we could still retain the 18 holes. After strolling over the links for an hour, we went into town to the Caledonian Hotel for lunch. Mine host, Kenny Ross, did us proud. By the time we had finished, it was three o'clock and we were all ready to brave anything which came our way on the flight back.

I changed course for our return trip, and made a landfall at Kinlochewe. Dropping down to 50 feet above the water we flew right down to the east end of Loch Maree, obtaining a magnificent view and then pulling up the Glen Docherty Pass and down the valley over Achnasheen, Garve, passing Strathpeffer on the left and up the Beauly Firth to Inverness, landing exactly one hour after take-off.

The directors of Highland Airways accepted my report and agreed we should make an official approach to the Stornoway Town Council. We would also ask the Air Ministry to survey the site in order to make sure that the golf course would be acceptable for licensing. Major Mealing of the Civil Aviation Directorate duly arrived from London and flew over with me, some months later. He was very pleased with the site and gave it a clean bill. Thereafter the fun started. The Golf Club did not want to give up the ground or have it altered. The Council were not prepared to make any contribution for the construction of the runways. Then when we were beginning to make some sign of progress, a pilot from Renfrew flew up and said he would give Stornoway an air service by using seaplanes. We considered the water was usually too rough for floatplanes and proved this, by later sending the *Cloud of Iona* flying-boat over to make tests. The report of the expert seaplane pilot Captain Scott of Saunders-Roe Limited, Cowes, Isle of Wight, confirmed our views. He also pointed out the hazard of flotsam and jetsam in the sea and even though the rough water was ruled out, it would cost a lot of money operating motor launches to patrol the landing area for each landing.

The west coast authorities would not believe this assessment and went on dealing with the Renfrew pilot whose name was Glen Roberts, known to his friends as 'Rocky', and that well described him. To cut a long story short, bickering over that aerodrome dragged on until four years later, early 1938, before we got the site approved by the owners and golf community. We could get no local financial support and so Scottish Airways had to finance the construction. It cost us around £8,000 to produce those four runways. They were not finished until the end of August 1939. The war came on 3rd September, and we never used that aerodrome. Our £8,000 airfield, unused, was torn up and a large modern airfield was built by the Government for the use of Coastal Command. I think we obtained compensation from the Government for the money we spent to no purpose.

It was not until 24th May 1944, towards the end of the war, that the Air Ministry allowed us to operate the first Inverness-Stornoway service. Out of all the governing local bodies I had to deal with, the west coasters were the most difficult. Time meant nothing to them, and they were not prepared to spend a 'bawbee'.

May 29th 1934 was drawing near. On that date we were to be invested by the Director of Postal Services with an Air Mail Contract and Air Mail Pennant, and on that day, I was to fly the first regular internal air mail service in Britain at ordinary letter rates. It was a red letter day for me, as it meant I had conquered all that I had set out to do in those early days when I was hunting around Kirkwall for capital to finance the company. We had now obtained the four essentials I had been looking for, finance, passengers, mail and newspapers.

The 29th May arrived and Sir Frederick Williamson and party were arriving on the night express from London to preside at the Air Mail ceremony, for after one year's operating at near 100 per cent regularity the Post Office had decided to entrust us with the Orkney Air Mail contract. The fleet of aircraft were lined up in front of the hangars and the press and postal officials were greeted by my directors and myself. *The Scotsman* of Wednesday, 30th May 1934, headed this occasion as follows:

Britain's First Airmail
Opening of Inverness to Orkney Service
Epoch Making Event

"A new epoch in British postal history began in Inverness to-day, when General Sir Frederick Williamson, K.C.B., Director of Postal Services, inaugurated the first inland air mail service in Britain, which will operate between Inverness and Kirkwall. Over 2,000 letters were despatched by the plane to-day, as well as the supplies of *The Scotsman*, which has been conveyed by the air service since its inception of over a year ago.

"The occasion was marked by a simple ceremony, and the unfurling at the municipal aerodrome by Sir Frederick of a Royal Air Mail Pennant, the first pennant authorised for an inland service. The pennant was attached to the flagstaff at the aerodrome and hoisted by Sir Frederick to the accompaniment of cheers. A letter from Provost MacKenzie to Provost Slater, Kirkwall, was handed to Mr. Measham for delivery. Twelve thousand letters were sent to Kirkwall to Inverness by the plane on its return journey."

The first half of July, I spent my time in Orkney with the monoplane *Inverness* touring the Orkney Isles and giving joy rides to test the attitude of the islanders to air travel, preparatory to opening a 'Round the Isles' service. These islands are so cut off and the small steamer which plies between them so slow that a plane can do in a few minutes what takes hours by sea. The islands visited were Rousay, Sanday, Westray, Stronsay and North Ronaldsay.

I made my headquarters in the island of Rousay, which is one of the smaller islands of the Orkney northern group. It is mountainous and fringed around the perimeter by gently sloping ground which is farmed.

Undoubtedly the outstanding air-conscious island was North Ronaldsay, the most northerly and isolated island of the North Isles group. Mr. Swanney, their postmaster and spokesman, asked me to give them an early air service.

"We can't give you an air connection without an airfield to operate from," I replied. "There is no field large enough here which could be used as a landing place. It would require two fields converted into one."

"Which two would you like?" he shot back at me quickly.

Thereupon, I spent an hour or so, looking around from the air and on the ground, and chose an excellent site alongside the Post Office which would provide the largest airfield of the North Isles group. I explained to Mr. Swanney that there was a lot of work to be done before we could use it. A 300-yard stone dyke, at least four feet high, had to be removed; parts of the ground required levelling and thousands of fair-sized surface stones required gathering up before it would be suitable for an airfield.

"I'm afraid it would cost us too much to prepare, for the amount of traffic we would obtain from the island," I commented.

"Leave that to me," said Mr. Swanney.

He thereupon sent runners to all the houses on the island and asked the inhabitants to report at the Post Office within half an hour. Meanwhile, I was asked into the house for tea and a very good one it was. I had barely finished when I was told the islanders had arrived. Indeed they had, almost every one of them, including the children.

The Postmaster stood up on a box and proceeded to say,

"I have called you all here because I have an important announcement to make. Captain Fresson has assured me that Highland Airways will give this island an air service to Kirkwall providing there is a suitable landing field. He has this afternoon, made a survey and has chosen two fields alongside the Post Office. These two fields belong to Farmer Rendall, is he here?"

"Aye," shouted a voice.

Said Mr. Swanney, "Are you prepared to allow your two fields to be used, and if so, will you allow the separating stone dyke to be pulled down, the ground levelled in places and stones cleaned up on the surface. If so, will you grant the use of the land for an air service free of charge?"

"Certainly," said Farmer Rendall of Holland Farm.

"Now," said Mr. Swanney, "who is going to help in removing the dyke, and preparing the surface? Hands up!"

Up shot a forest of hands, including the small boys.

"When will you begin?" enquired Mr. Swanney.

"Tomorrow," was the unanimous reply.

The next day was fine. At ten o'clock, 60 men and 20 carts were on the fields. Just before dusk, the job was completed. Schoolboys had joined in the work, mostly in the picking up of the loose stones scattered all over the surface. The day before there were two fields uneven of surface. That evening the day after, they were converted into a 28-acre airfield, flat, free from obstacles, the finest in all the

115

North Isles; 'made in a day'. What enthusiasm! I saw to it that the people of North Ronaldsay never had reason to regret the spontaneous effort of its populace, and many a time, in after years when they were cut off by storm with no contact with the outside world, Highland Airways and their successor's Scottish Airways planes, were always ready to go to the rescue.

I trained a team to catch our planes in, to prevent them being blown over, when there were high gales blowing and mountainous seas were pounding the coast line. We flew food and mails in to them even when the winds were topping 70 m.p.h. No steamer service could operate under such stormy conditions. Anyone wanting to get back to Kirkwall would be taken on the return journey. When we eventually opened the air service early in August, full loads of passengers were available, taking their produce, such as chickens, ducks, eggs, etc., in to the market in Kirkwall and returning on the afternoon service. We ran two services a day, three times weekly, to give the return daily service. Visitors and business people would go out on the morning service, stay the day and return on the afternoon plane, which had brought the islanders back. It paid our company and the islanders were more than satisfied with what their endeavour had brought them, for they were no longer isolated. Later the Post Office gave them a postal service. The air trip took a little over quarter of an hour as compared to most of the day by the old steamer service.

The other islands, Westray, Sanday and Stronsay, were also helpful but we were able to find single fields on those islands large enough for full load operations, and which only required a little levelling. All the farmers gave us free landing facilities, after the magnificent example set by North Ronaldsay.

The final and probably most important boon that the North Isles air service brought the inhabitants came about when the Orkney County Council, early in October, two months after the air service commenced, contracted with Highland Airways Ltd. to operate an air ambulance service. A great number of urgent cases were flown to the Balfour Hospital in Kirkwall, and a number of lives were saved.

With a view to educating the Aberdeenshire people to air travel, we started, at the end of July, giving short air travel demonstration flights at a country village in Aberdeenshire named Inches and other local towns in the district. While at Inches, I received an invitation to the opening of Dyce Airport constructed by Mr. Eric Gandar Dower.

The opening of Dyce Airport immediately began to create a problem. It appeared evident that the previous Caledonian Hotel arrangement that Highland Airways flew the northern routes while Mr. Dower flew the southern was not going to be implemented, for we had news that Mr. Dower was planning a competitive air service from Aberdeen to Kirkwall. To make matters worse, we were suddenly confronted with the stark fact that our airfield at Seaton was to be used for the Highland Show next year and we would have to seek another airfield to operate from. Mr. Gandar Dower was sounded about the use of Dyce, but we were met with a blunt refusal. Clearly it appeared to us that he was out to freeze us off the Aberdeen-Kirkwall run, for he knew as well as we did that owing to the lie of the land around Aberdeen, our chances of obtaining an alternative field to Seaton were most remote. I certainly knew it, as I had searched the countryside at all points of the compass without success before I found Seaton. It seemed to us a bitter blow. The Aberdeen-Kirkwall run which we had so successfully operated, and had educated the public to use, was now to be taken from us by the freezing-out process, for the want of an airfield. What bad luck and bad coincidence about Seaton, for the Highland Show only visited Aberdeen once every five years, and 1935 had to be the 'one year in five'. Another site just had to be found.

I decided to make a square search in our Moth, which we had recently purchased from Miss Pauer, its former owner. I landed in many fields and ended up at Kintore. There was a long field alongside the stream running alongside the railway to Inverurie, so I landed on it. It was a sunny Sabbath morning. I found the owner, but he said he could not spare the grazing. I explained our difficulty and asked him to help us.

"Why not go up and see Mr. Barrack about quarter of a mile up the road on the left which leads to Inverurie," he said, "there are two good fields there with a cemetery in between."

A good omen, I thought. At least, we would not require to look far in case of accident. I went up, walked over the fields and decided that, with several fences removed and a lot of levelling, we could make a satisfactory aerodrome. The cemetery did not bother us as an obstacle, but the main road telegraph wires would. They were a good 25 feet high and at least four feet deep with wires. They would have to come down. So along I went to the farmhouse, and asked for Mr. Barrack.

"I have been sent up to see you by the farmer next door alongside the village. I am looking for an airfield as I have got to get out of Seaton, owing to the Highland Show next year. This is the only place I can find, will you help me?"

"Ah, Captain Fresson, we have read a lot about you, won't you come in?"

I was ushered into the sitting room, and a bottle of whisky was produced. Mr. Barrack poured out liberal doses in each glass and by the time they were disposed of, we were getting along famously.

Mr. Barrack and his mother-in-law were prepared to help me when they got to know what a fix Highland Airways were in. We then walked out over the fields and I explained exactly what was required. Remembering the shot which so successfully registered at Wideford, Kirkwall, I said

"Of course gentlemen, we shall only require to use the field for an hour or so each day, so the grazing for the rest of the day would be yours."

I could see I had again registered a 'bull's eye', and that settled it. They asked me the terms, I told them what I was paying for Seaton, and they accepted the same figure. They were prepared to give me a long lease, I could build a hangar alongside the main road and, to accentuate their extreme goodwill, they would attend to the removal of fences and levelling without charge. Back we went into the house and clenched the deal over another strong dram. They were incensed over Mr. Dower's attempt to freeze us out of the Aberdeen-Orkney air route which we had established with the backing of the Aberdeen civic authorities.

"Gentlemen," I said, as I was about to take my departure, "you have been very good to us, and saved the situation for my company. I will not forget. We will have an agreement drawn up and I will bring it over early in the week for signature."

This agreement was duly signed; I managed to get the Post Office to drop the phone wires for 100 yards and bury them underground, and in a few weeks, the airfield was ready for use. (That gap in the telephone wires on the main road can be seen to-day, just opposite the Kintore Cemetery. Our hangar can also be seen from the road.) From that moment, a lasting friendship sprang up between Mr. Barrack, who was the actual owner of the land, and myself.

That winter, I got Mr. Reggie Bissett, who had the year before cleared the runway for me at Dyce for my commercial charter to Lerwick, to erect a 50-foot-span hangar which would house a D.H.89 Dragon Rapide, and we moved over from Seaton early the following year. Our Kintore Airfield was a better one than at Seaton, operationally, but unfortunately, it was ten miles further from the centre of Aberdeen and we had to operate a car service to carry our passengers in and out, which added to our operational costs. We also would

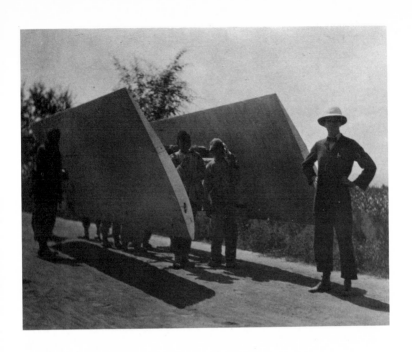

The Shansi aeroplane nears completion.

The aircraft before take-off in Shansi, 1925.

The first take-off at Shansi, 1925.

The aircraft in flight over Tai Yuan Fu,
Shansi Province, 1925.

suffer from the advertising value of Dyce, but the name of Highland Airways was, by now, well known, and that helped considerably to counteract that disadvantage.

During those early years, it seemed to me that I was always coming up against high walls that stood in my way to progress, but we survived all the problems imposed on us, until January 1939.

By now, our passenger traffic was increasing rapidly, along with the mail, *Scotsman* newspapers and freight. We accordingly considered testing out one of the new de Havilland 89 Dragon Rapides. They were faster than the Dragon and had a better reserve of engine power thus giving better single-engine performance, which would be a great asset on the Shetland run over so much open sea, and they carried a better load which was our immediate problem. We arranged that de Havilland would send up one of these aircraft and G-ACPO arrived at Inverness the third week in October 1934. I spent several hours testing this aircraft with particular attention to the distance this plane required for taking-off with full load and the run required on landing. Our fields would accommodate the take-off run, but as this plane was faster and had a higher wing loading, it required great skill in landing and pulling up in still air on the existing small airfields. The answer was, either lengthen our airfields, which would be extremely difficult and very costly, or persuade de Havillands to fit landing flaps which would permit a slower touch down and lower stalling speed. The proposition was submitted to the de Havilland Company and within six months they had a flapped demonstration Rapide ready for test. We tried it out and there was no question, our problem was solved. The flaps reduced our landing run considerably and we could operate this aircraft safely from our small aerodromes. I kept our Board conversant with what I was doing, and when they received my report, we immediately placed an order with de Havillands and our first flapped Rapide aircraft was delivered to us the following spring.

It was most successful, and helped us to more than hold our own on the Aberdeen run. We then decided to replace the slower D.H.84 Dragons with the Rapides. We also had standard radio installed and began to press the Air Ministry for direction-finding stations at Inverness, Kirkwall and Sumburgh, Shetland. In the meantime, the Air Ministry arranged with the Post Office to allow us to experiment with their shipping radio station at Wick. This station operated on quite a different frequency for shipping, but they agreed to alter their frequency setting for half an hour on certain days when we could experiment on homing. We experienced some trouble at first,

E

but eventually we made contact and the tests were most satisfactory. Arising out of this test, the Air Ministry informed us that they would install radio stations for aircraft under certain conditions. The main condition was that we would have to throw our airfields open to the public, and that meant letting Mr. Dower's company, Aberdeen Airways, into our Shetland airfield and, if necessary, into Kirkwall. We discussed this point at great length. Firstly, we were anxious to open the Shetland route and having regard to our air mail contract we naturally expected the Postmaster General to extend the contract to Shetland, and without radio navigational assistance, we were under no misapprehension regarding our inability to maintain the required regularity. But we were very conscious that our company had been refused the use of Dyce aerodrome. It was, therefore, with great reluctance that we opened Sumburgh aerodrome to public use. Had we known how we were later to be betrayed by the Postmaster General, after two years of nigh on 100 per cent service, we should have most certainly kept Sumburgh airfield private and let the Shetland air mail service slide.

From our experience of the winter months in the past year, we decided to carry on a daily Inverness-Kirkwall winter service. Our mail contract was only valid until the end of October and without a connection in the winter we would have to break the continuity and there was no telling what would then happen with threatening competition from Aberdeen. That was a wise decision as we were later given a permanent mail contract as far as Inverness-Orkney was concerned, and it was rumoured that, at the beginning of December, we were to be given the Inverness-Wick mails, which would be a substantial gain in prestige and load factor.

During the winter we had a different type of weather to contend with from that in the spring and summer. In place of continuous spells of fog, we experienced gales up to 80 m.p.h., heavy rain and sometimes low stratus cloud which had the same bad effect on us as fog, but fortunately that type of weather was not so frequent as the fog. One other difference was that, whereas one could usually climb above fog at 2,000 feet and fly in the clear, there was sometimes no getting above low stratus. As a rule, it was joined to higher stratus cloud. That meant instrument flying and its attending difficulties at that stage in our operations. We managed the high winds without much trouble. The Monospar monoplane was usually used under gale conditions as it had little or no tendency to blow over on the ground, whereas the Dragons could quite easily be blown over on their backs. When we had to use the Dragon aircraft owing to heavy loads which were beyond the capacity of the Monospar, we made provision for a landing party at Wick and Kirkwall and in the latter case, when the aircraft had to wait over for two hours before the return journey, a lorry had to be on the landing ground so that we could tie the aircraft down to it during the wait. The usual picketing was not strong enough in such winds. This system worked well and we never to my knowledge suffered any damage through aircraft being blown over.

The pilots had to be trained in special landing technique. The principal *must not* was not to allow the tail of the aircraft to drop after landing until the landing crew had got a good grip on the plane. Approaching the airfield at say, 50 feet, the motors had to be shut down, half-way down the strip in use, and by judicious use of the throttle, and keeping the nose of the aircraft very slightly down, we were able in winds of 60 m.p.h. and over to drop down almost perpendicularly, like a modern helicopter. It took a deal of practice, but all our flying staff had to learn the drill before being let loose in gales.

A month later, we were entrusted with the air mail for Caithness and Sutherland. The service commenced on 1st December 1934. We produced a special air mail cover for this occasion. On top of this development came the Orkney County Council air ambulance award to Highland Airways Ltd., for the transport, by plane, to hospital of all urgent hospital cases occurring in the Orkney Islands; this became operative in November 1934. Later this service was expanded to carry urgent Orkney cases to Aberdeen for specialised treatment.

As will be seen, 1934 proved a year of considerable progress. Highland Airways had now passed the fledgling stage and had become a factor that was creating considerable influence in the lives of the North of Scotland inhabitants. Southern national newspapers who had looked at me with pity and turned me down contemptuously when I called on them for their support in the days I was hunting for capital and support to launch Highland Airways, now became vociferous in their demands to have their newspapers carried by air to Wick and Kirkwall. They were no doubt well informed of the great increase in load of *The Scotsman*, which had occurred over the past 18 months to their detriment. Sole rights had been extended by our company for a further year, with the understanding that Mr. George Law of *The Scotsman* would consent to opening the door for outside interests at the end of the second year, *viz.* 31st May 1935. We had been threatened by several newspaper barons with court proceedings to force us, as 'public carriers', to carry their newspapers north. We had to inform them that we were not a public carrier, and that they had had their chance before I approached Mr. Law of *The Scotsman* and turned it down. We could not do anything for them until *The Scotsman* contract expired. They then threatened that they would operate their own planes, in which case we had to tell them they would not be allowed the use of our airfields. We suggested that they should have patience and await the completion of our *Scotsman* contract and we would be pleased to carry their freight, as from the 1st June the following year. I never thought that the day would come when a small limited company would be in the position of saying 'no' to the national press, and I don't think they thought it either when they turned down my approach to them in 1932, before Mr. Grant gave me that introduction to Mr. Law in Edinburgh.

The Aberdeen service was making good headway, but as most Aberdeen passengers wanted to stay over in Orkney and the Orcadians were the other way inclined, wishing a few hours in the Granite City and returning home for the night, we decided as from 1st October to alter our schedule and base the aircraft in Kirkwall, running an early service to Aberdeen and making our return departure from Aberdeen after lunch. This timing connected with the arrival of the southern train from Edinburgh and Glasgow and enabled passengers to reach Orkney the same night. This arrangement proved very successful, and our passenger load increased appreciably.

The end of the second year was upon us, and when the festivities were over, we addressed ourselves to the new problems ahead. Shetland with the attending mail contract was our objective, and of course Stornoway was very much in my mind, but most elusive. We had made no progress in spite of many visits to acquire an aerodrome in conjunction with the local authorities. However, we were constantly making a number of charter flights for which we had prepared the emergency strip in the tidal basin. They seemed to be satisfied with that, probably because they were not asked to put their hands in their pockets.

Night ambulance flights in those days called for a high degree of skill on the part of the pilot and were not entirely without risk. The landing grounds were small which meant that the aircraft had to touch down immediately on the approach edge, and with indifferent ground lighting, which consisted of two cars shining their headlights in the form of an L representing the boundary of the field and the vertical line of the L the direction of the runway into wind, required very accurate flying and a considerable amount of practice. It was not possible, owing to the expense, to arrange a proper flare path system on the islands which, of course, would have made night landings much easier. I had foreseen this problem, and arranged previously that our pilots and myself went through training in this sort of night flying at Inverness Airport, when it was known that the ambulance contract was to be given to Highland Airways. We made a number of emergency night flights using this technique and no damage was done to any of our aircraft. Such methods caused consternation to the pundits who were accustomed to operating under the modern slap-up conditions in the south.

CHAPTER SEVEN

DURING the previous summer, a very bad accident occurred with a D.H. Rapide aircraft belonging to Hillman's Airways Ltd., whose headquarters were at Romford, Essex. The aircraft was on a schedule run to Paris. About noon, holiday-makers on the sea front somewhere near St. Leonards heard the roar of an aeroplane just above them, invisible in the heavy mist enveloping the town. Shortly after, a loud report was heard out at sea and near into the shore. Boats sent out to investigate, came across the wreckage of a Rapide. The seven occupants were dead. An Air Ministry investigation subsequently took place and the cause of the accident was attributed to the pilot having lost control of the aircraft in cloud.

Shortly afterwards, a 'Notice to Airmen' was issued by the Civil Aviation Authorities that no pilot's air transport licence would be renewed unless the applicant went through a satisfactory instrument-flying test at R.A.F. Station, Hendon. My own licence No. 310, one of the early ones (at the time of writing there are now over 40,000) became due for renewal in May, so I had time to prepare myself for the conditions to be fulfilled. It was arranged for the two front seats in the Monospar cabin to be partitioned by a curtain between the two seats, thus segregating the pilot from the passenger on his right. In addition the pilot's cockpit windows would be blanked out with three-ply sheets cut to size. When that was completed, it produced the same effect as being caught up in dense cloud, as visibility was nil. On the other side of the curtain, that is the right-hand side of the cockpit, another pilot sat as an observer with duplicated controls and full vision, in case the pilot under test got into trouble, in which case, he would act should an emergency arise. The test comprised the following requirements:

(a) Take the aircraft off the ground on instruments.
(b) Climb to a prearranged altitude.
(c) Complete three left- and right-hand turns and continue on the same course.
(d) Complete three turns and proceed on a reciprocal course.
(e) Fly a triangular course of over half an hour and return on dead reckoning to as near the starting point as possible.

124

I had been doing a considerable amount of instrument-flying on the route, principally when it was foggy, so that I could get above the fog when the weather was clear each end of the route. The test showed up certain faults and I practised for ten hours. At the end of that time, I flew a plotted course blind from Inverness to Nairn, across to Cromarty and back to Inverness, landing up about a mile off the airfield at Longman. There was not much wind and the courses were previously computed for each of the three legs. That I thought was good enough and I awaited my test at Hendon with interest.

In the meanwhile, my other pilots were put through the same instruction and it was found to pay handsome dividends, as it gave them so much extra confidence when they encountered bad visibility. They always knew that, in a case of emergency, they could climb up into the overcast and return to base and clear weather.

About that time, we were informed that radio stations were shortly to be erected at Longman Airport – Inverness and Wideford – Kirkwall. We heard later on that the Sumburgh station could not be supplied until the following year. With radio station control, that meant we would be in a position to fly the whole Inverness-Orkney sector at altitude in cloud if need be, the radio station bringing us in overhead. We would let down through the overcast on a time and course procedure, known in those days as the 'Z' approach. To fly as accurately as this required modern blind-flying instruments. So, we began to install our aircraft with the Sperry artificial horizon which controlled the lateral and perpendicular position of the aircraft, and the Sperry directional gyro which indicated the number of degrees turned to right or left. While this instrument was unaffected by magnetic variation, it was subject to precession which necessitated a check and correction with the compass every 15 minutes. Unfortunately, the aircraft manufacturers did not provide for these instruments to be driven by an engine-operated vacuum pump. Instead, they chose to drive the instruments by two venturi tubes attached to the side of the aircraft. Under icing conditions, these tubes would become clogged with ice and the blind-flying instruments would cease to function. When that happened we only had the Reid & Sigrist turn-and-bank indicator to fall back on. As it was difficult to maintain an accurate course in cloud on this instrument for long periods, we usually made for the open sea if we were over high ground and let down under the overcast with the help of bearings from the nearest radio station. Subsequently we found a fairly good method of overcoming the freezing of the venturi tubes, by re-mounting them alongside and to the rear of the hot exhaust pipe.

I have mentioned these difficulties and explained them at some length so that the reader may be able to appreciate the difficulties which beset us in the early days of instrument flying. Of course we had no radio landing and approach system as is the case to-day. The radio station brought the aircraft overhead by a series of W/T[1] bearings or R/T[2], if no radio officer was aboard. After that, the pilot had to find his own way down and on to the airfield. It is too complicated to explain the 'Z' approach method we used, but with practice we got extremely accurate with the let-down and could get into our airfield with cloud a few feet off the ground and with visibility 100 yards or so. That is considerably better than can be done to-day with larger aircraft and their modern automatic approach radar equipment.[3]

By this time, our maintenance was reaching a stage which required a maintenance organisation operated by an engineer with specialised qualifications. Up to then I had been responsible for the work in conjunction with engineer Pugh. He was a first-rate chap on field maintenance but was not sufficiently qualified or experienced to organise and operate an up-to-date maintenance shop which would cover the complete overhaul of motors, and carry out the annual Certificate of Airworthiness overhaul required by the Air Ministry. We had been obliged to ferry our aircraft to the makers for this annual overhaul which was very costly. We accordingly decided to engage a fully licensed engineer to carry out this work and I was fortunate in locating George Griffiths, who at that time, was employed by the S.M.T. Aviation Department, Edinburgh, and who was looking for a change. He joined us around the middle of 1934. I have always looked upon that appointment as the most lucky shot in my life in business. Griffiths turned out a superlative craftsman. There was nothing he could not do. If he didn't know an answer, he found it out within a matter of hours. When we started using radio, we found ourselves in difficulty because we had no radio maintenance. Every time a set went out of action we had to send to the manufacturers for them to send a mechanic to put it right. After several of these visits, which were costly, Griffiths started correcting faults himself. He had watched and questioned the factory mechanics and had already grasped the fundamentals of our radio sets.

[1] W/T – wireless telegraphy in which the morse code was used.
[2] R/T – radio telephony allowing speech.
[3] Written before introduction of blind landing system.

I accordingly asked him if he would undertake a month's course at the Standard Radio Corporation's workshops if it could be arranged. He agreed and he took the maintenance course in London. On his return, he set up his own radio shop and carried out an efficient maintenance service until Theo. Goulden joined us a year or so later. Goulden also knew radio backwards and was a great asset to our company.

Griffiths had learned in a month what would have taken an ordinary person 12 months to acquire. He stayed with me until we were nationalised, after World War II, and within a few months under very difficult conditions left the nationalised corporation and joined Rolls-Royce at Hillhead near Renfrew.

Under the new maintenance arrangement, it was not long before it became apparent that Pugh and George Griffiths were out of tune with each other. It was, therefore, with great reluctance on my part, that Pugh was asked to find another job. In view of the loyal service he had given me to date, I had insisted that he should be kept on with Highland Airways until he could find an alternative and satisfactory appointment. He had done a good job for me and we parted good friends. I was sorry to see him go.

One day, it was announced in the Aberdeen press that Mr. Gandar Dower at Dyce Airport had floated an air operating company known as Aberdeen Airways Limited. It appeared that the so-called 'Gentleman's Agreement' which I had previously discussed the year before in the Caledonian Hotel was not going to be kept. Press announcements indicated this concern intended to operate alongside us on the Aberdeen-Kirkwall run and ultimately on the Shetland service. Our agents in Shetland informed us that Aberdeen Airways representatives had been making enquiries in Shetland, and in fact, had been trying to wrest the Sumburgh landing-ground from us by approaching the Sumburgh Estate Manager, Mr. W. Laidlaw MacDougall. They met with a rebuff as Mr. MacDougall remained loyal to Highland Airways.

Up to the middle of March, I spent a lot of my time at Kintore, overseeing the building of Kintore Airfield and the hangar which was to house our first Rapide on order for the Aberdeen-Kirkwall-Shetland run. During the middle of the month, Provost Smith of Stornoway along with Councillor Alistair MacKenzie, who subsequently became Provost, and a Miss Margaret McIvor, arrived in Inverness from the south and booked a charter flight over to Stornoway. I flew them over in the Monospar, landing on a tidal basin alongside the golf course at low tide. Work had previously been carried out to enable the aircraft to be taxied up to the golf club above high tide. Having picketed the aircraft down, I accompanied the passengers into town and spent four days with the Council, with the aid of Provost Smith and Baillie MacKenzie, trying to get them to move and start construction of an airfield on the golf course. They had control over the golf club but seemed either shy or afraid to use it. At the end of four days, I had not got any further, and as I had passengers for the return journey, took off for Inverness with a Mr. Hooper, a chartered accountant, and friends, who were resident in Inverness. Incidentally, Mr. Hooper was the first business man to fly from Inverness to Stornoway some months before, when he chartered the monoplane *Inverness* for the journey. It turned out that he had regular audits to do in Stornoway and as it only took him 50 minutes by air compared to all day and night by train and steamer, he found it a business proposition to charter a plane. We made many trips together.

I returned to Stornoway in April, having previously advertised a five-day visit for the purpose of giving short flights to cultivate air mindedness amongst the population of Lewis. I used the hard beach for this exercise, and operated between tides. I took my chief engineer George Griffiths over with me and we had a very successful tour carrying 250 passengers in three days' operations.

The result of the month's operations to Stornoway, and the frequent use being made of that very small runway on the tidal basin for charter flights, confirmed without doubt that an Inverness-Stornoway air connection would be a success. I still had not solved the problem of getting all the interested parties involved in the golf course to come to some common agreement over the alterations and the payment for carrying out the levelling and draining work required.

By the end of April, our airfield at Kintore was ready for operations and we shifted over from the old field at Seaton and started our summer service to Kirkwall some three weeks later.

We were worried about the competition which would begin almost immediately, as at that time there was not really sufficient traffic available for one airline, let alone two. The public had to be educated to this new form of travel and they still clung to slower sea transport. What were we to do? It was disgusting luck that we had spent so much time and money pioneering this route only to have a second party 'horn in' on us, thus depriving us of the chance of running this service, if not at a profit, at least not at a loss. I knew we were well backed by the North of Scotland Shipping Company, but there was no knowing how long they would be prepared to help subsidise a service which was losing money. On the other hand, the shipping company knew that if we withdrew and left the Aberdeen-Kirkwall run to the Dyce operators, they would gradually strip the sea route of their passenger traffic, so the result would be as broad as it was long for them.

In early April, we received an enquiry from United Airways Ltd., whose Headquarters were at Blackpool and London. They were backed by the wealthy Whitehall Securities Corporation, and wished to know whether we would be interested in joining their organisation but still retaining our identity.

We were interested in the enquiry and the matter was discussed at length by our directors. We came to the conclusion that a merger with such an influential concern might be the answer to our problem *vis-à-vis* the threat of competition from Aberdeen Airways Ltd. I was authorised to write and ask for an appointment suggesting Glasgow as the meeting place. A date was ultimately arranged and Mr. R. Donald our chairman and myself as managing director flew down in the Monospar to Glasgow on 1st May 1935, for a meeting in the Central Hotel with two directors of United Airways Ltd. We booked in for the night and awaited the arrival of the United Airways' representatives. They flew up from Blackpool arriving late in the afternoon at Renfrew. Mr. W. D. Roberts led the deputation, supported by Mr. A. R. Ballardie, the secretary to Whitehall Securities. The discussion began before dinner and carried on right through the meal and for quite a while after. Mr. Roberts opened with a general survey of the internal airways situation and described the picture they had in mind for future operations. We in turn presented our views and spoke from strength as far as the extreme North of Scotland was concerned. We possessed the airfields, mail and newspaper contracts and at that moment all the passengers and their goodwill. United Airways appreciated our desire to retain our identity and both Mr. Roberts and Mr. Ballardie thought it a good thing, since the name of Highland Airways now meant something to the travelling public, having created and established a feeling of goodwill. At that juncture, we hied ourselves down to a magnificent dinner in the 'Malmaison', as the guests of our visitors. On top of the whisky, the wine flowed in abundance, and both Donald and myself felt that there was little doubt that we were up against two men who could easily see us under the table. It was imperative to keep fit for the final discussion after dinner so we resisted the wine. After dinner we went upstairs to the lounge and, over coffee, got down to final business.

Mr. Roberts did most of the talking while his friend gave advice, when needed. I instinctively liked Roberts and Ballardie, and I could see that they were interested in our proposition. They definitely wanted us in their orbit – I could feel that – and for that matter, we wanted them to help combat the war that was building up in the north.

"Well, Mr. Donald," Roberts said when our talks drew to a close, "how much do you want for a majority shareholding in Highland Airways?"

Without hesitation he named a figure which would give our shareholders a 50 per cent profit.

"We weren't thinking as high as that," said Roberts, "won't you come down a bit?"

"No," said Donald firmly, "we don't have to sell but we would like to have you with us, providing you are willing to offer a worthwhile figure. We hold all the airfields. I think our offer very reasonable."

There was a long pause, Roberts looked up at his friend Ballardie, "I'm afraid Ballardie, we've wasted a good dinner," he said.

"Looks like it," said Ballardie gloomily.

We talked on for a bit longer and having thanked them for a very nice dinner, suggested we would be off to bed as we had to make an early start for Aberdeen in the morning. Mr. Roberts then suggested that we put our offer to them in writing, along with an undertaking that we were willing to sell on the understanding that we would continue to operate the North of Scotland routes under our own management.

"If you will do that, we will then put the proposal to our principals, Whitehall Securities, and will let you have our final answer at an early date."

We retired to bed jubilant. There was little doubt that the offer would be confirmed and new vistas would be open to us; we would be able to join up with the southern end of the group by operating a service to Glasgow, which would in turn, join up with a network throughout England, the Channel Islands and the Continent; and most important, we should be in a very strong position to combat the Dyce competition.

Our board approved our negotiations and our offer was duly sent. We received a reply by the third week in May accepting our terms.

We now felt more than ready to go into action and the whole of our attention was turned to making our company the predominating air carrier between Glasgow and Shetland. Our first move was to build the up-to-date maintenance workshops at Inverness and to substitute D.H.89 Rapides for our D.H.84 Dragon aircraft. To do this we would also require new hangarage at Inverness as the new type of aircraft did not have folding wings like the D.H.84, and so our existing sheds were not of sufficient span. However, the old sheds converted nicely into workshops and so were not wasted. In those sheds we soon built up a first-class organisation under George Griffiths' direction and our spare stores were the best that could be obtained. We wanted for nothing, down to the last bolt. Also, we added an engine test bench with instruments which enabled us to carry out our complete engine overhauls and we could repair any damage that our aircraft might sustain. Up to now, all this work had had to be sent to the south and not only was the transport expensive, but a lot of valuable time was wasted.

We took on further engineers to cope with the extra work, two of whom were outstanding. A. MacLennan, who came from around Fochabers, was an expert woodworker and he became the foreman of aircraft repairs. The other, Bert Farminer, had been brought up in aviation. When a boy of 14, he had joined the Tom Sopwith sheds at Brooklands in 1912. What he did not know about rotary engines was not worth knowing.

On 31st May, I duly reported to Hendon for the Instrument Flying test. The aircraft on which the test was to be carried out, was a Lynx-Avro with a hood over the rear seat which I occupied. In the rear seat was an R.A.F. instructor, who put me through the mill. On landing he pronounced me as competent and said the Air Ministry would be notified regarding the endorsement of my Transport Licence.

Towards the end of July we received notification from the Air Ministry that Major Mealing and Mr. Duncan from the Signals Department in London were visiting us with a view to siting the radio stations along the air route. I met them in Aberdeen and flew them up to Shetland and Kirkwall. Major Mealing approved the Sumburgh landing-field and Mr. Duncan in striped trousers, bowler hat and umbrella, to the great amusement of the locals, wandered around the bleak Shetland countryside looking for a position to site the radio station. Major Mealing said that he always did that, and was quite impervious to the amusement which he caused to the locals. The radio site chosen did not turn out to be very practical, because it was washed away the first season and had to be moved to higher ground. On the way back to Kirkwall, the weather was far from good, we had to negotiate a big fog bank off Fair Isle. Major Mealing said he could quite understand why we were so insistent on having radio service on this inhospitable portion of the North Sea. I could guess how he was feeling, as of course we were flying on dead reckoning and if the fog got worse over Orkney, it would not be easy to locate Kirkwall. However, we arrived all right in Kirkwall with the conviction of our Air Ministry officials fully behind us on the need for radio communication, and they used their influence to speed matters up on their return to London.

We stayed the night in Kirkwall and flew on to Thurso next morning, as Major Mealing wished to look at a site that Aberdeen Airways had chosen to use as a landing-field, and desired to obtain a licence for. We had flight tested that field a year before, but turned it down as being unsafe. He was not very impressed but a licence was ultimately granted. The run was very short and only one runway at that, east to west. A year or so afterwards, there were some nasty incidents on that air strip involving a complete write-off of one aeroplane. It was raining heavily at this field, which was about three miles from Thurso on the Castletown main Wick road. We had given up using Thurso, as we could not find a safe airfield to operate from.

After Major Mealing had completed his work, we went into Thurso to see James Wilson who owned the Royal Hotel.

"Hello, Captain Fresson," he said when he saw me, "glad to see you. What brings you here?"

I introduced my companions and when he heard that their visit was in connection with providing Thurso with a landing strip he was elated.

"Come in gentlemen," and he took us into the lounge and said, "you must be a bit dry after a hard morning's work. Waiter, bring three large whiskies and soda."

Major Mealing's face took on a sudden warmth. We chatted a while and went in to lunch. Mr. Wilson had started life selling ginger-beer and aerated water from a barrow and he now owned the Royal Hotel, which he had recently extended and almost completely rebuilt with accommodation for over 100 guests.

As the years went by, the coaches came north every summer in ever increasing numbers and Mr. Wilson was rapidly becoming a very wealthy man. He was naturally, also keen to build up an air passenger clientele and he was looking to Aberdeen Airways to provide these passengers. I had told Mr. Wilson repeatedly that Highland Airways would provide all the air communication he required, provided the council would construct a reasonable airfield which we would hire from them. This never came about although there was an effort made around 1938 which fell through. We had searched the Thurso area very thoroughly but had been unable to find a large enough field which would give the safety margin we required. That afternoon we flew back to Inverness in time for my friends to catch the half past four train to London.

Mr. Duncan was looking out of the carriage window waiting for the train to start.

"I'll do all I can, Fresson, to get the Inverness-Kirkwall and Shetland radio stations under way," he said. "You certainly need them on that route. It's a wonder how you have flown so regularly and without accident for so long without such aids."

"I must admit, it has been pretty soul-destroying at times," I said.

Major Mealing then said that he and Duncan would be up again later on.

"I want to go over that Stornoway site with you, so we'll meet again soon."

With this build-up of evidence, I was hoping that Major Mealing would be able to make some impression on the Councillors and loosen up their pockets when he returned. But as will be seen, I hoped in vain. It appeared that the local rulers were still sold on the uneconomic flying-boat service, which they hoped to obtain without any cash outlay. They were hoping some other company would come along and solve this situation. But they waited in vain – our services were running to good capacity from Aberdeen. The distance of Kintore from the town did not seem to deter the passengers. Inverness planes were invariably filled to full capacity, what with rapidly increasing mail and newspaper supplies. We were now permitted to carry outside newspapers, the second year's *Scotsman* contract having terminated.

The merger with United Airways brought us into working agreement with Northern & Scottish Airways Limited, Renfrew, which succeeded Mr. John Sword's company, Midland & Scottish Air Ferries at the end of 1934. George Nicholson was the managing director and William Cumming was their very able secretary. Already, I knew them well. They operated the air services from Renfrew to Campbeltown and Islay and were beginning to extend northwards to the Outer Hebrides, Barra, South and North Uist, and hoping, like ourselves, finally to link up with Stornoway. So they were also an interested party in the establishment of an airfield there. We had both discussed the question of a seaplane service with Mr. Roberts of United Airways. He thought we should survey the route in a flying-boat and as the company were connected with Saunders-Roe of Cowes, Isle of Wight, who built small flying-boats, it was agreed that an amphibian would be made available and sent up to Renfrew as the kicking-off point.

One morning my phone rang.

"Hello, Fresson, is that you? This is George Nicholson, Renfrew," a voice said.

"Yes, George," I answered.

"We've just got word that Saunders-Roe are sending up the *Cloud of Iona* with Captain Scott in charge and Captain McIntosh (ex-Imperial Airways) as second in command."

"That's fine," I said, "when do they arrive?"

"Over the week-end, and we intend setting off for the west coast on Monday after lunch. Can you come along?"

"Certainly, I can and will," I answered. "I'll meet you at the airport club, in time for lunch."

I arrived by air at half past twelve, and the *Cloud of Iona* was sitting on the tarmac, ready for us. I made for George Nicholson's office and instantly recognised Captain Scott. With him was Captain McIntosh whose name I knew well. He was one of the 1920's pilots who had designs for flying the Atlantic from East to West.

We took off after lunch, Captain Scott and McIntosh in the front

134

cockpit and George and myself in the cabin, which seated six persons. It was a cloud-free afternoon and we climbed high to cross over the lower Argyll Mountains to reach the coast at the north end of the island of Islay. I was invited up to the cockpit after a while and Captain McIntosh went back and sat with George Nicholson. What a wonderful sight it was; I had never seen that part of the coast before. The broken coastline and innumerable inlets and small lochs, the blue sea in the distance and the heather coloured mountains under-neath looked superb. On reaching the sea, we turned northwards and flew up to Mallaig, where we alighted on the water, the wheels having been wound up. We looked for a sheltered bay, but there was nothing within ten miles of the next opening to the north. I jotted down Captain Scott's report on the Mallaig landing, and we took-off again, this time headed for Kyle of Lochalsh. Soon the famous Cuillen Mountains came into sight in the far distance and we dropped off height with the islands of Muck and Eigg coming up on our port side. Soon we ran into the Sound of Sleat with Loch Hourn on our right. In front of us the mountains, some 2,000 feet high on each side of the Sound, seemed to converge into a tiny gap like the eye of a needle as we approached. On we flew, and the mountains appeared to be touching each wing. Suddenly, we were over the Kylerhea ferry and the horizon opened up, and turning to the left there was Kyle of Lochalsh, directly ahead. What a breath-taking trip that had been, with the clear sky and sun shining on the mountains in the south-west.

We circled the port and as there was no shipping abroad, made a perfect landing opposite the hotel. We tied the 'boat up to one of the wharves and scrambled ashore. We checked with the port authorities that the flying-boat would be safe for the night where we had moored her, and with our suitcases in our hands, made for the hotel and booked in for the night.

"Kyle of Lochalsh," said Captain Scott, "would be very suitable for flying-boat operations, but there was a big hazard caused by the flotsam and jetsam floating in the water. It would need a motor launch to patrol a sea lane for each landing."

A very expensive proposition, I thought.

We found the hotel to be very well furbished and the flight had given us a thirst so we retired to the bar, and planned our operations for the morrow. We decided to fly up to Portree, make a landing in the harbour, if possible, and then cut across the centre of Skye and over to Dunvegan Head and across to Loch Maddy. From there we decided we would make for Stornoway that night. Such were our

plans but it did not work out that way. We retired to bed early after
a very good dinner and agreed to meet for an eight-thirty breakfast.

Next morning at breakfast, I had a nasty feeling when I observed
the type of clouds hanging around that there was a depression
advancing on us. Captains Scott and McIntosh arrived and they
were of the same opinion as myself regarding the weather. We
hurried our breakfast and decided to get on the move as soon as
possible. We took off at around half past nine and headed up the
Sound and across the lower end of Raasay Island into the Sound of
Raasay. The overcast was undoubtedly getting lower, the further
north we went. We pulled in to Portree Harbour and flew around a
bit looking for suitable sea lanes and dropped down in the harbour
and went ashore. Our flying-boat was no stranger here as the Duke
of Hamilton had given joy rides in the *Cloud of Iona* at Portree the
year before and had taken up a large number of passengers.

We got on the phone to Lochmaddy for an actual weather report
and it was bad. Cloud base estimated 400 feet, one mile visibility,
heavy rain and a south-westerly wind blowing at least 40 m.p.h.
Captain Scott asked me if I knew the coastline over the other
side.

"A bit," I said, "I have landed at North Uist once."

"What do you think of making an effort?"

"If you can get clear of Skye without having to go into cloud," I said, "I think we can make it, but it is going to be hellish bumpy."

"Right oh," said Scotty, as he was known to his friends, "let's get going." By the time we were airborne the wind had freshened a lot and we headed up the valley to Carbost and then up Loch Snizort, hoping to cut across the Vaternish Peninsula at Loch Losait. The air was getting very rough and we were just skimming the base of the clouds at 400 feet. We scraped through to Ardmore Point with the hull of the boat just about kissing the peat. And on that five miles, Captain McIntosh had to help at the dual controls to keep the 'boat right way up the turbulence was so great. George and I were strapped into our seats. I gave Captain Scott a course for Weavers Point Lighthouse at the entrance to Loch Maddy 16 miles away. The wind was now at gale force from the west and the sea was running high. As we only cruised at around 90 m.p.h. I estimated we were not doing more than 45 m.p.h. against the gale over the sea. I calculated we would pick up the coast in about 24 minutes. The visibility had now dropped to not more than half a mile and we flew on into the storm, still being thrown all over the sky. I didn't like it so low down, we appeared to be only 100 feet above the raging waves. Almost to the minute, we picked up the coast of Uist and a few minutes later our lighthouse hove in sight and we turned into Loch Maddy. There the sea was protected by the land and was calmer. We landed in front of the pier. Although the water was sheltered here, nevertheless the flying-boat was being rocked quite a bit. We made signs to some fishermen standing on the wharf. Shortly a motorboat put out, towed us to a safe mooring and then took us ashore. It had taken us a little over 40 minutes to fly the 40 miles from Portree. It had seemed like two hours and I was glad to be down.

The storm grew fiercer and by the afternoon there was a gale of around 60 m.p.h. blowing and the rain was coming down in sheets. There was nothing we could do so we sat down in the hotel lounge and played poker.

As I have said there is no accounting for the weather on the west coast, it can change so quickly. So, next morning, Captain Scott was surprised to see the sun shining again and the wind down to a respectable 20 knots from the North West. We got going soon after breakfast and made several landings off Lochmaddy Wharf. It was quite good for seaplanes but here again there was flotsam, consisting of cans and shore debris. We concluded that the landings would have to be effected some miles away from the village where the water was cleaner and the flying-boat would then have to taxi to the pier to discharge and pick up passengers.

We left for Stornoway around eleven in the morning, and covered the 58 miles in just under the hour. There was a fair headwind to contend with. However, the turbulence had subsided and we had a pleasant flight. We landed in the bay at Stornoway and were soon ashore. I took my friends along to see Kenny Ross at the Caledonian and introduced them. George Nicholson had not met him; he hadn't as yet, apparently, got so far north with his plans.

"Well, Captain Fresson," said Kenny, "it's a surprise seeing you land here in a flying-boat."

"Yes, Kenny, it sure must be, but we are trying the route out from the seaplane angle, as we cannot make any headway with an airfield."

"Come along in, gentlemen," said Kenny Ross, "no one comes to Stornoway without a good welcome."

We were soon sitting down to a series of rounds, waiting for lunch to be served.

After we had eaten, I took Scott and McIntosh along with George, to see the golf links where I usually landed. We walked the whole area over and there was no doubt whatsoever in the minds of our friends that here was the answer to the problem. It was definitely a landplane route.

"Stornoway Harbour was too unprotected from high winds for seaplane work," Captain Scott told me.

I went along and saw one or two of my councillor friends and told them that we had tried out the seaplane possibility, but we wouldn't take it on, so the sooner they got busy building their airfield the sooner they would get an air service, which everyone by now knew, had to come.

We left at around four in the afternoon and headed over the Minch to Ullapool and amidst great excitement of the villagers, alighted off the pier in calm water. The whole village turned out. It was the first time they had seen a flying-boat. The tide was low and we had a difficult scramble to the top of the pier and hied ourselves over to the Royal Hotel for tea. Captain Scott thought the facilities at Ullapool good for a seaplane but I doubted it in high winds, as I knew to my cost how fierce the gusts were at the bottom of those hills opposite.

After tea, we took off from Loch Broom after quite a long run as the water was fairly smooth, climbing up to the Braemore Pass and then down the valley to Garve. I shivered to think what would

138

happen if one engine failed over that rough and rocky terrain, because that 'boat would not hold height on one motor.

We flew around Inverness and decided to land on Longman airfield instead of the Firth, as there were no boats available or suitable moorings. So down went the wheels and we made a smooth touchdown on our home airfield. George Nicholson decided to return by the night train to Glasgow as he had no interest in the northern operations and next day my wife took his place.

We left after lunch for Kirkwall. Captain Scott was not too certain of getting the *Cloud of Iona* off the Longman airfield with us on board, so he took off alone and landed in the Beauly Firth. He taxied up to a broken-down pier at Clachnaharry and we crept over the rickety structure, and somehow or other got aboard. Again the weather was good with little wind, but there was a slight swell on the sea and that helped a quick take-off. We headed north, and flying at a high altitude we passed Helmsdale. Captain Scott was behind in the cabin with my wife and myself and Captain McIntosh was piloting. My wife commented that this was the way to fly.

"A landing ground as far as you can see," she murmured.

She had barely got the words out of her mouth, when a terrific report occurred and the plane started to vibrate dangerously. Captain Scott, who was sitting alongside me on the port side with his feet up on the front seat, leapt out as if shot from a gun, disappeared through the narrow entrance to the cockpit and was in his seat in a matter of seconds. In the meantime, McIntosh had shut off both motors and was diving towards the sea. We had just passed Wick and had lost a lot of altitude, when Scott opened up the port motor full bore and eased the nose of the plane up to the horizontal. McIntosh shouted to me to come forward.

"Is there a sheltered bay near here?" he asked.

"Yes," I answered, "Sinclair's Bay, about three miles ahead." He passed the information on to Scott. We were losing height slowly and it was anybody's guess whether we would reach the Bay. We shot by Duncansby Head Lighthouse and landed about a mile off the sandy shore to the west. I was then told that the airscrew on the starboard motor had parted with the top of a blade, which completely upset the balance of the motor. In cases like that, it has been known for the motor to be torn from its mounting by the damaged airscrew. We could not taxi towards the shore on one motor because we only went round in circles.

"What's to be done," said Scott, "can you see a boat around?"

We searched the horizon without any success.

"Have you got a hack-saw in the tool kit?" I enquired.

"I don't know," he said, "have a look Mac, will you?"

A search fortunately produced one.

"What are you going to do with that?" queried Scott.

"Saw the unbroken propeller blade down to the same length as the damaged blade," I said. "That will reduce the vibration and you might then get enough power from the starboard engine to enable you to taxi ashore."

Mack and I clambered on to the starboard wing, where the engine was mounted, and got down to sawing about a foot off the sound propeller blade. That done, we scrambled back and Scott started up the motor. The vibration was considerably reduced and by running the starboard motor twice as fast as the port engine, the 'boat got under way and we steered for the shore. There was some vibration, but not enough to worry about. We cast anchor some 50 feet from shore, in about two and a half feet of water. The beach was desolate and a long way from help. We held a council of war. It was decided that I should take my trousers and shoes off and wade ashore and see if I could find a cottager who might be able to help us. About half a mile inland I found one and the owner came back to the shore with me. Captain Scott asked him if he could get some men to help pull the *Cloud of Iona* up above the tide, if he let the wheels down. The man said he thought he could find half a dozen bodies and went off. In the meantime a crowd seemed to appear from nowhere – the feminine sex predominating. Scott asked me to take the ship's papers and our baggage ashore. I only had short aertex pants on, and in this garb started a number of trips to the beach. I took my wife ashore on my back on the first trip, and then went backwards and forwards for the rest of the gear. After a while I noticed the crowd began to shriek with laughter as I turned to make for shore. This went on for a few trips when Captain Scott told me what was wrong. Unbeknown to me, my pants had slipped quite a bit and I had been creating quite a diversion with the women onlookers. My last trip out was to collect my trousers, shoes, socks and jacket. As I turned towards the seaplane, I noticed it turning around, and before I could reach it, it was moving out to sea with my clothes aboard. A small fishing boat had come up behind while I was ashore and Scott had arranged for them to tow the seaplane back to Wick Harbour, I learned afterwards.

Here was a fine predicament. I was practically naked, and stranded on the beach. There was no transport, and the John O'Groat's road was a mile away across the marshes. Gwen took off a woolly jumper she had on and I covered my shoulders. It was beginning to get chilly. I couldn't stay on the beach all night, so decided we would have to make for the road; one of the crofters said he would raise a car to take us into the Station Hotel at Wick, some six miles away. It was rough going for my bare feet and I was grateful when the road was reached. Within a matter of minutes the car arrived and we set off. On arrival at the Station Hotel entrance, there were three elderly ladies sitting in the sun porch. There was nothing to do, but to make a dash for it. I told my wife to go in and arrange for a room for the night and I followed her in my semi-nudity. When the three ladies saw me, they let out a trinity of squeals and held their hands high in the air in seeming horror. Could it be, they had never seen such a scantily clothed male before? I was past them in a flash, leaving them in a state of complete hysterics, genuine or otherwise I never found out. That was a good story for Wick, and I heard about it for a long time afterwards.

The result of that experience was that I caught a severe chill and was confined to bed for a couple of days. On the morning of my recovery, an engineer arrived with a spare airscrew, by air from Renfrew, and he proceeded to the harbour where the *Cloud of Iona* had been towed to set about changing the damaged propeller. It was ready by a little after noon. Now came the problem of getting the plane off the water. It was too rough outside the harbour and the length of run inside to the narrow opening in the harbour groyne was not much more than 300 yards. With the aid of a slight wind from the east, Captain Scott thought he could make it alone and with a small petrol load. So we had to hunt around for cans to drain petrol off. This accomplished, the motors were started and well warmed up. The seaplane was then pulled right up to the jetty. We held our breath as the motors were opened up and the seaplane started to gather way. If Captain Scott failed to clear the concrete groyne on the far side of the harbour he faced certain death in a terrific crash. He headed for the centre of the entrance through the groyne but as there were not more than a few feet clearance each side of the wings, it was unlikely he could pass through the eye of such a small needle. He had to be off before he got there. Nearer and nearer he got. We all held our breath.

Gwen said, "He's going to crash."

I thought so too, but he just made it. The boat came off about 40 yards before the groyne and cleared it with a good ten feet to spare. We all felt limp as we walked back to the hotel. I phoned Kirkwall and told the traffic officer to send the Dragon we had stationed there, over to Wick to take us to Kirkwall that afternoon. With that done, McIntosh thought we were due for a little 'pick-me-up' and Gwen and I agreed. Also I thought it would help the chill along that I was throwing off.

After lunch, we went up to Hillhead field and waited for Captain Rae, who was resident pilot at Kirkwall, to arrive. We had not long to wait and we were in Kirkwall within the hour. We found Scott and the *Cloud of Iona* waiting for us on the Wideford airfield.

"That was a narrow shave," I said to Scotty, "I didn't think you were going to make it."

"I felt," he said, "after I had covered half the run that she would just make it, otherwise, I should have shut off and postponed the take-off until the sea outside had calmed down sufficiently."

"Yes," I agreed, "an experienced pilot can usually tell if his aircraft is going to get out of a tight place. We often have the same problem here at Wideford, when the ground is soft and muddy in the winter."

We planned next day, Sunday, to fly up to Fair Isle and Shetland, and have a look round. That night I was not feeling so well again, the temperature came back and I was laid up next morning, to my great annoyance. I really wanted to have a go at landing on Fair Isle, or at least on the sea adjacent to it. Scotty said he had to return south next day and so it was that day or never, so he and McIntosh set off on their own. They were back at lunch time. The weather was not good, a heavy sea was running off Fair Isle which made landing impossible and the wind was rapidly gaining strength, so they decided to call the Shetland section off. They left next morning for the south. So we bid each other goodbye. They were a couple of really nice guys. Scottie and McIntosh both insisted we should look them up when we next ventured down to London,

"Don't forget," were their parting words.

We promised we would, but we never saw them again.

We returned home on the afternoon service a couple of days later and my first job back in Inverness was to communicate with the Stornoway Town Clerk in writing and ask him to advise his Council that they could wash out any idea of a seaplane service as far as we were concerned and to request him to try again and get some solution to constructing the golf course airfield. It didn't do any good; they just withdrew into their shells and still did nothing. There was no escaping the fact that the onus would be on us if we were to establish an air connection to Stornoway, so we too decided to sit on the fence and await events.

On 3rd March 1936, the Inverness radio station was ready for testing and Kirkwall was ready a few days after. I carried out the air to ground tests which were completed within the week, and the stations were ready to go into service the second week of March. What an enormous difference that made to our flying technique. The whole character of our flying changed in bad visibility. We were now able to climb to a safe height which would put us well above any mountains along the route and home straight on our destination. More often than not, we got above the clouds at 5,000 feet in winter and at other times we settled down to fly through them.

In May 1936, we advertised the commencement of our Shetland run on 3rd June. A few days before that date an advertisement appeared in the Aberdeen and Shetland press announcing the opening of a similar service by our competitors the day before we were advertised to start. I immediately wrote to Aberdeen Airways, Dyce, a letter pointing out that Sumburgh airfield was not open until 3rd June, and refusing them permission to land until the airfield was officially opened. Foolishly, I did not send Jim Black our Sumburgh agent instructions to immobilise the airfield by placing obstacles over the landing area. I don't think, at that date, we had fully appreciated the type of forceful competition we were up against. Our letter went unanswered and an Aberdeen Airways plane landed at Sumburgh with passengers the day before we were due to start, thus jumping our wicket and claiming to be the first company to operate the Aberdeen-Shetland service. The public reacted to that one with unconcealed disgust, but there were people in Shetland who appeared pleased, especially some of their Councillors, who seemed to discount completely the work I had put into organising the Shetland route, and the time and money spent on its development by Highland Airways.

However, we had the advantage of being able to place a Rapide aircraft on that run which the competing company were apparently unable to match at the time. The speed of the Rapide and its extra safety over the stormy open sea leg, plus the more efficient heating system installed in the plane, appealed to the public, and we did not suffer very much from loss of traffic, at least to begin with. We were to be subjected to another jolt the following year and this time the shaft was an official one.

Our Shetland service from Kintore airfield commenced on 3rd June with myself as pilot. We had a full load of passengers and the weather was good. Climbing to 6,000 feet we reached Sumburgh, by way of Kirkwall, in one hour forty-five minutes. There was a representative gathering to welcome us at Sumburgh airfield, including some members of the Shetland County Council. The Rapide proved itself splendidly on that run. Its rate of climb was very much faster than the Dragon, likewise its cruising speed, and the cabin was better upholstered, so much so that the passengers made a point of expressing their appreciation. Captain Adam Smith piloted the return flight. I stayed over in Shetland with my very good friends Mr. and Mrs. Bertie Ganson, whose firm represented us in Lerwick and provided the road transport to and from Sumburgh airfield, some 25 miles from Lerwick.

We now had three very skilled pilots who maintained the services close on 100 per cent. I now had less time for flying, as the management was developing into a full-time job, so I discontinued regular service work. However, I acted as relief pilot along the routes, when needed, and attended to all the charter flights, which were numerous, involving journeys as far afield as London, Edinburgh, Glasgow and Stornoway. The latter town was becoming a very busy leg. Around this time, I stepped up the North Isles and trans-Pentland service by stationing an aircraft at Kirkwall, plus a resident pilot and engineer. This aircraft became very busy and operated a late Kirkwall-Shetland flight, in addition to the morning service. Commercial travellers found it convenient to fly up late in the day to Shetland from Orkney which enabled them to begin their work early the following morning. Conversely, travellers from Shetland took advantage of the return flight, to position themselves in Orkney ready for the following day. There were also a number of private ambulance flights cropping up from time to time, and this arrangement found favour with the Orkney County medical authorities, who made full use of being able to transport dangerous cases rapidly to Aberdeen Hospital.

CHAPTER EIGHT

EARLY in March 1937 we received the first ambulance call from Stornoway. It was for a sick person arriving from hospital in the south, who wished to avoid the long rail and steamer journey across the Minch. The patient was comfortably flown over from Inverness in 50 minutes. The chairs had been taken out of the cabin and a mattress placed on the floor and made into a comfortable bed. Certainly the hard beach at low tide and the tidal basin alongside the golf course had proved their worth as emergency landing facilities over the past three years and demonstrated conclusively how necessary an airport was for Stornoway.

I stayed the night and took the opportunity of calling on the Stornoway Trust Committee accompanied by the Provost and Town Clerk, who owned the ground of the Melbost Golf Course. In all, I had made not less than 50 chartered flights between Inverness and Stornoway up to that time, and at last the value and the necessity of air travel had begun to penetrate the minds of those who had the control of the only land which was suitable for the construction of an airfield. Resulting from that discussion, we had at last got them to concede that they were prepared to release the golf course, or that portion of it which would be required for the construction of an airfield.

At the end of March, we were booked to fly the Secretary of State for Scotland, Sir Walter Elliot, and his advisers to Wick, Kirkwall and Sumburgh, and return. Mrs. Elliot and Dr. Shearer of the Ministry of Health were amongst the party. It was the first time that a Scottish Secretary had ever used air transport to visit the out-lying boundaries of Scotland and the flight thus created history. I found Sir Walter and his wife charming people, and after his trip with us he became a regular supporter of the future development of Scottish air travel. I later learned that the decision to fly was made after a rough trip in the fishery cruiser aboard which the party had set out from Edinburgh to Inverness. It was a fine day. We flew high and the air was calm, so Sir Walter and party had every reason to suppose that air transport was not only faster, but more comfortable than rolling about in a ship at sea.

145

Our traffic on the long-distance sections was now increasing. Many more bookings were being made by residents in the south and it was evident to me that railway influence with travel agents all over the country was making it difficult for would-be southern passengers to book at their local travel agents on our routes. That state of affairs could mean loss of business. There appeared to be an agreement between the travel agencies and the railways, prohibiting them from effecting bookings which were not approved by the railways, and our company, so far, had not been approved. So all southern bookings had to be made the hard way, that is, by letter, telegram or telephone to Inverness. We then either had to send the tickets on to the would-be passenger, or hold them for their arrival. It also meant that passengers had to remit the value of the reservations made direct to us. All this lengthy and irritating procedure could be avoided if the railway authorities could be persuaded to authorise travel agencies to book for us.

I decided to tackle the matter, and wrote to the Superintendent of Traffic at the L.M.S. Railway Headquarters at Euston, enquiring whether they could see their way to accommodating us, and expressing my willingness to call on them to discuss this matter, should they desire to see me. In due course a reply came back, intimating that one of their senior executives, Mr. W. P. Bradbury, would be glad to discuss the matter I had raised, if I would call on a certain date at his Euston office. At the appointed time I was ushered into Mr. Bradbury's office, and after shaking hands, he introduced me to another person by the name of Wing Commander Measures. At that time, the British railway group were about to float an air company to be known as Railway Air Services and the Wing Commander had been appointed as their air superintendent. Accordingly, he was there to take part in the discussion to protect the new rail air company's interests. Mr. Bradbury was a tall man of lean stature and appeared very human and pleasant. We were later, destined to become very close friends.

Mr. Bradbury opened the discussion by saying that they had considered the Highland Airways letter regarding the travel agency bookings but that they found some difficulty in granting permission, in view of the fact that we were in direct competition with the railway, which ran from Inverness to Wick and Thurso, and which, incidentally, before the air service started, carried all the Orkney traffic to those ports.

"That is so," I suggested, "but if the public wish to use the faster mode of transport, they will fly irrespective of your withholding booking facilities and that doesn't help you; in fact, it only creates public resentment towards the L.M.S."

He appeared slightly taken aback at that interpretation of the position.

"What about the Inverness-Glasgow service the press report that you are about to commence?" he enquired. "Will you want the same facilities for that run?"

"Certainly," I replied, "if you are prepared to grant them, but for the moment I am chiefly concerned with the traffic north from Inverness."

He went into a huddle with the Wing Commander, and finished up by telling me that they would agree to my proposal for the northern routes, but not for the Inverness-Glasgow run, should we commence to operate. I took that proviso to mean that Railway Air Services would be casting their eyes on that one, which in the end turned out to be a correct prophecy.

They said goodbye to me and I left for home, thinking that I had not done too badly for a beginning. What I did not realise then, were the far-reaching changes that were about to occur following that meeting. From Mr. Bradbury's conversation, one could read between the lines that they were very knowledgeable about our operations. I was perplexed as to where they had obtained so much information from. We found out shortly after.

For many months we had noticed a short stocky man, wearing a bowler hat, standing alongside our hangars at Longman Airport, Inverness. George Griffiths, our chief engineer had also noticed him and had called my attention to his behaviour. Day in and day out, he was always there and never missed a day, fine weather or foul. The only difference in the latter case was that he always came armed with an umbrella. He carried a pencil and notebook and always appeared to be writing. We wondered what interested him so much. Eventually, we became suspicious. No one would surely waste so much time as he did, without some purpose. I told Griffiths to put one of our boys on to following the man with the bowler hat back to town, to find out where he came from. To our astonishment, it turned out to be the railway headquarters in the Station Square. Next day, I was down at the airfield while the morning Orkney plane was being loaded and passengers going aboard. I stood a few yards away from the 'little man', where I was not too conspicuous. As soon as the mailbags were being loaded on to the plane from the trolley, he began to write. When the loading finished he stopped writing. Then the passengers came out, ready to embark. Out came the notebook and pencil again, and more writing went on as the passengers stepped aboard.

"Good gracious," I thought, "he's noting the aircraft load. What's he up to?"

I walked up to him:

"You appear to be very interested in the mail and passengers going aboard that plane?"

He turned and gave me a blank look, but said nothing.

"Why do you take the trouble to make notes of our aircraft loading?"

"Because the boss told me to," he replied.

"And who is the boss?" I interrogated.

"The Traffic Manager," he answered, "I've been told to do it every day."

"Are you working for the railway?"

"Yes," he said, "I'm in the Traffic Office."

"You've been doing that for a long time."

"Yes, over six months now, and it's jolly cold work sometimes."

"Well, little man," I said, "you've been very honest; go back to your boss and tell him we don't like the railways snooping around here. If it continues, we will have to call the police."

He scuttled off, and we never saw him or to the best of our knowledge, anybody else, taking loading notes again. So that explained it all. Those figures were being transmitted to London and Mr. Bradbury was the recipient. No wonder he could tell me a thing or two.

A year or two later, I pulled Bradbury's leg about the incident. He laughed, and then told me another story, this time against myself, which occurred at Stornoway the previous summer. He and the Wing Commander had visited the Western Isles by surface transport, spying out the land on the islands to which Northern and Scottish Airways were operating, namely Barra, South Uist and North Uist, and they had finally landed up at Stornoway, where they were checking the air potential and a possible site for an airfield. They had been told that I had spent years at that game and had decided on the Melbost Golf Course. Mr. Bradbury went on to say that one sunny afternoon they were walking around the golf course, when they espied a Rapide coming in from the East. They watched it circle the town, dropping off height.

"Do you think that plane is going to attempt a landing here, Measures?" Bradbury asked.

"No, Sir, I shouldn't think so, there's not enough level ground here for a seagull to land on."

They were standing by the golf hut in good view of the tidal basin. To their astonishment the plane approached the northern end of the basin and Measures said,

"Good God, that Rapide is going to try and land here after all; look out, there's going to be a crash."

"Isn't there a sufficient run over there?" Bradbury asked the Wing Commander, pointing at the tidal basin.

"What, for a Rapide landing at 70 m.p.h.? Not in your life, he'll never do it," he answered.

"To our utter amazement," Bradbury continued, "that pilot made a beautiful landing and with quite a bit to spare. Wing Commander Measures couldn't believe his eyes."

"My God," he said to me, "I've never seen a Rapide landed in such a small place before. Come on, let's go and quiz the pilot."

"We were both dressed as tourists," Bradbury continued, "and we went up to the pilot and had a chat with him asking him what he thought about the golf course for an airfield."

"Very good," he said, "I'm trying to get the rights, as we wish to run a service to Stornoway."

We told the pilot that we were tourists and were most interested, as the steamer and rail connections were so long and tedious.

"You made a wonderful landing with such a short runway," we said.

"Oh," the pilot said, "I'm used to that, I've done it many times before."

On hearing that the plane belonged to Highland Airways, we plied him with many more questions, couched of course in tourist language.

"Obliging chap that pilot," Bradbury said to me, "he told us all we wanted to know!"

"You're returning to Inverness this evening?" we asked.

"Yes, in about an hour's time."

"Well, we'll wait and see how you get off." He bid us goodbye and left for the town, with his passengers.

Mr. Bradbury was laughing by this time, having come to the end of his narration.

"What are you laughing at?" I enquired.

"You were the pilot," he replied.

"Good Lord," I said, as it all came back to me, "those two figures, one in a straw hat and the other with a cap, and both dressed in tweed jackets and flannel trousers. Who was your pal?" I asked.

"Wing Commander Measures," he replied.

"Well you fooled me all right," I had to admit. "I had little idea when I met you in your office for the first time, that I had actually been in conversation with you two before."

"We know," Bradbury said, "we were laughing about it after you had left."

A month or two later, we were surprised to receive a letter from United Airways, now part of British Airways, informing us that they had received overtures from Railway Air Services Ltd., who were now operating a number of air routes throughout the country, proposing a merger of Northern and Scottish Airways, Renfrew, and ourselves with the railway octopus. They asked for me and our secretary, Willie Hamilton, to attend a meeting in London to discuss the proposal. They told us that the recent formation of British Airways involved operations to the Continent, and that they, British Airways, thought a partial link-up of the internal routes to the Railways Air Service would enable them to concentrate more on their new task.

As the meeting progressed, it was obvious that there would be advantages in being tied up with such a powerful group; I had in mind again Aberdeen Airways, who were becoming a nuisance to us on the Aberdeen-Kirkwall-Shetland run. At the same time, I did not wish to lose my control of the northern routes to their air superintendent, who let alone being wholly unknowledgeable of the local requirements, had as far as I could judge no technical experience of operating aircraft. When asked for my views on such a merger, I said I was quite content to go on under the British Airways set-up. As far as I remember, George Nicholson of Northern and Scottish Airways, who was also present, expressed the same views. The problem was left to Mr. Roberts, the chairman of our board who also spoke for the new company British Airways, to settle. Willie Hamilton and I returned home and became engrossed in other matters, not giving the idea any further thought.

To my surprise two months later, in early May, I received a chit from old man Roberts, as he was known to us, saying that he would be visiting us along with Wing Commander Measures to inspect our organisation at Inverness, Wick and Kirkwall and would like to return by way of Thurso. Would I have a plane ready and stand by to fly them up. I showed the letter to Donald and Willie Hamilton.

"Looks as if they are going in with the railways after all," they said.

"Funny thing, they didn't write to us, and say what they were doing," I replied. "We can only wait and see. No doubt Mr. Roberts will wish to discuss whatever they have up their sleeve."

On their arrival, Roberts said that they had been considering the

Railway Air Services offer but that nothing would be completed until we had had an opportunity of finally discussing the matter again at boardroom level. I took our friends down to Longman in our car and they commenced to go through our sheds and stores. Measures was making criticisms of our methods – why hadn't we this and that, and why didn't we do this or that, all of which would have meant the employment of many extra bodies at heavy expense. By the time we had got to the end of our tour, I had formed the opinion that Wing Commander Measures would have us run our organisation on R.A.F. lines, but without the Government purse to pay the piper.

The weather was not very good up at Orkney. There was heavy fog over the Pentland Firth and I flew above and homed on Wideford radio station, dropping down over the sea on the north end of the airfield, and then into land with a ceiling of around 300 feet. The same process of inspection and comment went on at Wideford and at our town office, before going to lunch at the Kirkwall Hotel. We left around three o'clock for Thurso. As there was no radio at Thurso, I decided to try and fly under the fog as I didn't like to chance breaking cloud at the other end without knowing exactly where I was. As it happened, the weather was clear over there and it was a pity I didn't find that out by telephone before we left, as it would have made the flight that much easier. The trouble was, I was worried and my mind was full of doubts about getting mixed up with the railways. It was clear that they had a very different outlook on operational methods from my own. Moreover, I did not wish to lose my identity and authority to possible bureaucracy, restrictions and planning unsuitable to the requirements in our part of Britain. We had to remain flexible and British Airways had not disturbed our *status quo* in that respect. As a result, our services were increasing and we were not losing money like most of the other independent air services in the south.

Mr. Roberts said they wanted to see the Old Man of Hoy, that remarkable rock formation standing some 100 yards off the perpendicular cliffs of the island of Hoy. The pinnacle towers 100 feet or more in the air and has the features of a man's head on the top, looking out over the Pentland Firth like a sentinel. It can be readily seen from the Thurso shore on a fine day. We flew out over the township of Stromness and rounded the north end of Hoy. Very soon the Old Man came into sight and as we passed it, Mr. Roberts and the Wing Commander obtained an excellent view. We were flying a few hundred feet above the sea and within 200 feet of the Old Man's profile, and it presented a wonderful spectacle. Old man Roberts

was just saying what an extraordinary freak of nature that such a realistic profile could be carved out of the rock by the wind and rain, when we suddenly ran slap into the fog. I continued flying but now on instruments, altering course a little to the right to make sure we would miss Dunnet Head on the cliffs east of Thurso. Occasionally, there was a glimpse of the water. I expected that we should run out of it as we neared the other side. Suddenly a voice sounded in my ear,

"Doesn't look too good, does it?"

"I expect it's only local," I said.

After ten minutes, we were still in it, when the same voice came up again,

"Don't you think we had better turn back?"

I then realised, he had the wind up.

"I'll keep on a bit longer," I told him, "we can always climb above it and continue on to Inverness if the worst comes to the worst."

I took a quick look at him and his face betrayed his anxiety. My other passenger was quite demure. What a difference, I thought, between those two. Just then we flew out into the clear and we were about a mile off-shore in Scrabster Bay, making for Thurso dead on course. They spent an hour or so in Thurso, after which we left for Inverness and the south.

There were many meetings in London after that exploratory trip. Shortly afterwards, Wing Commander Measures visited us again with the intention of inspecting our arrangements at Sumburgh. By then, we had our hangar built facing south-east. Measures considered we should have sited it facing west.

"All the gales come from that quarter," I told him, "anything up to 80–100 m.p.h. The roofs would soon be off when the doors were opened to get the aircraft out." I added, "One has to know the local conditions," just to show we were not so stupid.

No more was said. By then, I had definitely got the impression that everything we did had to be turned around, in order, I supposed, to assert authority.

It was decided by British Airways that we would merge with the railway group the following August. We were to remain a separate company and were to operate under the name of Scottish Airways Limited. George Nicholson at Renfrew and I would remain as directors and be in charge of the same areas as hitherto, but the Wing Commander was to be the 'overlord'. British Airways would hold half the shares and the railways the other half. I did not like the set-up at all, and I knew I was going to have trouble with Measures. His views and mine were clearly miles apart.

At that stage, I was beginning to wish I had tied up with Mr. Gandar Dower. At least we had the same views on resisting bureaucracy and useless extravagance, which was looming on my horizon. Also, Mr. Dower and I, outside business, were the best of friends. At least I thought so.

May 1937 was the month of the Coronation of King George the Sixth, and on that day, the 13th, I looked up Sandy McLaren, the local representative of Star Photos, Perth, who kept the daily newspapers well supplied with photos of Highland Airways' developments.

"What about coming to Fair Isle with me today, Sandy? We'll take a good supply of the Coronation newspapers and there should be some good photographic material if we can make a landing."

His eyes sparkled over such original possibilities.

"I would most certainly like to accompany you," he said.

So downing tools on whatever work he was doing, he rushed off to get his camera and slides filled, and said he would meet me at the airfield in half an hour's time.

It was a brilliant day and I had been meaning for some time to try and effect a landing on top of the cliffs at the south end of that island. I had crossed over by boat in the summer last year and had found this possible landing place, the only one on the whole island.

It was precariously situated some 200 feet above the sea and the cliffs surrounded three-quarters of the perimeter. So if I overshot on landing, it meant disaster and a plunge into the sea 200 feet below. I had a little over 300 yards to play with. Sandy was down on time with camera plates and a good supply of the various 'dailies'. We bundled them into the Monospar, which I decided to use for the job, and we flew off. We landed at Kirkwall for lunch and set off for Fair Isle around two-thirty. It was fine up to North Ronaldsay, but after that when we started crossing the sea, it turned hazy. We spotted the island some 15 miles away, looking gaunt and rocky, like a lone sentinel stuck out in the middle of the North Sea. There was a slight wind from the north-east, which was in our favour for the landing. Soon, we were circling the island – Sandy was sitting alongside me.

"There's the landing strip, Sandy, on the south end and to the east of the lighthouse," I said as we came down lower to have a good look.

"You've not much room, Captain," said Sandy, "and those cliffs, they look forbidding."

"Yes, I know, but don't worry. If I can't make it with certainty, we'll return to Kirkwall. Strap yourself in," I said, "and keep quiet, I'm going in on a dummy run, to get the touch-down point in my

mind. We've got to land within 20 yards over the nearest cliff edge."

Down and down we went, the engines ticking over slowly. I pulled the nose up so that the plane was nearly at stalling speed and then opened the engines up a bit. The cliff loomed up ahead, sharp as a razor on the top edge. Must take care I don't touch the wheels on that edge, I thought. Suddenly the plane started to sink, and the cliffs rose up in front. I froze at the thought of smashing into them. At the same time opening the motors full out and slightly dropping the nose to pick up flying speed, I let the monoplane fall away to the right in a slight bank and as we came parallel to the cliffs, I commenced climbing again to safety.

"Whoof," Sandy said, "that was a near shave!"

"Yes," I answered, "there's a bad air sinker along those cliffs. We were lucky to get out of that one."

We started the run in again, higher up this time as the cliffs came near, and at the same spot the sinker started its evil work, but we were high enough and with a little motor running we touched down within a few yards of the cliff edge and with full brake we pulled up a little way past the centre of the run and turned north towards the stone cottage, and cut the engines. Within seconds there was a milling mob around us. The entire population had come to look at the very first aeroplane to land on their island, and to most of them it was the first aeroplane they had ever seen on the ground at close quarters.

As we opened the canopy and stood up to get out, a loud cheer went up, and I saw old Mr. Stout the Postmaster of the island, whom I had met on my earlier sea trip and who manned the boat to take me ashore off the steamer *St. Magnus*. He was pushing his way through the crowd to greet me. Sandy McLaren was thrilled at the prospect of a good all-time first photographic scoop. As I got off the plane, Mr. Stout had reached us and gave us a warm welcome.

"You couldn't have chosen a better day to come," he said, "we are celebrating the Coronation with a big tea party and we all hope you and your friend will stop and share it with us."

"We'll be very glad to, won't we Sandy, so long as you don't make it too late. I don't like the look of the sky, I think bad weather is not far away."

Mr. Stout agreed with my assessment, and said they would commence tea at four o'clock.

"That will be fine, and we will leave not later than five. We've brought you the Coronation newspapers as a souvenir, so perhaps you will distribute them in a manner fair to all, as there are not sufficient to go round the whole population."

"Right, Captain, I'll see to that."

I caught a glimpse of Sandy plying his trade in real style, with a number of the local beauties lined up for a front page news picture. It was soon four o'clock and we were ushered into a fairly big cottage and a sumptuous tea was provided, with crowds waiting outside to take the second and third shift. The King and Queen were toasted in good 'tea-total' style and everyone made merry, some playing musical instruments. I have never seen such a happy lot of people; and there they were confined to an island of very small dimensions. The southern half only was habitable, as the northern end was mountainous and was only good for sheep grazing. After a lot of speech-making and reference to our arrival, I gave them a talk on my ideas for the construction of a better airstrip in the middle of the island. Time for departure drew nigh, and we were both presented with a present for being the first aerial visitors. My present was one of the famous scarves and I believe Sandy McLaren received a pair of the locally knitted gloves. We were also presented with one of the new threepenny bits each.

I was anxious to get off; during our tea spell the weather had deteriorated and we did not carry radio in the Monospar. I had plenty of room for take-off and was not worried. We shook hands with old Mr. Stout, the lighthouse keeper, Ingram I think was his name, and some of the other inhabitants and climbed into the plane to the accompaniment of cheers and calls of "Come back soon."

I had told Mr. Stout that I would pay them another visit, next time I wished to test a Dragon out on that small strip, so that if anyone was taken seriously ill, we could rescue them and take the patient into hospital at either Lerwick or Kirkwall. We were airborne long before we reached the cliff edge. The wind had increased and that helped our take-off considerably. We circled the island and dived at the crowd, scattering them in all directions before turning the aircraft on to course for North Ronaldsay, 35 miles away. The visibility had dropped down to a couple of miles and the sea was getting up, with white horses clipping the tops of the waves. There was absolutely no hope of rescue if our engines failed. We felt very much alone out there with the weather clamping down on us.

I now had a three-quarter cross-wind to contend with, so I headed the aircraft more to the south to take up the drift and to make sure that we hit the Orkney North Isle. We plugged on through the murk in silence, flying low at around 500 feet. In murky conditions one can see further at low altitude than higher up, and I wanted to be sure that I saw the islands as soon as they came into view. In 20 minutes I discerned land; we had hit North Ronaldsay bang in the middle. That pleased Sandy McLaren for he said,

"Good navigating, Skipper."

We turned on to a more southerly course and very soon ran into better visibility and made Kirkwall 15 minutes later.

Early in June that year, we opened up a new service between Inverness and Aberdeen. The air journey took 40 minutes and altogether roughly an hour between town centres, compared to the rail time of over four hours and three hours by road. The fares were kept uneconomically low to begin with, so as to compete with the first-class rail fare and attract passengers. We operated the service so that Invernessians could spend a day in Aberdeen shopping and as an encouragement to the business fraternity. However, it did not catch on. I put it down to the good road communications. With petrol at one shilling and fourpence a gallon, my would-be passengers could motor there and back in the day, allowing plenty of time for shopping at a quarter the cost of our cut-price air fare. I suppose the same went for the business travellers. We withdrew that service at the end of the following year. It had the honour, or dishonour, as the case may be, of being the only one we threw overboard.

One morning in the middle of the summer, we read in the daily papers that the Fleet was coming north and intended carrying out naval manœuvres in the Moray Firth for a few weeks. The political situation in Europe was going from bad to worse, and we wondered whether the announcement had any bearing on the European situation. Was this display of might intended as a warning to Hitler who was raging through Europe? We had almost forgotten about it, when one day a telegram arrived stamped 'On His Majesty's Service' at the top of the envelope. I opened it and the contents read, somewhat as follows: "You are notified that from 'such a date', naval exercises will be carried out in the Moray Firth until further notice. Your company are instructed not to fly over the Moray Firth route to Wick and Orkney. You should divert your aircraft inland behind Dornoch and fly overland to Wick and Orkney. Signed, 'Tidewater', Invergordon". I read, and re-read it, and wondered why we should be thrown off our direct route, for a more difficult one. We only flew over the sea between Tarbatt Ness and Helmsdale, which represented the estuary of the Dornoch Firth. That surely could not be sufficient reason, to my mind, for asking us to fly a longer and more expensive course inland, which would add to the flying time of the out and return flight, thus throwing our timetable out.

157

I took the telegram to Mr. Donald and Mr. Hamilton.

"What do you think of that?" I asked, "and who is 'Tidewater'?"

Willie Hamilton said that 'Tidewater' was the naval telegraphic codeword for Invergordon Naval Command. I discussed the objections I had to this autocratic demand and our chairman, Mr. Donald, agreed with me.

"But I'm afraid you can't do much about it," he added.

I went back to my office, and waited until next day, when I sent a telegraphic reply stating

"Reference your telegram signed 'Tidewater', regret we are unable to divert our aircraft from the direct course. Our route from Tarbatt Ness to Helmsdale only utilises a minute portion of the North Sea. Request you to arrange your western boundary two miles off the coast. You will then still have the whole of the North Sea to manœuvre in. Signed Highland Airways."

A week went by and we heard nothing further. Shortly afterwards, I attended one of our monthly board meetings with British Airways in London. One of their directors, Major McCrindle, came over to speak with me after the meeting. I knew him very well and we were on good terms. He was a charming man, and I believe a barrister by profession.

"What have you been doing to upset the Navy?" he enquired. "I was out to dinner the other night, and one of the senior officials of the Home Fleet, whom I know, was there. He asked me, 'Who is that man Fresson you've got up in Inverness?'"

"Why do you ask?" I enquired.

"He's got the whole of the Admiralty in an uproar," and he told the Major about my telegram.

I explained to Major McCrindle about the peremptory telegram, ordering us to divert our services inland. To have complied would have caused us considerable upset and would have cost quite a bit in hard cash.

"And for what purpose?" I asked him. "The Navy have got the whole expanse of the Moray Firth to carry out their exercises. Surely they don't want to run their ships ashore by manœuvring right up to the cliffs along the coastline, along which we fly. All I've done is to suggest that they arrange a corridor, two miles off the coast, which they will probably observe anyway, in the interests of their own safety."

"I see," said the Major, "Well, they seem very upset. You should have sent the telegram to us for attention. We could have put it through more diplomatically. However," he smiled, "don't worry yourself, I know one of the Heads of the Department concerned and will have a word with him."

We left it at that.

Shortly after I was back in Inverness a letter arrived from Invergordon, written on flagship notepaper and signed by the Admiral's secretary, inviting me to lunch aboard his flagship at a certain time on a certain day. To say the least, I was somewhat startled and taken aback. I hurried down to Mr. Donald's office (my office was in the premises of Macrae and Dick Ltd.) and said,

"What do I do with that one?"

He read it and passed it across his big desk to Willie Hamilton on the other side, to read.

"You've got yourself into the lion's den this time," Donald said. "You'll have to accept."

So I wrote a polite answer, and told them I should be very pleased to present myself at the appointed time.

Promptly on the day at twelve-thirty, I was being piped aboard the flagship as if I were an Admiral, and an officer met me at the top of the gangplank asking me to follow him. He took me down to the wardroom full of senior officers having their appetiser before going in to lunch. I was presented to the Admiral's secretary who took me under his wing and introduced me to several officers. I soon found my feet. Suddenly the Admiral appeared and one of the officers took me over and introduced me. He enquired if they had looked after me, and on being assured, called several officers over and we got down to business before going in to lunch. I told him that I had seen Major McCrindle in London at our last Board meeting and that I was sorry to learn that my telegram had been the cause of embarrassment but I suggested that my request was a very reasonable one. Surely the Navy would not wish to exercise close inshore, and therefore a two-mile corridor might reasonably be conceded. I explained the upset and cost Highland Airways would be put to if forced so far off course. We should have to claim for any such losses, would the Admiralty pay? The Admiral asked one of his officers to produce a chart of the Helmsdale-Dornoch area, and when it arrived they were able to assess the picture after I had laid our course off on the chart. It could then clearly be seen that we would not interfere in any way with their exercises should they accede to my request. The Admiral said that they would discuss the matter further at lunch, when other interested officers would be present. The lunch was a very nice one; the atmosphere, which was at first a bit chilly, warmed up and the other officers heard what their Admiral had to say. After some discussion the Admiral turned to me saying,

"I think, Captain Fresson, we can fall in with your wishes, but please see that your pilots clearly understand that they are liable to be fired at if they wander off the corridor."

I gave him and his other officers my assurance that their orders would be met. After lunch, having expressed my thanks for their consideration, I took my farewell from His Majesty's Navy, and returned to Inverness feeling very well lunched and well done by!

Mr. Donald and my good friend Willie Hamilton, were surprised to hear the successful results of my mission.

"It's not usual that the Navy can be budged," he said laconically.

I wrote to Major McCrindle telling him how well they had treated me aboard the flagship, and that the Navy had agreed to my suggested air corridor. So all was well that ended well, and although bureaucracy had been breached, no one had any hard feelings. I gave my pilots very strict instructions regarding adhering to that corridor; in fact I instructed them to fly over the edge of the cliffs after reaching Helmsdale, and to take special care on the Tarbat Ness-Helmsdale leg.

"Steer for Dornoch after leaving Inverness and that should prevent any misunderstanding with the Navy," I told them.

The month's naval exercises went by without any incident.

During the second half of the year 1937, we received a shock, for it was announced that the Shetland air mail contract had been awarded to our unwelcome competitors at the cut rate of 1¾d. per pound of mail. Inasmuch as the Post Office were paying Highland Airways 4d. per lb. for the Inverness-Kirkwall section, a little over half the distance of that to Shetland, the absurdity of the tender from Allied Airways should have been obvious to the authorities. For at that price, the air company were subsidising the carriage of H.M. Mails. We were amazed at the Post Office policy, for had we not forfeited our exclusive rights to Sumburgh airfield in order to obtain a radio station, without which it was not possible to provide the regularity which would enable the mails to be carried by air? So, through our public-spirited action, not only had we lost the mail contract, but were faced with passenger competition and the passengers were not all that plentiful.

Our directors and myself rightly considered the Post Office had double-crossed us. Another grievance was that the Postmaster General had called on us to provide a satisfactory operational record for 12 months before we were entrusted with the first internal air mail carriage in the British Isles. No such conditions appeared to have been imposed or insisted upon with our competitors.

Later in the year, after many meetings between British Airways and Railway Air Services, it was agreed that the railway interests would acquire a half interest in the Scottish air companies, which meant that on 12th August 1937, Highland Airways and Northern & Scottish Airways lost their identity and the two companies became welded together under the name of Scottish Airways Limited with registered offices at Renfrew. The amalgamation brought powerful backing, but we lost a lot of our independence.

Mr. Roberts, our chairman, remained in office, as also did the other British Airways directors, including Major McCrindle. The railway directors were Mr. W. P. Bradbury, W. Yeaman, L.M.S. Scottish Region Manager and Mr. J. W. Ratledge of David MacBrayne & Company Limited. George Nicholson and myself retained our directorships as before. On 12th August (Thursday), we held our first Board meeting at Renfrew and after Mr. Roberts introduced us all to the new members of the Board, we got down to work. Wing Commander Measures was appointed managing director of the new company. I would have preferred that George Nicholson and myself should have become joint managing directors, as I could not see how a newcomer could possibly cope with the complexities of the operations Nicholson and myself had grown up with. After all, the routes operated were organised by us. As it was not to be so, we had to make the best of a difficult job. The major issue discussed was the *modus operandi* of the new company. It was agreed that George would carry on as before with the southern section and I would remain boss of the northern section.

It was at this meeting that I first became aware of the difference in financial stability of the Western Isles services. Whereas Highland Airways had been making ends meet and were beginning to show a profit, Northern & Scottish had been in the red for a long time. Their traffic density did not appear as great as ours, but their operating mileage was much longer. Further, they were using a more expensive operating type of aircraft than we were and all this added up to a not too rosy picture. It was at this juncture that I submitted to the new Board that our accounts should be kept separately and shown separately at each Board meeting. In due course, it was frequently murmured by one of the new directors that the more affluent 'brother' was helping to keep the poorer one.

Mr. Bradbury, at the end of our first meeting, invited my wife and me to spend a long week-end with Mrs. Bradbury and himself at

Rothesay, where they were staying. It was a lovely sunny day and we gladly accepted. We drove down to the Greenock ferry in my one and a half litre Riley, and we made the journey in record time. I don't think Bradbury was feeling too safe, as he gently enquired whether I thought I was piloting a plane! However, we had a very pleasant crossing over to Rothesay and on arrival at the hotel we met Mrs. Bradbury for the first time. During that week-end, Bradbury and I were able to get together on future procedure. I told him I thought the managing director arrangement had weaknesses but as long as the Wing Commander would not interfere in technical matters, I for one would do my best to play ball. Bradbury appreciated my frankness and said that the appointment had been made as Measures had to co-ordinate the Railway Air Services with our operations and see that there was no overlapping or other divergencies.

We left on Monday morning, the Bradburys returning to London and we to Inverness. On the whole, I now felt pleased with the way things had worked out and above all that we now had the railway goodwill with us, instead of in opposition. That would smooth out many a past headache. Also, I had I felt sure, a friend in Mr. Bradbury and as he was a senior official in the L.M.S. Railway, I thought that if I ever found myself in genuine difficulty, his help would be at hand.

In the middle of September, my wife and I left for the south by car and we stopped off at the George Hotel, Perth, for afternoon tea. There was a point I wished to clear up about the Inverness-Glasgow service I was planning for next spring, so I took the opportunity of calling William Cumming, the secretary of the new company at Renfrew, on the phone before continuing our journey. During our conversation, I was told that it had been decided that the Inverness-Glasgow service would be operated from Renfrew.

"Who told you that?" I asked.

"The Wing Commander," he replied.

"How did that happen? I've been working on that route for the past year and I want it integrated with the Kirkwall-Wick-Inverness run, timed to leave Kirkwall early in the morning, so that the Kirkwall passengers can spend a day in Glasgow and return at night."

"Sorry, old chap, but those are the orders," he replied.

"Where can I get Measures?"

"He's in London as far as I know."

"What's his phone number?"

He gave it to me and I got on the phone to the Wing Commander.

By then I was really ready to jump off the deep end. I was beginning to see how the Renfrew set-up was working. Consultation was going on without my being present. Eventually, Measures' voice came through.

"That you, Wing Commander?"

"Yes, Measures speaking."

"I've just been speaking to Cumming and he tells me you have instructed the Renfrew end to operate the Glasgow-Inverness service?"

"That's correct," he answered.

"Why have you done that? Everyone knows that run has been in my mind for a long time. I want you to alter that decision, it's most unsatisfactory."

"I can't do that," he said, "we want the service to tie up with the south."

"But I want it to tie up with the north," I replied.

By this time, the 'Wingco' was getting as heated as I was, and he said it was too late to alter the decision.

"Why wasn't I informed about it?" I howled.

"I never knew you were interested."

"But I told you long ago."

"It's no use continuing this conversation, we will have to talk about it later," he said.

I rang off.

"What's the matter?" my wife said when I joined her, "you look pretty het up."

"I should think so," and I told her what had happened.

I felt sure in my mind that the decision had been engineered by Renfrew and I was determined to get to the bottom of the matter.

I brought this matter up at our next board meeting and it was finally agreed that Renfrew would operate the service for the coming season and that we would take over the following year. The traffic results would be compared and the final decision would rest on which way paid best. That appeared reasonable, so there I left it. What I liked the least, was that such decisions could be reached without any consultation with myself. I decided to get this put straight at the first opportunity.

Early in the autumn, a new pilot arrived to take charge of the Kirkwall station. Captain John Hankins was a senior pilot and had been recommended by George Nicholson to take on that onerous job. Talking with him one day, he brought up the question of Fair Isle and asked if I would take him over and show him the landing drill on that island, so that he would be in a position to pick up any ambulance cases which might arise. I agreed, because I knew he was an experienced joy-riding pilot, and was therefore proficient in short landings.

We set off on 11th November, a fine day, and I made the second landing on that island within six months, this time with Dragon G-ACIT as that aircraft would be used for the ambulance cases. This time there were no downward air eddies over the approaching cliff face, but also, there was no N.E. wind to help shorten the landing. Nevertheless, we managed to pull up by the usual swing to the north during the middle of the landing run towards a wire fence, instead of the 200 feet cliff drop into the sea. We went up to the middle of the island with Mr. Stout and a few of the islanders to settle on the site for a strip which the locals had undertaken to hew out of the hillside in their spare time. Mr. Stout invited us to stay for lunch and we were served with some very tender Fair Isle mutton. The islanders were excited to see me back. We explained to Mr. Stout the procedure to obtain an ambulance flight if needed. Also, I introduced Captain Hankins, who told me he was prepared to undertake flights to Fair Isle now that he had seen me land. I explained that Captain Hankins was in charge of Kirkwall, and how to get in touch with him in the case of emergency. We left for Orkney after lunch and more presents were handed us. The Dragon got off easily and I had no fear about ambulance or emergency flights being undertaken with it.

On 19th November, I flew over to Stornoway for our final meeting with the Stornoway Trust Committee, about starting work on the Melbost Airfield. I carried with me copies of the agreement, and I returned with the documents signed. Nearly five years I had been working to obtain that agreement and now it was in my pocket. We had obtained a long lease, on condition that we agreed to shoulder the cost of construction. There was, however, protection for Scottish Airways should the long lease be broken, and with that safeguard, we were prepared to go ahead.

The L.M.S. at Glasgow recommended a civil surveyor, a Mr. Warren to carry out the survey and on 2nd December 1937, he and several members of his staff arrived in Inverness. I met them off the train and we lost no time in taking off for Stornoway. For good measure, there was a 50 m.p.h. wind blowing from the north and we ran into heavy snowstorms across the mountains. We flew at 5,000 feet on an instrument course and ran into better weather over the Minch. I spent the day with Mr. Warren, going over the golf course and marking the four landing strips we would require.

I returned in the evening as I had to fly to Kirkwall next morning to bring a party in from Metal Industries at Lyness to Inverness in time to catch the southbound express. The wind had abated quite a bit for the return journey, and the flight was uneventful. The Lyness charter was carried out without incident, the fully loaded plane getting off easily on the downhill run. The Lyness landing strip had more than justified itself and the air connection was a great boon, Mr. MacKenzie told me, to their company.

We were near the end of the year and I finished it off by taking the scheduled morning service to Kirkwall, fully loaded with passengers and a big stack of His Majesty's Mail. I looked forward to the New Year with some misgivings. I was still suspicious of the new set-up, but I felt that I had the sympathy of the chairman and British Airways directors to see that I did not become engulfed in muddled thinking. I also had the support of Mr. Bradbury, should any be needed, and I had won my point at the Board meeting, that I should be present at all meetings on policy held at Renfrew.

CHAPTER NINE

THE opening months of 1938 were exceedingly stormy, gales and high winds prevailed. These were not the only storms on the horizon, for the situation was growing steadily worse in Europe.

As the Nazi war machine grew in might, so individual countries were beginning to be overrun. Life, however, went on as usual in Britain and it was not until Munich, later in the year, that our citizens began to realise that all was not as well as it should have been. However, with Mr. Chamberlain's flight to Germany and his meetings with Hitler, the public appeared reassured with the message on his last return that 'We would have peace in our time'. As we all know now, this promise was bust wide open a year later.

There was a similar militant movement on my own home front. Renfrew and the new operations director were still a constant source of worry to me, in their ever increasing interference and tendency to arrive at policy decisions without consultation with myself, in spite of the board ruling. I was placed well out of the way in Inverness, and also heavily engaged in flying owing to the surging increase in traffic which necessitated many duplicated flights. Accordingly, I was unable to spend a great deal of time in the south. By the spring matters had got to such a pitch that I requested the Glasgow operations manager to come up and see me. I insisted that orders should not be given without my consent, especially as they affected the northern section, and unless these practices were stopped I would have to make a major issue of the matter. It appeared to me incongruous that the southern management, who were making a heavy loss, should be dictating to me, who at least enjoyed a clean balance sheet. Matters improved after that set-to, and relations became less strained and more co-operative.

At the beginning of January, the surveyors from Glasgow arrived for a second time, and I flew them over to Stornoway, to continue their survey of the Melbost Golf Links Airfield. I remained with them for a few days and assisted in laying out the runways we should require, for we had decided on a new technique. Up to now, it had been customary to level off the whole of an airfield area, but from experience gained in the Orkney North Isles, where we had to be satisfied with narrow strips of ground, pointing into different wind directions, it occurred to me that we could save a lot of money if the Stornoway Links were laid off in four different strips, 150 feet wide, pointing north/south, north-east/south-west, east/west and south-east/north-west. We had also found from experience that we could land and take off in cross-winds safely up to 45 degree angles and the four strips never at any time presented a greater wind angle than that. I accordingly, requested the chief surveyor, to survey and cost the two projects, namely for levelling the complete area and alternatively, levelling the four runways 150 feet wide. When the survey and costing was completed it was found that the saving in cost by employing strips, amounted to many thousands of pounds. I now had to convince our Board that flying would be safe using air-strips, instead of the conventional airfield. That, I succeeded in doing.

The project was accepted and the airfield constructed on these unconventional lines. I believe it was the first airfield of its kind, and set the pattern for future airfield construction. It was wholly taken up by the R.A.F. and F.A.A. during the war and all modern airfields are constructed on the same principle today. The survey and costing took a long time and there were other delays which put back the commencement of constructing the airfield until the latter part of the year.

It was finished in August 1939, but never went into use. The outbreak of World War II prevented us from opening the Inverness-Stornoway run which we had advertised for 1st September 1939. Our new unused airfield was taken over by the R.A.F. and completely reconstructed on a vast scale with tarmac runways. It played a major part in wartime operations for Coastal Command.

Our air service did not commence until towards the very end of the war in 1944. Although all my hard work and patience had had to wait so long before we obtained any benefit from that airfield, at least we had the satisfaction that we had led the way in helping the war effort in no mean way.

As January progressed, so did the speed of the winds, and at the end of the month the Island of Foula was reported running short of food. The supply steamer which provided connection with the outside world through Walls, Shetland, had been unable to make the crossing for nearly a month. The Shetland authorities asked us if we could help and I sent Captain Wilson up to Sumburgh in a Rapide to organise a food drop, as there was no known place where we could land on the Island of Foula.

He took with him a number of home-made parachutes which we roughly constructed from old flour bags. The parcels were in packages

weighing five pounds and each parcel attached to a 'chute. I told
Captain Wilson to see that the aeroplane door was removed before
taking off from Sumburgh for Foula and to pick up Captain Johnson,
who was stationed at Kirkwall, to attend to the dropping of the food
parcels. Captain Johnson was to lie on the floor and have his legs
strapped to one of the aircraft chairs, as a safety precaution. There
was a gale blowing itself out when the Rapide aircraft arrived over
Foula and Captain Wilson told me on his return that the air was
exceedingly turbulent low down over the island and they had great
difficulty in manœuvring into position to effect the drops.

He selected a portion of moorland for the drop near the cottages
at the southern end of the island and the ten packages, each con-
taining five pounds of food were successfully dropped. All were
observed to be collected.

In all, 400 miles were flown by the time Captain Wilson returned
to Inverness that night. He deserved great praise for carrying out
the food drop successfully under such stormy conditions, as also did
those who assisted him. Only recently, I read in the daily press
that Foula was again cut off, this time for a much longer period, and
they were completely out of supplies. Yet in this modern age and with

State-run airlines, no steps were taken to bring air relief, such as our commercial company successfully carried out 25 years previously. One is left wondering why, when equipment and techniques are so far advanced compared to that of the 'pioneering 'thirties'?

The gales persisted and continued into March, so much so that one day the mail steamer could not make the voyage from Mallaig to Stornoway. The Inverness Postmaster rang us up to enquire whether we could fly the stranded mails over. I was a bit sceptical, the wind was blowing at 70 m.p.h. and almost directly ahead on the flight over. That would mean two hours' flying at altitude, and there was no radio station at Stornoway to home on. I hesitated over taking the valley route in that gale. In the end, I decided to have a go; I thought the publicity would be good for the company; so I told the Postmaster to send the mails down to the airfield and we would get under way as quickly as possible. However, I warned him that I might have to turn back.

I took off with a very heavy load of mail, and I took Goulden, our radio mechanic, as my radio operator for the return journey above cloud. Wind usually increases in speed with altitude, so I decided to fly low on the outward journey. As soon as we got into the Ullapool main valley, we were trounced badly by most vicious bumps. I knew the journey was going to be a rough one, but I hadn't bargained for what we were getting. Ploughing through the bumps which were like sledge hammers, with the outer wing struts bending with the strain, we commenced rounding the bend at Braemore Pass where the road bends sharply to the left and runs up the valley to Dundonald and Little Loch Broom, when without warning, a master gust hit us. The plane shuddered, and I thought it was going to break up. It all but stood on its tail and I could do nothing with the controls. I thought we were lost. Never in my 41 years as a commercial pilot have I ever encountered anything like that hammering in the air and I have been through some pretty bad ones in my time. My radio engineer poked his head through the cabin door and said

"Are we going to crash, Captain?"

Taking a mighty quick look at him as I was wrestling with the controls, I saw that his face was as white as a sheet. There wasn't time to answer. I had to get that plane back on to an even keel while it was still in one piece. After what seemed an interminable time, gradually the controls commenced to function again, and the valley dropping down to Loch Broom came into sight. I immediately pushed the nose down and dived for the Loch, clipping the tree tops down that valley. At last, we reached Loch Broom and flew low over the water and below those murderous blasts which were coming down the mountainsides higher up.

Once past the Summer Isles, the going was much better over the Minch, and I heaved a sigh of relief when the cliffs of Chicken Head were sighted. The mail was handed over to the 'postie' in the mail van, waiting at the Melbost Golf Club House nearby. We scrounged a lift into Stornoway for a rest before wrestling with the return journey.

As the gale would now be behind us, I decided to climb to 10,000 feet in order to get above the frightening turbulence experienced on the outward journey. With my radio operator as the only passenger, the aircraft was lightly loaded and so climbed quickly and we were soon in the calm air. What a contrast to the outward trip. We reached Inverness 93 miles away, in half an hour, with the help of the gale on our tail. Had we been going the other way, into the gale, it would have taken us over two hours.

Before leaving for the town, I suggested to George Griffiths, our chief engineer, that the plane should have a thorough check in view of the buffeting it had received. No damage could be found, which spoke well of the de Havilland stressing. Nothing on earth would ever induce me to fly low through that valley again, in the teeth of a gale of the magnitude we had experienced that day. The delivery of the stormbound Stornoway mail was a feather in our cap with the Post Office and it was the talk of Stornoway. It appeared that the population were puzzled at receiving their mail early after lunch, instead of the following morning, which was usual, as the mail steamer did not arrive in Stornoway until evening. All the same, I felt the G.P.O. did not deserve that effort and risk which had been taken, having double-crossed us on the Shetland air mail contract the year before.

In the spring, we would be running to our summer timetable, and we completely reorganised our Shetland air communications. The Aberdeen run was altered to start at Shetland in the early morning, arriving in Aberdeen just before midday, via Inverness. The return journey was scheduled to depart from Kintore at 12.40 p.m., reaching Sumburgh at 3.35 p.m. To do this we built a hangar at Sumburgh and stationed an aircraft there, with pilot and engineer. In addition, on 3rd May, the Glasgow-Inverness service was inaugurated. The plane called at Perth on the way, and proceeded on to Kirkwall and Sumburgh, arriving at 12.35 p.m. A quick turn around was organised, and the southbound passengers departed at 12.45 p.m. arriving at Glasgow at quarter to five, after calling at Kirkwall, Wick, Inverness and Perth. Thus, Shetland was served by two services and although they were operated at close on 100 per cent regularity neither, strangely enough, carried the mail.

The month of May had not advanced far when a serious state of affairs came to my notice. One morning the Renfrew plane arrived completely iced up and I was told that it practically fell into Inverness Airport. I did not see the pilot on that occasion. The aircraft could not proceed in that condition to Shetland, so we had to provide a substitute plane at short notice, which was not easy. A few days later, it happened again. This time I found and questioned the pilot. He told me he understood that the managing director, who had no practical experience of flying, had issued instructions to the operations manager at Renfrew that the passengers were not to be subjected to the frightening experience of flying in cloud and pilots were accordingly instructed to climb above the clouds after leaving Perth, to get over the mountains. At that time of year, 10,000 feet or considerably more had to be reached to get above the overcast. On many days it was impossible to climb sufficiently high to get above cloud, but in the process of trying, the aircraft got badly iced up, with the results observed at Inverness. This dangerous practice had to stop. We could not afford a fatal accident on that or any run. I complained to Renfrew without any effect. They simply said they had their instructions and if the pilots ran into icing, they were to return to Perth. That alternative would ruin the regularity of the service and was wholly unnecessary.

We in Inverness knew a safe and proper way to fly that sector with the aircraft we had available, and which did not possess de-icing equipment. We called it the 'dog's leg' route, because we flew to Perth on two courses, which drawn on paper looked like a dog's leg. That way, we rarely encountered icing because we did not have to fly at an altitude higher than 5,000 feet, but it usually meant cloud flying most of the way. It appeared that the only measure left to avoid the danger was to convert the pilots of the southern division to our way of thinking, and when they learned that we had experimented with the 'dog's leg' route via Drumochter Pass at 5,000 feet altitude, without running into icing, they gave it a try and decided to ignore the instructions they had received. In future and for the rest of the summer, that's the way the Perth-Inverness sector was operated without difficulty. Nothing was said, so we let sleeping dogs lie.

The opening of the Renfrew-Shetland service was celebrated by the Town Council at Scone airfield, Perth, and a luncheon was given in honour of the occasion. Many well-known people attended.

Speeches flowed galore and after lunch an air trip was given over the city of Perth from Scone Airport, to prominent members of the Council and community. To my surprise, I was asked to pilot the plane, which I did with pleasure. I stayed overnight and joined the northbound service next morning. Captain David Barclay, who was piloting, invited me to fly the plane as far as Inverness. I well remember it was a beautiful day at Perth, blue sky and brilliant sunshine. Half-way over the mountains, we ran above cloud at 7,000 feet and it continued that way to Inverness which was completely overcast.

In the middle of June, word was received that the Stroma Island strip was completed and I flew up with a Mr. Muir as passenger in the Moth to inspect the work. The islanders had made a good job and levelled off some 400 yards of moorland. They had removed the top layer of peat and uncovered a firm clay and gravel surface, along the entire strip. The wet part had been drained and the islanders must have put in a tremendous amount of work to prepare that strip, all by hand. It went to show how people living in the remote parts of our islands appreciated and yearned for air transport, as was the case a few years before when North Ronaldsay hewed out their own airfield. We had a gathering in the Islander's Hall and I thanked them for the work they had so freely given, and told them that I would give them the utmost support for any air transport required.

The third week in August, we had an interesting charter flight, which was the first of its kind. A firm of fish curers in the Island of Stronsay, North of Kirkwall, had a branch in Stornoway, and they required six of their senior fish girls flown to Stornoway for an important job. To travel by surface transport would have taken over two days. By air, it took one hour and twenty minutes. The flight was mostly over sea, the only land we flew over was the Cape Wrath peninsula which was only 15 miles wide. The girls had never flown before and were looking a bit nervous, but as soon as we were on our way flying at 2,000 feet in smooth air, they had such a splendid view of the Orkney Isles that they soon forgot about any squeamishness. By the time I landed them at Melbost, they didn't want to get out. We left Kirkwall at 11.00 a.m. and landed at Melbost at 12.15 p.m. Transport was ready and my passengers were in town at 12.30 p.m., ready for work after lunch. No wonder the fish curer jumped at the price I offered him for the charter since he had saved two days' wages for six employees, and the cost of surface transport to Inverness and across to Stornoway, which would have come to about double the sum for the air charter. The girls were thrilled with their flight when they alighted. I thought at the time, they

172

would be good publicity agents for the Stornoway-Inverness service when it started.

During September, terrific controversy started about an airport for Thurso, and pressure to provide an airfield was brought to bear against the Thurso Town Council. The Air Ministry, at the request of the Council, had sent up one of their surveyors to inspect several sites proffered, and one had been chosen at Dixonfield Farm, which was owned by Sir Archibald Sinclair. Obviously Thurso was very much out of the air picture at that time. Air traffic had increased enormously in the past three years and most of it was going through Wick, plus the mail.

Thurso enjoyed a large summer tourist trade, and the Royal Hotel had recently been enlarged and refurnished by Mr. James Wilson, its owner, to provide 75 rooms. The small field operated by Allied Airways was unsuitable and dangerous for heavily loaded aircraft and in any event was a closed shop to outsiders. So Thurso could not even receive charter flights from the south, besides having no regular air route from the south to accommodate its passengers. In spite of all this, the Thurso Town Council still jibbed at providing a municipal aerodrome. Once the Air Ministry had settled the location which would be acceptable, the battle really started. The town finance Scrooges lined themselves against the business community and were locked in deadly combat. Mr. James Wilson led the business community and they demanded action. They worked out the cost, including the purchase of the land and the constructional costs, and having obtained Scottish Airways support, who agreed to rent the airfield and manage it, submitted an extremely good business proposition to the Town Council, and asked them to go ahead and get on with the job. Still the finance committee would not move. To-day, Thurso has no airfield, and is not likely to have, as Wick airfield was reconstructed by the Air Ministry during the war, and now serves the whole of the North of Scotland.

One of the main reasons I wanted an airfield at Thurso was on account of weather. Frequently it was extremely difficult and even risky trying to land at Wick. Situated bang on the north-east coast, the town was subject to sea mists and low cloud which frequently settled over the area, whereas Thurso did not suffer so acutely from that type of weather. In addition, as I have already said, Thurso was developing a very good tourist trade, more so than Wick, and naturally, we wished to capture that business. Lastly, there was a demand for a service direct to and from Inverness and the Orkneys. However, it was not to be, and Wick retained all services.

On 10th October, for the second time, Mr. Walter Elliot, Secretary of State for Scotland as he was then, used Scottish Airways for his northern tour. He flew with me to Wick and Orkney and we renewed our acquaintanceship. I gathered from what he said that it was the intention of his Department to use air transport in future when and where practical. The flight was successful inasmuch as it enabled the Secretary to carry out his mission in one day and return to Edinburgh on the late afternoon train. That, of course, saved a lot of time compared to his old method of travel by fishery cruiser or train. It was also an advantage to Scottish Airways as such publicity certainly encouraged air-mindedness with the public.

In the early autumn, I transferred Captain Hankins back from Shetland to Kirkwall to continue the management of the Orkney station. The traffic had now developed to such an extent that I needed someone in charge who could also manage the technical problems which were arising with the aircraft operations. Captain Hankins installed himself in Tankerness House in the main street just opposite Saint Magnus Cathedral. It was very old and full of historical charm, and I spent many pleasant visits there.

The New Year was not far away and had we but known it, 1938 was to be the last year we should be allowed to operate as free agents and free from bureaucratic control. The year had been one of continued expansion and consolidation. Our traffic and freight had increased substantially since our tie-up with the railway group the previous year. By now, the name of Highland Airways had been completely superseded by Scottish Airways and most of the friction which had manifested itself during the first 12 months had disappeared and we were working as a team, which was all to the good and as it should have been.

I had been hard put to it, what with the work of management and flying many duplicated services, to take care of the upsurge in reservations, but the results were worth the effort. The comparisons of traffic figures are worthy of note. For the first year 1933, we carried 1,400 passengers. For the 11 months ending, November 1938, 7,500 passengers were transported on Scottish Airways northern routes. That figure did not include the passengers travelling on the Inverness-Perth-Glasgow route.

The mail figures were even more outstanding: 1933, 10 tons, end of November 1938, 80 tons. I have no records of the newspaper loads, but since the second year was completed under contract to *The Scotsman*, we were carrying most of the national daily newspapers and the *Aberdeen Press and Journal*. The daily loads were always extremely heavy and more often than not we were obliged to put on a separate aircraft to take care of the mail and newspapers. From a trickle in 1933 of 60 lb. a day, I should say 600 lb. daily would scarcely have covered the 1938 loading.

These remarkable results had been obtained in four and a half years and had only been attained by the extraordinary high percentage of regularity of flights. Only one year out of the four did the annual regularity fall to 97 per cent – for two years it was 98 per cent and one year 100 per cent, which meant that not one single day was missed during a whole year's flying. I am afraid that standard is not maintained to-day, 25 years later, in spite of the great advances in technical equipment. Great credit was due to our pilots for such a record of regularity and safety. They flew through a high percentage of extreme weather. For posterity, I quote their names in order of joining the company:

Cyril Coleman, Greenshields, Adam Smith, Johnny Rae, John Veasey, Johnny Fielden, John Hankins and Johnson, with a little help from myself!

The pilots certainly could not have carried out their onerous task without the backing of a fine engineering and maintenance organisation behind them, led by George Griffiths and assisted by Bert Farminer, Arthur Dodds, Archie MacDonald, A. MacLennan and our radio engineer Goulden, who maintained our radio sets to a very high standard of efficiency. It was remarkable how few failures we had with our radio, upon which the lives of the passengers and air crew often depended in bad weather. I must not forget the traffic and office staff headed by Miss MacDonald and Sandy Cumming. At any time, all of them along with the engineering staff would work overtime without increase in pay to further the efficiency of the company. The sense of *esprit de corps* and loyalty was intense. They were a great team of which I was proud.

So we leave Stage One of the 'Birth of Highland Airways' and turn in 1939, with controls and a second World War to face up to, in which Scottish Airways played a very important part.

CHAPTER TEN

DURING the middle of January 1939, the Air Transport Licensing Authority under the Air Navigation (Licensing of Public Transport) Order 1932 sat in Edinburgh to deal with the applications by Scottish Airways, North Eastern Airways and Allied Airways (Gandar Dower) Ltd., to operate air services. The proceedings opened up on Monday, 16th January, and were presided over by Mr. A. M. Tristram Eve, K.C.

Scottish Airways were asked to state their case for the applications for a number of services including Inverness, Shetland, Glasgow, Inverness, Aberdeen and Stornoway with intermediate landings. The application was opposed by Allied Airways and North Eastern Airways. Our examination lasted all Monday and a part of Tuesday. After that, Allied Airways and North Eastern Airways were called to present their cases. After the last applicant had been dealt with, local witnesses from the North of Scotland were called, representing local authority.

The chairman indicated the Tribunal's provisional views "subject to all proper conditions being attached to the licences".

"Ideally, civil aviation north to Inverness and Aberdeen both inclusive should be operated under single control, subject to the safeguards and interests of the public, which may be imposed. In this we agree with the contention of Scottish Airways. Scottish Airways claim they should have the monopoly of civil aviation in this area to the exclusion of Allied Airways. We think that a case has not been made out by Scottish Airways to exclude Allied Airways from this area."

The chairman went on to say:

"In default of single control, we are of the opinion that a case has been made out for the granting of licences to Scottish Airways and Allied Airways to operate services respectively from Inverness and from Aberdeen, and that these licences should, subject to minor exceptions, be exclusive to each respective company.

"We appreciate also that conditions in aviation change rapidly. We have in mind the possibility on those and other routes of night flying, of the utilisation of more rapid machines, of the extension of ground organisation and of landing grounds and other factors which

176

may affect these licences. Our views, therefore, are to be taken as expressed upon the facts as existing today and on the evidence now before us."

Later on in the month, we were informed that our applications as applied for were granted, but with the exclusion of operating in and out of Aberdeen. Thus the cuckoo was left sitting in the pioneer nest. One concession given to Scottish Airways was that we would carry the Aberdeen-Shetland mail from Kirkwall to Shetland every other day, and Allied Airways would be responsible for the carriage on the alternate days. This in effect was tantamount to the ruling of King Solomon, when two mothers claimed the same baby; in this case, the baby was actually cut in half and each mother took a cut. We did not like the idea of being a 'mother' at a cut rate paid by the Post-master General under the uneconomical acceptance of Allied Air-ways' bid to grasp the mail from Scottish Airways. We would have preferred a passenger to take up the weight utilised by the 'unwanted portion of the child'. To make matters worse, there were many days when Allied Airways either could not or would not operate from Kirkwall to Shetland. We were then called upon to carry the mails on that sector and this caused us considerable embarrassment, as we were frequently fully booked by passengers. I noticed that such occasions usually occurred on the days when the weather was extremely bad along the Aberdeen-Kirkwall route, which was of course without radio assistance. In the end, I gave orders that passengers were not to be unloaded for mail, which we had not contracted to carry, and in such cases the mail had to remain in Orkney overnight and we took it on the next day. The new licensing arrangements carried on until 1st September 1939, when war was declared and we and Allied Airways were called upon to operate under Air Ministry direction.

I have said early in this narrative that the airfield site I originally chose at Kirkwall was situated at the farm of Hatston, but that I was unable to obtain the use of the land, although the tenant farmer was agreeable, owing to other interests which were likely to be affected by the opening of air communications. I had always hankered after getting that ground for an airfield as it was situated at sea level, whereas Wideford was 200 feet above, and often in fog when Hatston was in the clear. So, when a London representative from the Admiralty called on me at Inverness at the end of January, asking if I could advise them of a suitable site in Orkney, for the construction of a Naval Air Station, I immediately recommended Hatston Farm.

He told me that they wished to construct four air strips and one had to be at least 1,500 yards long. I worked out that, continuing the north-east/south-west air strip into another farm to the north-east, all the requirements could be met at Hatston with the possible exception of the approach to the east/west strip, which was downhill. My visitor, Commander Heath, said he would like to charter a plane to fly him up to inspect the site.

"That's easily arranged; I will fly you up myself," I replied.

A telephone call to Whitehall soon confirmed permission and we set off in Dragon G-ACIT.

I was requested to make dummy runs from the eight points of the compass over the Hatston site with a view to testing the approaches. When that was completed, we landed at Wideford airfield and went into town for lunch. We returned to Hatston Farm in the afternoon to walk over the ground and my Admiralty friend expressed the view that the site might be satisfactory. I warned Commander Heath about the boggy state of the ground in Orkney during winter months and recommended that hard-tarred macadam runways should be constructed. The Commander looked at me in amazement,

"I have never heard of anything like that in airfield construction before," he said.

"I am sure you haven't," I replied, "it is new thinking on my part after five difficult winters at Wideford airfield struggling to take off with heavy loads in a sea of mud. The Navy will never get away with the standard grass airfield in Orkney."

They accepted my advice and as far as I am aware, that was the first airfield constructed in the British Isles which was provided with hard strips for take-off and landing. When construction was completed Hatston airfield caused some concentrated thinking in the R.A.F., for many senior officers arrived in Kirkwall to inspect the finished job. Within a couple of years, the hard strip became standard practice for the wartime airfields constructed all over the country.

Commander Heath returned to London. Within a week he was back and accompanied by Admiralty surveyors. The second time we flew up in a Rapide and repeated the dummy runs and approaches with the faster aircraft. We transferred their theodolites and surveying equipment into the waiting car and left for Hatston. On the way I booked them in at the Kirkwall Hotel.

The result of that survey was entirely satisfactory. I was asked to advise on the direction in which the four runways should be sited. They agreed three but queried the east/west strip as the approach towards the east was downhill. I was thinking that, if hostilities did not take place, we might be able to rent that airfield from the Navy, in which case our operations in and out of Orkney would be considerably eased and be far safer. Accordingly I was all out to help the Naval authorities construct such a splendid airfield. So I answered quickly,

"If there is a strong wind from the east, then the strength of the wind will counter the slope downhill. On the other hand, should only light winds be encountered, then there is nothing to prevent the pilot landing on the north-east/south-west strip."

They accepted that viewpoint. It was subsequently proved after the airfield became operational that the naval pilots encountered no difficulty in using the downhill strip once they got used to gliding down the approach hill low over the surface, as the slope corresponded to the glide path of the average aircraft in use in those days. Shortly after the survey party had returned to London, I received word that the Admiralty were going ahead with the plan and construction began in the early spring.

The airfield runways were finished just in time for the early phase of World War II. The hangars, maintenance shops and personnel quarters were still in course of construction for some time after 3rd September 1939. An arrangement was made between the Admiralty and Scottish Airways that they would use and manage Hatston in peacetime, but that never came about inasmuch as construction was finished at the same time as hostilities began. We, however, hoped that as we had given the Admiralty so much assistance with Hatston airfield we should be allowed the use of that airfield in the event of hostilities. That view was at first accepted, but we ran into trouble with the Commanding Officer who succeeded Commander Howe, R.N., who was the first Commandant of this air station at the outbreak of war.

During the summer of 1939, the war atmosphere continued to develop as the weeks went by, but it appeared remote and one's daily life continued as hitherto. In Orkney, our ambulance service was doing good work and was often called upon by the Orkney County Council. In the evening of the last day of February an urgent call was made at nightfall for medical assistance at the Island of Sanday. The night was dark and a young gale was blowing, also to make matters more difficult there were heavy rain squalls. Nevertheless, our Station Manager, Captain John Hankins, decided to answer the call to fly a doctor out to the island. Apart from the difficulty of finding the island in the dark without radio or proper airfield lighting, the available run on the landing field at Sanday was not more than 300 yards, and the only lighting would be car headlights. This flight

I consider was the highlight of all our urgent ambulance flights and I have always admired the skill and courage of Captain Hankins in undertaking that call.

The flight created quite a stir in the Orkney Islands and it was not long before all the islanders knew about the good work Captain Hankins did that night on Sanday. It was all in keeping with the Scottish Airways motto – *This plane must get through.*

We were now getting near the summer season schedule. A new service was under way, which would link London to Orkney in six hours. The service was planned to depart from Orkney at 6.25 a.m. arriving in time to connect with the North Eastern Airways plane at Perth, departing 9.00 a.m. for Edinburgh, Newcastle-upon-Tyne and arriving at 12.30 p.m. at Croydon Airport, London. The north-bound flight by Railway Air Services would leave Croydon just before midday and reach Inverness/Wick and Orkney in time for dinner. Another feature of that service would enable the public to spend half a day in Glasgow and return to their homes the same night. Fares were kept low to encourage people in the north to spend half a day in Glasgow or Perth for business, shopping or sight-seeing. The plane reached Glasgow just after 9.00 a.m. departing on the return journey north just after 3.00 p.m. It was subsequently decided that the last year's schedule of Glasgow-Perth-Inverness-Wick-Orkney and Shetland would also be maintained. Thus, the public travelling to and from Glasgow and Orkney had two services per day, which is outstanding compared to present day schedules. There is no doubt that the service frequency has suffered with modern planning and that the North of Scotland was considerably better served in that respect in pre-war years. We carried all passengers who wished to travel, and more important, at the time they wanted, so the modern claim that better service is offered today is incorrect in so far as frequency is concerned.

The London service was not very well patronised at first. In any event, not so many people were travelling from the north to London but we found the Inverness passengers interested. Unfortunately, owing to the outbreak of war, the service did not operate long enough to assess its true value.

On 1st June, I carried out a charter to Orkney, carrying four passengers to attend a meeting and dinner-party, which took place in the Kirkwall Hotel. My wife and I were the guests of our good friend Mrs. Mackay the owner. It did not really get dark in Kirkwall at that time of the year and our passengers appeared in no hurry to return. We did not take off until one o'clock in the morning for the return flight. The light was eerie and it was like taking off into another world especially as we climbed, when wonderful pastel shades appeared on the horizon.

We flew at 3,000 feet and I was wondering what the landing was going to be like at Inverness as we had no landing-lights out. After passing Wick it started to get darker and by the time we were down to Tarbat Ness we were flying in moonlight. There was no wind and the whole picture, I can well remember, was like a fairyland. We could see the airfield at Longman, Inverness, quite distinctly as we passed over. Most of my passengers appeared asleep behind, excepting my wife, who sat just behind me in the starboard front seat. She was apprehensive about the night landing. I turned, shutting off the motors and commenced the descent and approach in from the sea. The lower we got the darker it appeared, and I switched on the aircraft landing searchlight, which picked up the dyke alongside the Moray Firth, after that the going was easy and we made a good landing. My passengers had done so well at the party, that they took quite a bit of waking. I think they would have been quite happy if I had left them in the cabin for the night.

Shortly after that trip, an urgent call came in from the Stornoway fish curers to ferry 12 lassies between Wick and Shetland. I had only one aircraft available, so having delivered the first six at Sumburgh I had to turn around and return to Wick for the second lot. I was in the air for five hours and twenty minutes and all the girls arrived on time. I believe one or two of them had previously made the trip with me on the first 'fish girl' flight direct from Kirkwall to Stronsay a year or so before.

We were given an Air Ministry contract as the political situation worsened to carry out Army Co-operation flying at Inverness, Kirkwall and Shetland for 297 H.A.A. Battery. The aircraft had to fly on certain courses and at different altitudes up to 10,000 feet while the A.A. guns practised training. These exercises went on from one to two hours and became very boring.

As the war clouds gathered momentum and the Nazis swallowed up Austria in their rampage over Europe, so did the Army Co-operation work increase. We were stepped up to three nights a week and I was kept very busy. High-altitude spotting and gun-siting was the order of the day, and I can remember one evening was so clear that flying at 10,000 feet over Inverness and towards Loch Ness I could see the mountains alongside the Corran-Ardgour ferry south-west of Fort William some 70 miles away. It was a wonderful sight which never repeated itself. We would repair to the Ack-Ack Mess after these flights and the details of the exercise were discussed and procedure for the following exercise would be mapped out. It was very necessary for the pilot to know the drill the gun crews were involved in, as the flying had to be co-ordinated to give the gun crews the maximum value of training. I am happy to know that we did the job well and it was to be hoped that the instruction was such that it accounted for a record bag of Germans at a later date.

Monday, 31st July, proved a red letter day for the island of North Ronaldsay, for at long last the Post Office, who had been considering the question for the past two years (in tortoise fashion) at last decided to grant the island an air mail service. I chose our Dragon G-ACIT for the job as it was that plane which had an honourable mail record.

It was a bad day along the route from Inverness, with thunder, lightning and heavy rain. But the weather at North Ronaldsay was kinder and I arrived over the landing ground to find the whole island out in force to welcome the mail and myself, for they knew the amount of effort I had made to improve their communications with the outside world. Before the advent of the air service, they used to be cut off for days and even with fine weather it took hours to reach Kirkwall, whereas, with the air service they enjoyed, the journey only took a matter of 15 minutes or so. Now their mail would

Tai Yuan Fu.

16th October 25

This is to certify that Mr. E.E.Fresson has just completed his
Contract with us to our entire satisfaction.

Last year Mr. Fresson came here to organise a Factory and manufacture
Aeroplanes.   The first machine has been produced and flown by
him and he is now leaving us at his own wish.

All business transactions entered into with Mr.Fresson have been
carried out in an honest and business like manner and we are quite
satisfied with him in every respect.

Shansi Govmt. Arsenal & Mint.

...................*M.S.Li.*...................

Director.

Chinese Translation.

Completion note of Fresson's contract from the
Shansi government, 1925.

The S.T.4 Monospar at Inverness, 1933.

North Ronaldsay islanders going to Kirkwall market.

Presentation of pennant at the start of the first air mail service from Inverness to Orkney, 1934.

Inauguration of the Shetland air service, June 1936.

arrive regularly and on time, so it was not difficult to understand their joy. How tragic that, having waited so many years for the privilege they received that day, after only one month's operation up to the end of August, it was suddenly taken away from them. For at the outbreak of war on 3rd September the island services were closed down by the Air Ministry and all North Isles landing fields were immobilised by building stone cairns over them. Then after the war when Scottish Airways had spent several months with the Orkney County Council surveying the islands with a view to laying down permanent airfields, they were denied a resumption of the pre-war services owing to nationalised bureaucracy.

We in Scottish Airways and its directors were concerned that we were providing an air service which was of life or death importance to those islands, and which paid its way with the type of aircraft we used, in conjunction with other local routes such as the trans-Pentland service and an Orkney-Shetland service for the business community. The islanders accordingly lived to curse the day when Socialism, which was supposed to exist for the people, sold them down the drain. Since then, I believe, depopulation of the Orkney Islands has become a very serious matter and all on account of reverting to outmoded transport.

We were glad to see the month of July end, for it was a month of almost continued fog and we were all feeling the strain of maintaining our service at 100 per cent under such conditions. We little knew it at the time, but August was the last month of 'peace in our time' which Prime Minister Chamberlain promised us on his return from his second abortive trip to Munich and Berchtesgarten after his talks with Hitler.

The North Isles service traffic was booming and on the 12th of the month we carried no less than 26 passengers in the day which was a record for such sparsely inhabited islands. This success, however, was short lived because on Sunday, 3rd September 1939, Mr. Chamberlain announced that we were at war with Germany. We sat in our drawing room at Mid Kerrogair listening to the radio and the Prime Minister's scathing attack on Germany's bad faith. It was a lovely summer's day completely spoiled by the gravity of the situation.

CHAPTER ELEVEN

ON Monday, 4th September 1939, the Air Ministry ordered the cessation of our air services and withdrew the radio facilities along our routes. Thus, the naval base at Scapa was cut off from rapid communication with the south.

For Scottish Airways, war meant considerable changes including our freedom of action. The closure of our air communications affected the Admiralty badly and we were soon faced with the problem of service personnel turning up for transport to their units, and technicians on their way north for urgent duties in Orkney and Shetland. Urgent signals were despatched to the Air Ministry. In the meantime, I assumed the responsibility of retaining one Rapide aircraft, G-ADAJ, for Admiralty and Scapa communications.

A spate of charter flights occurred, which was tantamount to a regular daily service. It took exactly ten days to solve that Gilbertian situation. It subsequently transpired that the Air Ministry had notified our Renfrew Operations Office three days after the outbreak of war that the Orkney service should be resumed as early as possible, but without radio facilities. For some reason, which I was unable to discover, that message was not passed on to Inverness, and it was some ten days after that I received direct instructions from Mr. Collins, Air Ministry, to resume the Orkney service as soon as possible.

As Scapa Flow was to the Navy, so the airfield we had built at our own expense in Shetland was to the R.A.F., who immediately requisitioned it, together with our 50-feet span hangar. A squadron of Gladiator fighters was sent to Sumburgh to give air cover and patrol the northern sea approaches from Europe to the Atlantic. For the past three years, we had been exhorting the Government to give financial assistance for constructing airfields at Wick and Shetland which would be of urgent and strategic value should war break out.

The aviation magazine *The Aeroplane*, backed by its well-known editor C. G. Grey, joined forces with us in urging the Chamberlain Government to act, but no notice was taken of those exhortations. Scottish Airways were accordingly forced to proceed on their own in order to provide an air link with Shetland. At considerable expense they had an airfield constructed which provided an 800-yard run in a north/south direction and 600 yards east/west.

That airfield was of sufficient dimensions for the operation of Gloster Gladiator fighters. So owing to commercial enterprise the Royal Air Force was able to provide immediate air cover to the Northern Defence Group immediately war broke out. In addition we had a 50-feet span hangar which was invaluable for the maintenance of the R.A.F. fighters.

No official appreciation to my knowledge was ever extended to the company or myself who located, surveyed, established and financed such valuable defence facilities in the early and critical stages of the war.

More confusion followed shortly, for on 27th May 1940 I received a 'call-up' notice from the R.A.F. under my Reserve commitments, to report to Gillingham, Kent, in ten days' time. I immediately notified the Air Ministry department who were responsible for our operations of my call up, and that I would be leaving Inverness to take up my Reserve R.A.F. duties in ten days. There was a lot to be done in a little time. My house had to be let and a thousand and one things to be sorted out. Over and above all the worry there was the daily flying to be done in spite of a great shortage in flying staff. Also someone had to be found to take my place and there was no one with the first-hand experience and knowledge which I possessed. On the day before my departure with luggage packed – and sleeper booked, ticket issued and within a few hours of boarding the express train for London – an urgent departmental signal was received, instructing me to remain where I was.

In due course, I was instructed to stay in Inverness and take charge of the air communications for the North of Scotland on behalf of the Air Ministry. That meant everything had to be unscrambled, including the persuasion of the prospective tenant of our house to cancel his lease, which he was naturally reluctant to do.

The wartime increase in passengers, mail and newspapers for the forces in Orkney and Shetland increased to embarrassing proportions, and we were at our wits' end how we would carry the loads with the few small aircraft we had at our disposal, together with the small staff left to us.

In 1940 and approaching my 50th birthday, I had perforce to rejoin the regular pilots' roster, which duties I continued to carry out for the duration of the war, in addition to the responsibilities for the management and operations of the air-routes.

With the advent of winter and deteriorating weather conditions, the absence of radio facilities was bearing hardly on our pilots and myself in maintaining the regularity which was called for under war conditions. If the Admiralty did not receive its air mail at Scapa Flow, or couriers were delayed, it could have serious results in the conduct of the war effort. Against this apparent stupidity of those responsible for this situation I was told by a high-ranking R.A.F. officer that the Germans flying up the European coastline could be heard using their radio for local operations in plain language. So I wondered, why deny such urgent facilities to us? Without radio stations to home on, we were forced to fly at low altitude. I have described in earlier chapters the risk involved in that sort of flying and the danger of collision involved in being forced up into the overcast, without the pilot being able to determine his exact position for the descent. A further obstacle was also placed in our way. We were denied the coastline route which we had always followed in the early days before radio stations were provided. That forced us into flying over high ground inland, which made it virtually impossible for us to operate when the cloud base was down to 500 feet; such conditions, incidentally, were ample for the coastline route. Unless we could get those crippling conditions altered, it was clear to us that we should not be of much use to the war effort, as we would be grounded many days of each month. If that happened, the Admiral in charge at Scapa would be mostly affected, so I finally decided, why not present the problem to him?

An appointment was made for the afternoon of 13th October 1939, through his secretary Lieutenant Commander Laybourne and I was duly presented to Admiral French on board the *Iron Duke*, Scapa Flow. He was very sympathetic and helpful. He listened to the problems placed before him,

"If we withdraw the restrictions we have placed on your company operating along the coast route when the weather and cloud conditions are down to 500 feet, would that be of any assistance?" he enquired.

"It would indeed, sir," I answered, "but we would still be back to 1933 methods of crawling along at low altitude in bad visibility, and it is not an easy or particularly safe approach to Orkney under these conditions. The regularity would still be affected, though in a lesser degree."

He could not hold out any hope for the resumption of radio navigation, which led me to wonder if the Admiralty were responsible for the impasse, but he did say that he would authorise the coastal route to be made available to us under low cloud conditions without further delay. That at least was something gained. Our conversation had been prolonged and it would be dark long before I could get back to Inverness. Night flying was prohibited, besides being very restricted without radio. I was, therefore, obliged to remain the night at Scapa Flow and Lieutenant Commander Laybourne made arrangements for me to stay on the s.s. *Voltaire* which was used as a guest ship for Admiralty personnel and visitors.

There were a number of interesting naval officers at dinner and later in the wardroom we chatted about the war and other matters well on into the night. Retiring around midnight, it was not long before I was in a sound sleep. It had been a long day. I was awakened in the very early morning by the sound of numerous feet clanging about on the steel decks and orders being shouted around. This went on for an interminable time and I wondered whatever the Navy were up to at that unearthly hour. Gradually the noise subsided, and I fell asleep again.

An orderly brought me a cup of tea at eight o'clock.

"Whatever was going on in the early hours?" I enquired, "the noise was enough to wake the dead!"

He appeared reluctant to answer me.

"Didn't you hear, orderly?"

"Yes, sir, I was up helping."

"Helping, whatever were you helping, at that unearthly hour?" He hesitated,

"A terrible thing happened, sir, the *Royal Oak* was blown up last night in the Flow, and there's a heavy death roll. The wounded were brought here and to the hospital ship. It was terrible to see them, sir," he said, "covered in oil and choking, and others badly hurt by the explosion. I'm not supposed to tell you all this, sir," he went on, "so please don't mention it to anyone here."

I gave him my word and immediately got up to shave. It was not until after breakfast and when being ferried over to Scapa Pier in a naval launch that I fully realised the horror of what had happened. The sea was covered by a film of black fuel oil. Countless bodies floated around with debris, soaked in black oil and it was clear that the death roll had been heavy. What on earth could have been the cause? Nobody appeared to have a clue. It was not until some time after that we learned that a German U-boat had managed to breach the defences and had plugged at least five torpedoes into the *Royal Oak*, around one-thirty in the morning of 14th October 1939, at a cost of 786 officers and men.

Apparently, there was a gap between two block ships at Kirk

Sound, and with great skill the U-boat Captain, Lieutenant Prien, steered between the block ships through the narrow gap presented in the dark. It was reported shortly afterwards by Lord Haw Haw over the German radio, that the crew could see a man on a bicycle going home, they were so close to the shore. For quite a while, no one could guess how the U-boat could have got in, and what was more incredulous, got out and away again. There were rumours that the commander must have followed on the stern of a warship through the boom of one of the larger channels, but that did not explain how the U-boat got away.

Arriving at Scapa Pier, I was soon in the air on my way back to Inverness, stunned by what I had witnessed. Three days later, Scapa had an air raid and the *Iron Duke* on which I met Admiral French four days previously was damaged by near misses causing her to settle on the bottom in shallow water. She continued, however, to do her work throughout the war in that condition. A few bombs also fell on South Ronaldsay, blasting holes in farmland.

By the middle of November, the lack of radio navigation assumed an urgency not hitherto appreciated by officialdom in London, for on the 16th of that month I was detailed to fly Group Captain Croke to Shetland, on an urgent R.A.F. mission. We assumed at the time that it was something to do with the limited airfield facilities at Sumburgh Head, for it was obvious that if the Northern Approaches were to be fully covered and patrolled, a far larger airfield would be needed than that provided by Scottish Airways.

We landed at Hatston Naval Air Station in Orkney for lunch and continued the journey to Shetland afterwards. A few miles north of North Ronaldsay Lighthouse, with 56 miles of open sea in front of us and a very narrow landfall at the other end, we ran into a wall of cloud which stretched right down to the sea surface. There were no means of knowing or finding out whether these conditions continued all the way to Shetland, and it was quite obvious that if they did we stood a pretty hopeless chance of finding Sumburgh Head and landing, and perhaps a very good chance of running slap into the vertical cliff face of Fitful Head, west of our airfield, which reared up to over 900 feet. We accordingly returned to the island of North Ronaldsay and landed. My passenger was not at all pleased over the interrupted journey and enquired the reason. I explained the position to him and he was amazed to hear we had been deprived of radio navigation since the outbreak of hostilities.

"I mean to find out who is responsible for this chaotic state of affairs when I return to London," he said, "here we have air communications engaged on a most important job in the defence of the North and yet are denied the means of operating in bad weather."

And look into it he apparently did, for within a short time we had the radio stations restored, enabling us to reopen the Shetland route which had remained closed since the commencement of hostilities. However, we had to use coded messages which slowed us up a bit at first, but we soon got accustomed to it, and at any rate it was a reasonable price to pay to regain the directional bearings.

Our landing field at North Ronaldsay was situated on the south end of the island and adjacent to the Post Office and the local store, both of which were operated by Mr. James Swanney, who incidentally was also our agent. The service to North Ronaldsay had not been restored after the outbreak of war and so they did not see us very often. Mr. Swanney soon arrived enquiring if he could be of assistance. I explained the circumstances and he invited us into his house. We were met by Mrs. Swanney who soon produced tea and cookies. While we settled down to this pleasant interlude, Group Captain Croke became interested in what Mr. Swanney had to say about the changed life the air service and air mail had brought to the island.

"Just to think, Group Captain," he said, "we waited over four years for our air mail, which started at the beginning of August 1939, only to lose it as soon as the war started, a month later. Without our air service to Kirkwall, which we had grown accustomed to for the past four years, which enabled us to get into Kirkwall in the morning and return at night, we feel completely cut off."

I sympathised with them deeply; having been so clearly associated with the islanders, I knew how much they had lost in amenity by the withdrawal of air communications from that lonely and cut-off island.

After an hour or so, the weather appeared to improve so we bade farewell to the Swanney family and took off on another attempt to reach Sumburgh. We soon picked the low cloud up again out to sea, but in patches this time and after five minutes or so flew out into the clear, when we were able to see Fair Isle looming ahead on the starboard side, looking dark and foreboding in the misty conditions.

I sighed with relief at having run clear of that low cloud, but my relief was short-lived – for suddenly to the south of Fair Isle I spotted a big monoplane a bit higher than we were. I called to the Group Captain behind me and he came forward and took a look. We both agreed it looked like a German Dornier Do17 light bomber and we were just mincemeat for him, for we carried no armament. Suddenly the dark-looking monoplane turned towards us – had he spotted us we wondered? Hoping the stranger had not, I dived quickly for sea level with the intention of flying low to Fair Isle. Our plane was camouflaged and at sea level we stood a chance of reaching the island without being spotted, and of effecting a landing on the south end until the Dornier had passed on. But that was not to be, for as we commenced to go down, so did the other plane which by now was much nearer and heading towards us. We held our breath, for there was little doubt that we had now been observed. The Dragon biplane's flying speed was far too slow even to try and keep on the unarmed tail of a Dornier. We had to reach Fair Isle. It was our only chance. I opened the engines flat out, skimming a few feet above the waves. There was just a possibility of reaching the shore before the enemy caught up with us. We had all but reached the rocky coastline when the intruder came within shooting range. The bullets would soon start tearing us to pieces now, I thought, with the per-spiration streaming down my cheeks, when suddenly we both ex-claimed,

"It's an R.A.F. Anson."

What a relief that was.

The incident showed how extremely moist air could magnify an aircraft flying some miles away, for neither of us had any doubt, when we first saw the Anson, that it was a far larger aircraft. The incident had certainly put the wind up us. Had it been an armed enemy plane, I very much doubt whether we should have escaped with our lives. The Anson apparently recognised us as a friendly aircraft, for it veered off and resumed its southerly course, no doubt to continue its patrol for U-boats.

On arrival at Sumburgh airfield, our manager there, Jim Black met us. I thought he was looking curiously at us, for I said,

"What's wrong?"

"You look a bit shaken, Captain, was the weather very bad south? It has been a shocking day here."

"Yes, we did run into bad weather north of Ronaldsay, but after an hour's wait there, it cleared up."

After introducing the Group Captain we told him about our experience with the Anson.

"Come along to the house," he said. It was a stone cottage situated by Verkie Pool and was I believe like our agent's house at North Ronaldsay, the local Post Office which Mrs. Black operated. There was a wharf nearby which the local fishing boats used. Apart from that, there did not appear to be much happening that would distinguish one day from another – except maybe, a howling storm, which would whip the sea into a boiling cauldron.

We stayed overnight in Lerwick 25 miles away. Our Lerwick agent, Bertie Ganson of Ganson Brothers Ltd., sent a car to fetch us, and my passenger enjoyed the marvellous view which presented itself along the coastline to Lerwick, for the road winds up and down hill and often along sections of road cut out from the hillside.

We left Sumburgh next day in time to catch the night express from Inverness for London. Group Captain Croke had heard of the inland route which had been transferred to West of Hoy, Thurso, Kinbrace, Dornoch and Invergordon. We had flown up the coast route owing to low cloud conditions, so, as the following day was clear, I flew low over the back country behind the Caithness and Sutherland mountains which stretched along the coast from just above Latheron to Dornoch. That run involved the journey around Hoy in Orkney, and an excellent view of the Old Man of Hoy was obtained. We flew low across the moors south of Thurso and the 500 feet plateau beyond Kinbrace could be seen as we were passing Achintoul Lodge which Mr. George Law occupied in the early days of the war.

That route was an excellent one for safety as the war hotted up and German aircraft became more numerous. Our aeroplanes were camouflaged earth and green colour and the top wings merged with the peat and heather surroundings. Looking down from a height, it was very difficult for enemy aircraft to spot us. On many occasions, I received a radio message from Orkney to return there as enemy aircraft were reported in the vicinity, shortly after we left for Inverness. If we were over half way across the Pentland Firth, I pretended I hadn't received the message, as it was safer flying over those moors than risking the return Pentland Firth crossing which would show up my plane clearly to the enemy.

There was a small cottage at the bottom of the escarpment some miles south of Kinbrace. It was miles from nowhere, and I always used to fly low over that cottage on the northbound run and give the good lady who lived there a wave. She would come rushing out of the back door to respond. Sometimes I used to drop her a morning newspaper. I felt sorry for her in such uninhabited and lonely surroundings, and hoped my morning aerial salutations brought her a little relief from boredom.

We were nearly into December and the so-called phoney war dragged on while the Nazis finished off Poland. We brought the New Year in with misgiving. Poland could not hold out much longer and, it is said, we were not strong enough or properly equipped to make a

diversion in Poland's favour, along the Maginot Line, so we waited for the Nazis to make the first move.

In the meantime, Hatston airfield had been mostly completed and a fine air station it was. It was commanded by a very nice officer named Commander Howe. He was aware that I had a hand in the siting and construction of the Hatston Naval Air Station and he was also aware of how inadequate our landing field at Wideford had become with the enormous loads we were having to cope with under wartime conditions. He accordingly kindly gave us permission to use Hatston airfield providing that we conformed to Naval movements taking priority. That assurance I gladly gave and what a difference a full-sized airfield made to our operations and to the peace of mind of our pilots.

After seven years' use of the Wideford airfield, we were obliged to face up to the fact that its usefulness had become inadequate for modern needs. We, and the public, owed Wideford and its generous owner, Mr. Anderson, a great debt of gratitude, for it had served its purpose in establishing the passenger and air mail service to the Orkneys. It had also served in developing the aircraft loads from a trickle in the beginning to the rushing stream which was now on the point of flooding its banks. So, it was with many pangs of regret that

I advised Scottish Airways to discontinue the lease of that airfield as soon as the new R.A.F. aerodrome at Grimsetter, nearby, was constructed the following year.

On landing with the mail plane at Hatston towards the end of the first week in January, a naval Petty Officer was there to meet me as I descended from the aeroplane. He informed me that Commander Howe wished to see me in his office. He greeted me with

"Hello, Captain Fresson, I've got a job for you to do."

He had with him a high-ranking naval officer to whom I was introduced. His name was Admiral Somerville. He was of medium height with a typical seafaring look and possessed a charming personality.

"The Admiral wishes you to fly him up to the Fair Isle. We hear you have made several landings there and as Admiral Somerville's visit is urgent and of great importance to the war effort, will you take the job on? Our pilots have flown up to Fair Isle and say there is no place where they could land."

I agreed to take on the flight, but said it would be necessary to wait until the wind conditions were right. A few days later on Tuesday, 10th January, we phoned Hatston from Inverness that the Inverness Meteorological Office had informed us that we might expect slight easterly winds in the Fair Isle region, and as that was satisfactory, would they let us know when I arrived at Hatston on the normal service if Admiral Somerville would be available.

Prompt on arrival at Hatston airfield, there was the Admiral with Commander Howe waiting for me. Having ascertained how long the visit would take on the island, it was arranged with my traffic officer to have the southbound passengers delayed until three-thirty in the afternoon. Arriving over the island, I circled the landing place at 1,000 feet. Admiral Somerville was sitting just behind me and when the ground was pointed out to him, he exclaimed like others had done

"Surely it's not possible to land there?"

He had observed that the ground was encircled for three parts of the perimeter by cliffs and that there was a nasty drop into the sea if we overshot. He was assured I would not take unnecessary risks and if the approach looked risky, we would return to the base. I was flying my trusted Dragon G-ACIT and I could land that plane on a pocket handkerchief.

As we dropped lower, I observed to my dismay that the wind was fairly strong and not in the right direction, coming too much from the north. Fortunately the neck of ground connecting the landing area to the rest of the island was on the north so it was decided to land on one wheel and turn in a slight circle as we touched down, so that when the second wheel was on the ground, we were heading for the narrow neck into wind. This way we made a good landing – but I confess, the strong cross-wind take-off worried me, also the backing wind, as that meant the approach of a depression and probably bad visibility for the return journey. However, I kept all that to myself and accompanied Admiral Somerville on his search of the island. An introduction was made to Mr. Stout the island's chieftain and the lighthouse keeper, whom I had met on my first survey of the island by steamer some years back. It appeared that the Admiral was looking for a suitable site for the Navy to construct a radar scanner and we were all sworn to secrecy. We were taken to the top of a hill in the centre of the island, and on the way up I discovered a site that had good possibilities of being constructed into a landing strip. It headed north-east by south-west and was just right for prevalent winds. We hadn't been out an hour, when it began to rain. My foreboding about the depression appeared correct. We had landed at 11.30 a.m. and it was nigh on one o'clock before we got back to the village on the south end of the island. The Admiral had found a suitable site for his radar scanner. We were invited to one of the houses for lunch, and a wonderful lunch it was. Soup, chicken, canned peaches and local cream. Our hostess had gleaming ginger hair and Admiral Somerville teased that poor woman until she was blushing furiously. At the end of lunch, we were presented with Fair Isle hosiery gifts. We were looked after so well, that by the time we were ready to take-off at 3.00 p.m., I felt like having a good afternoon siesta.

During lunch, the weather had deteriorated badly. We said goodbye to our very hospitable friends and clambered aboard. There was no doubt in my mind that the Admiral had thoroughly enjoyed his impromptu outing, when he was able to drop the mask of officialdom and rank. We made a cross-wind take-off and rose in half the distance available. Passing over the sheer cliff edge, the air was very turbulent as we commenced a climbing turn on a south-westerly course.

It was raining heavily and the visibility was down to a mile or so. I hated that stretch of lonely water to North Ronaldsay without radio bearings to help me. It was so easy to fly past the north end and miss the Orkney Isles, and we had not too much petrol to go looking for them. The tanks had been kept purposely low so as to facilitate a quick take-off under such restricted conditions. As usual, when the visibility was bad over the sea, I borrowed Francis Chichester's technique, which he employed on his famous island hopping from New Zealand to Australia, by steering a deliberate error to one side of the target and after a calculated elapsed time, steer at right-angles to the course. In this particular case it meant steering ten degrees south of the true course, which if continued would take me to the left of my target the Orkney Isles. I calculated the point of turn-off so that it would be roughly abreast the Island of Stronsay and to the east of it, after half an hour's flying. By such means, one would avoid missing the northern tip of North Ronaldsay, and getting lost over the ocean.

It was an eerie and lonely feeling groping one's way across the sea, low down and hemmed in by mist with no shipping around. Every way seemed the same way, and one had to stick rigidly to the planned flight and to the compass course set. At the end of the half hour after being airborne, we turned west and within five minutes picked up the island of Stronsay. Within 15 minutes, we had landed at Hatston airfield. Admiral Somerville thanked me for carrying out a difficult job for him and bade me farewell. I was never to meet him again as he was shortly afterwards transferred to the Mediterranean. I was sorry, as he had been such good fun.

Picking up my waiting southbound passengers, I delivered them at Inverness in good time for the afternoon express.

Shortly before hostilities commenced, and during breakfast at our house at Mid Kerrogair, Dalcross, near Ardersier, there came a knock at the front door. I answered the knock, and found two individuals, who after greeting me said they were from the Air Ministry and wished to know if I could advise them where to find a likely site for an Air Ministry R.A.F. airfield near Inverness. They said they had been advised to call on me. It had so happened that, for some months, we had come to the conclusion that our airfield at Longman had become obsolete with the heavy increase in traffic and aircraft loads, and a thorough search of the district had been made for a new site. Longman would have cost too much to extend as it involved buying up and closing down two farms. I had chosen the ground on which my present house was situated, but there again it belonged to the Earl of Moray. The question, should I disclose the Dalcross site? The farmer wanted to get me out of my house as the lease was up, so it occurred to me that it might be possible to make a deal with these people that if they took over the land, we might retain our house. So I said to them

"We have the very place for you, capable of indefinite expansion;

if I disclose it, would the Ministry consider my interests in the matter?"

They said they were unable to answer that question, but would make enquiries and call back and see me.

They came back within a few days and said the Ministry were prepared to do all they could to preserve any reasonable interests if it was within their jurisdiction. My mistake was not to get it in writing. Accepting their word, as we were also keen on getting a full-size airfield for Inverness, I said to them

"Gentlemen, you are standing on the very place."

"What, here!" they exclaimed in surprise.

"Yes, come and look." I took them into the fields in front of the house and pointed as far as they could see to the east and west and certainly a mile to the south.

"The ground is undulating in places, and there are woods here and there, but that is no difficulty for modern machinery. One thing, however," I warned as a parting shot, "you will require tarmac runways, because the ground will become very boggy in winter. The drainage fall is very slight."

Off they went and we saw them for several days, marching over the fields before they returned and said

"Thank you, Captain. This is the place and you have saved us many weary days of search."

"Good, now tell the Air Ministry my interests are twofold. I wish to retain the lease of this house, and we would like the rights for Scottish Airways to use the airfield on terms to be arranged suitable to both sides."

They promised to hand this information on and later other and more senior officials came to see me and said that as far as they could see there would be no objection to my retaining the house on lease. As for using the airfield, they felt sure that in peacetime an arrangement could be come to with the Ministry.

Towards the end of 1939, we heard that the land had been requisitioned and that work would commence on construction shortly. It was after my arrival back from Admiral Somerville's Fair Isle trip, that we woke up one morning to the sound of tractors going and terrific thumps on the ground. Looking out of the window to see what was going on, there was a tractor with chains pulling our beautiful sycamore trees down and tearing up our 100 years' old lawn. I rushed down in my dressing-gown and got hold of the foreman and asked him to stop such senseless destruction, until I could get a message through to Air Ministry in London.

"The garden," I told him, "does not come within the area required for airfield purposes and at any rate, this house is for my use."

"Sorry, Captain," he said, "I am only carrying out my instructions."

However, he gave me until lunch time to try and get an official ruling from the Air Ministry.

The phone wires buzzed that morning, but to no purpose. The area of my house, they told me, was to be used for the erection of hangars.

"But," I answered, "the arrangement with your representatives who called to see me six months ago, was that my interests would be covered."

"Sorry," they said, "we have a war on our hands, and Dalcross is a first priority airfield."

So that was that. Not only did I lose the trees, but I lost the house and had to be out by the end of April. Every morning for the next few days, we awoke to the crunch of falling trees, and by the end of the week our beautiful old garden was no more. I had then to get busy to find another home and that came about in the most fortuitous manner.

Early in 1940, an official request came through for a charter from Stornoway to Inverness. It was a blind take-off in fog from Longman and no hope of landing there on the return. I made sure that our emergency field at Culloden Moor was fog free and took off using the boundary fence again to keep the plane in a straight line. There were still no white lines on Longman airfield to assist fog take-offs. On the return journey, we landed high up on the moors not far from the old battlefield. Alongside the Culloden Moor landing field, there was a house and petrol pumps, belonging to one of the most worthy citizens of Inverness, Willie Michie.

He was a first-rate humorist and in his job as chief auctioneer for Fraser's Auction Rooms would keep the bargain hunters in stitches of laughter during the sales by his witty remarks. Along with his charming wit, he was an excellent connoisseur of a good dram. On descending from the plane, one of my distinguished passengers confided that he had a bottle of a 'first-class Scotch Blend' and as we had a wait before our road transport would arrive, he suggested breaking the bottle.

"We haven't any water or glasses," he said, "can you take it neat?"

"Oh! that's easily remedied, come along to the house by the petrol pumps and I am sure Willie will fix us up and enjoy a dram himself."

On knocking at the door, Mrs. Michie answered, and said her

husband was out, could she be of help. I told her we had just arrived from Stornoway and as our car had not arrived, might we use the phone. Also could we have a few glasses and some water? She acquiesced and showed us into her sitting room and while I was phoning, Mrs. Michie went to see about the water and glasses. On rejoining my three passengers, the chappie with the bottle was looking glum.

"She's brought each of us a tumbler of water," he complained, "and there is no room for the whisky."

"Oh dear, that's sad, I must get that sorted out."

Ringing the bell, Mrs. Michie returned looking quizzical. I explained our difficulty and she blushed with embarrassment.

"I'm so sorry," she said, "I didn't know you had a bottle with you. I will get a jug immediately."

She came back with a half-full jug and we were able to pour the water in the tumblers back into the jug.

That whisky really tasted good. It was an excellent brand, and coming after the tricky flight and with the cold dank air outside, it was a great booster. Shortly after, Willie returned. On introducing him to my companions, the owner of the bottle invited him to join us in a 'hootie'. As the warm liquid disappeared down Willie's throat, he confided to us that his wife had told him of the embarrassment she had caused us and he added

"Just to think that such a thing could happen in ma hoose."

We talked on for a bit waiting for the car when Willie asked me if I was still living at Dalcross.

"Yes, but not for long now. The Air Ministry are turning us out and I've got to find another in double quick time."

"Would you wish to buy one?" he enquired.

"Yes, at the right price."

"Well, you go and see Mrs. Gordon Cumming at 12 Mayfield Road. I hear she is thinking of selling her bungalow. It is very nice with a good garden and garage."

Just then our car arrived and we bade the Michies farewell. I promised to get in touch with Mrs. Cumming at once.

The next day, we went around to see her. Yes, she was willing to sell if she could get her figure. I asked what she wanted and she told me. My solicitor friend, Harold Georgeson of Wick got busy with the negotiations and within a month the house was ours. We moved in early April. It was with great regret that we left our very nice residence in the country. However, it was really for the best, as the war soon started to hot up and it was far more convenient for me to be in town than nine miles away, especially in times of emergency, or when V.I.P.s were coming and going, and also with emergency charter flights cropping up at any odd moment.

My next important passenger was Mr. Clement Attlee. He flew north with me to Orkney on 30th March 1940. I well remember the trip. He sat in the front seat of the cabin just behind me, and on one or two occasions I tried to engage him in conversation on the way to the Pentland Firth. The windows of all passenger aircraft, under wartime regulations, were painted over and only the cockpit windows were clear. The passenger in the front seat could look out by bending well forward and I thought Mr. Attlee might be interested to see the mountains we were passing over. He appeared to look very white and tired.

Passing over the southern shore line of the Pentland Firth on our way to the west end of Hoy, a large battle cruiser appeared ahead, dead on our track. Standing naval orders said 'Aircraft were not to fly directly over warships' so I commenced to veer off course to the east. Suddenly signal lights commenced blinking away frantically on the cruiser. I had no signalling light installed on my aircraft to reply with, even if I had understood the flashes, which I didn't. We had nearly got abreast of the cruiser, when she suddenly started shooting us up with her anti-aircraft guns. Suddenly we were surrounded with white bursts which rocked the Rapide severely. I called to Mr. Attlee and told him we were being fired on, and to hold on tight as I was about to put the plane into a steep dive. He leant forward quickly and took a quick look, as I pushed the nose of our aircraft down. We were flying, my logbook tells me at 2,000 feet. We came out of the dive at a few hundred feet over the sea. By that time the firing had ceased and we scuttled low down around The Old Man of Hoy and into safety. Mr. Attlee looked whiter than ever, and became a little unbending, engaging me in conversation about the shooting.

On landing, I reported the incident to the Commander at Hatston, who promptly got busy to find out the ship responsible. There was quite a flap on in view of the importance of our V.I.P. I learned later it was an Australian cruiser who had opened up on us because we had not answered their signals. All the same, their aircraft recognition should have been better than it apparently was, because a Rapide biplane was unlike any of our own or enemy war aircraft of that period. However, they didn't hit us, which showed up their inaccurate aerial gunnery and there the matter ended as far as we were concerned. I accepted it along with the many other risks our pilots and myself took in operating wartime air communications.

April was a particularly bad month for weather, in fact the weather had been continuously bad all the winter. Snowstorms especially were prolonged with heavy gales. That winter without radio was exceptionally hard on all pilots, and as I look back on the effort made by all and the continuous nervous strain imposed on the aircrews, the highest praise is due to those concerned, viz: John Hankins, Henry Vallance and Bernard Wilson.

The 30th of April was another eventful day for myself. The Orkney Isles and the Pentland Firth were covered in low cloud and drizzle. I was returning from Orkney with a full load of passengers flying low over the water around Hoy, with visibility around a mile.

Suddenly we ran into a clear patch and found ourselves bang in front of two warships carrying out target practice. To make matters more alarming, we were between the warships and the target. No notice had been given to our operations room of this hazard. I took quick action. The only chance of dodging those shells was to drop down to sea level, which we did pretty quickly, and we flew along touching the wave tops with the shells passing overhead until we were well clear of the warships.

The war took an important change early in April, for the Germans attacked Norway, and sent a landing force to Narvik in the far north to protect it, for that port was of supreme importance to the Germans, as it controlled the shipment of iron ore supplies which came from the hinterland mines, over the Swedish border. Trondhjem was also overrun. The attack was very sudden and at the time was described as the 'Rape of Norway', a country which had for many years been on the best of terms with Germany.

At that time, I flew to Shetland a party of important Norwegians who would make their way across to Norway by sea and effect a secret landing. I surmised that these V.I.P.s were charged with the formation of the Norwegian Patriots' underground. As time went on, we were to play an important part in flying members of the underground to and from Shetland R.A.F. base. The R.A.F. would attend to their transportation to and from secret landing and embarkation spots along the rocky Norwegian coastline. We used to get quite familiar with the couriers' faces and then one day we would not see a particular face any more. It was not hard to guess what had happened. They were extremely brave people, we all learnt to admire and respect them in their dangerous work.

On 10th May 1940, sparks really began to fly. The war was now rapidly shifting westwards, for Holland and Belgium were attacked by the German armed forces. There was a terrific stir in this country and all our aircraft, except Dragon G-ACIT, were mobilised and despatched to France to assist at the evacuation of Dunkirk. Later the operation was considered too dangerous for unarmed and slow aircraft such as our Rapides, and within a few days, on 2nd June, they were returned to base.

We had a fortnight's respite before our aircraft were again commandeered, this time to assist in the evacuation of France. I was left with Dragon G-ACIT in Inverness to carry the Scapa Flow passengers, mail and documents, not forgetting the couriers.

On 16th June 1940 Rapide G-AFOI left Heston for Bordeaux with a Ministry of Supply party, who would endeavour to obtain a large quantity of industrial diamonds before France was overrun. On arrival at Bordeaux, Pilot Captain Donald Prentice arranged a dead-line for their departure the following day, in view of the imminent approach of German forces. The defeatism prevalent in the French Officers' Mess, caused mainly by conflicting radio broadcasts in French and German, did not contribute to their ease of mind the following morning. Incidentally, the Rapide crew of three slept in the aircraft cabin overnight (with the radio operator's socks drying on the fixed aerial!). At noon, the Ministry of Supply party arrived and they took off for the open sea following the River Gironde. Their fuel margin to reach England was very small. Pilots of varying nationalities with aircraft of varying degrees of age or airworthiness had 'nobbled' all available fuel and some had crashed on the runway.

Approaching Biscay, Captain Prentice concerned himself with petrol and decided that they must refuel at Nantes, or face the possibility of ditching in the Channel. Approaching Nantes, the pilot did a few circuits, but no German movements were observed. The aerodrome was deserted. They helped themselves to fuel and took off over the sea to England. Engine trouble developed, and eventually flying on one engine, Captain Prentice diverted to Jersey. A Jersey Airways D.H.86 was discovered in a hangar; it had been in for Certificate of Airworthiness. No Jersey staff were available, so the crew 'borrowed' one of the engines. John Rawse the engineer, did a marvellous piece of work. There was great enjoyment the morning after when the 'borrowed' engine was run up. The Ministry of Supply team by this time had deserted the sinking ship. The Rapide crew then got involved in the evacuation of Jersey and, loading a party of varying nationalities, set off for Exeter where they arrived safely.

It was a great piece of work for the pilot, engineer and radio officer, as an engine change was a major operation, more especially as the D.H.86 engine installation was different from that of the Rapide.

Airfield building in the North of Scotland which, as I have already said, we had constantly advocated from 1935-39 as a necessary defence project and for which we pressed the Government unsuccessfully to interest themselves by giving financial pre-war support, now became a mad rush in wartime, and at double the cost. Wick airfield had just been completed with a turf surface, which was the normal practice of construction in pre-war days. As soon as winter set in, it rapidly became a quagmire and became unserviceable. We had been accustomed to such conditions for years using smaller types of aircraft, but for the R.A.F. with larger and heavily loaded aircraft, they just could not leave the ground in the winter when the turf was waterlogged. A hurried scramble ensued to construct the hard tarmac strips. We were constantly taking off and landing in a sea of mud alongside the hundreds of Irish labourers and machinery engaged in the construction of the air strips. One would have thought that even officialdom would have learnt their lesson over Wick and proceeded to construct hard tarmac strips at Dalcross, Inverness, which was at that time under construction, especially after my warning, but not so however. With ostrich-like habits, the Air Ministry failed to apply the lesson which should have been learned, or pay any heed to my earlier advice, and Dalcross was opened with the customary grass surface. The R.A.F. moved in and within two months or so, history repeated itself. Most of their aircraft stuck in the mud, just as happened at Wick, for it rained and rained during that winter of 1940. We continued to operate from Longman, Inverness, which fortunately had a hard gravel sub-soil.

During these troublous times for the R.A.F., the Hatston airfield with its hard tarmac strips was functioning daily without the slightest difficulty. I believe a deputation from the R.A.F. again visited the Naval Station of Hatston and left duly impressed, for shortly after, tarmac strips became standard in R.A.F. airfield construction. Aircraft were becoming larger with the advent of the multi-engined bombers which would carry extremely heavy loads of bombs. A hard and smooth surface for take-off and landing was therefore essential. It was then that the old-fashioned grass aerodrome ceased to exist.

After Dalcross airfield was modified to have hard runways, Sumburgh airfield situated at the southernmost tip of Shetland remained the only grass airfield in the North of Scotland. Once its role in the war effort was decided upon, reconstruction commenced during the early part of 1941. It was a difficult airfield to reconstruct as its level area was very limited. Consequently, it amounted to a major engineering job and costly alterations had to be made to the surrounding country. On the north side, the Pool of Virkie, which was a tidal basin, had to be filled in to a great extent, and a great number of high sand dunes levelled. To the south lay the beach alongside the North Sea and to the east, Sumburgh Head rising to some 300 feet with a lighthouse on the top of it. To the west, lay Fitful Head towering to over 900 feet some four miles away with the ground sloping up gently from the airfield. So to construct the north-east/south-west strip, a cutting of 200 feet wide and some 40 feet deep had to be made, through the sloping ground to the sea coast at the southern end of the site.

The construction took over a year to complete, but when finished it was a fine airfield for post-war Shetland, which could never have come into existence had it not been for the war, as the cost of construction was enormous. Had the work been carried out before the war, when I was urging the Government to build airfields, it would have cost a third of what it did under war conditions with highly paid Irish labour. With the completion of Sumburgh airfield, we were assured of a chain of modern post-war airfields to operate from.

During the invasion of Holland, Belgium and France, the Germans had used aircraft extensively for dropping saboteurs in the rear of the Allies, and landing Junkers aircraft in fields with troops aboard. To make sure this did not happen in the North of Scotland and the Western Isles, the authorities erected poles along the roads, on the beaches and possible fields near the towns so as to prevent such landings, so they thought. Actually, if the enemy had wished to carry out landing operations, they could have crashed-landed their aircraft without injury to the air crew or troops aboard, or for that matter, dropped the troops by parachute. I suspect, therefore, that the immense amount of work employed on this stunt was more for psychological reasons *vis-à-vis* the local population. Even the road across Rannoch Moor, which was too narrow for aircraft to land on, received its share of many miles of poles at extravagant cost. However, be that as it may, I received a call to fly a party of surveyors over to the Western Isles, with a view to organising the immobilisation of the beaches, along the western side of Barra, South and North Uist.

We set off on 27th July 1940 to carry out this work. The sun was shining which made the trip not only pleasant but enabled us to make quick progress with the survey. A local architect, Mr. Hamish Paterson, a member of the Royal Engineers, was in charge of the survey party, and I of course knew him quite well. We spent the day, beginning at the island of Barra, flying up miles of hard sand beaches. The area was vast and it was soon obvious that the project was absolutely impractical. It would have taken a small army years and half the forest trees in Scotland to complete the job. We landed at our rough landing field at Sollas that evening and went to Lochmaddy to stay the night at the local hotel. We planned to finish the survey of Harris and Lewis next day and fly straight back from Stornoway to Inverness.

It was not to be, however, for next morning when we awakened the island was covered in thick fog. We had no radio officer with us which would have enabled us to climb above the fog and make the direct flight back to Inverness. Radio communication had been restored a week or two before, but all messages had to be sent in code, otherwise I could have operated the radio myself and obtained my own bearings. We were, therefore, stranded in Lochmaddy with nothing to do but play billiards and walk around the village. That night we had a really big party with the locals, the fog swirling around outside. We retired to bed, hoping the morning would break clear.

Not so, however. If anything, it was even thicker than the day before. We could not see 20 yards ahead. To make matters worse, our host informed us that the whisky stocks were running low. With the war on he said to me, he didn't expect such a big demand on his resources without notice.

"Hasn't the local store got a case left?" we enquired.

"No," he said, "I had that off him yesterday."

Our hearts sank. What was there to do in fog-ridden Lochmaddy, without a dram to keep one going in the evening, my passenger bemoaned.

"Let's go out to the landing strip," I suggested, "and ask the radio superintendent to despatch a message to Renfrew to send a radio officer up on the Renfrew-Sollas service, for around midday the fog will likely lift 100 feet or so, thus allowing the service plane to get in on radio bearings."

Out we went in the local taxi. Sure enough, on the west side of the island the fog was up quite a bit and one could see possible breaks with the sun trying to get through. Our message went off and a reply soon came through that Jimmy Mitchell, our chief radio officer, who was on the 'Jersey forced landing', was coming up to assist us. The plane got down quite well with about a mile visibility, and we greeted Jimmy Mitchell as a long-lost brother.

We got our plane started, and took off. Climbing on an easterly course, we were swallowed up in fog in a few seconds. One thousand feet and we were still in it. At 1,500 feet the sky got lighter and at 2,000 feet we broke out into blue sky and sunshine. It was a beautiful sight with the white cloud carpet below us and deep blue sky above. After 20 minutes or so we caught a glimpse of the island of Raasay through a hole in the fog. That meant that we were just east of Skye, and ahead were the Easter Ross mountains covered in cloud. We were flying at 6,000 feet which was high enough for safety, so I carried on through cloud. The radio officer at Sollas had obtained a weather report for us at Inverness, giving an overcast sky but good visibility. At an estimated position half-way across the mountains, I asked Jimmy Mitchell to get me a bearing on Inverness airfield.

He started to tap away on his key. I waited and still the tapping went on. After five minutes or so, I called back,

"What about the bearing, Jimmy?"

"I can't get one," he replied.

"Why not?"

"Inverness have asked me for the code word for the day, and they say the one I have got is incorrect, so they won't give a bearing."

"What in hell has happened?" I queried, "didn't you get the code word when you left Renfrew?"

"Yes, but they must have given me the wrong one."

"Have another go," I said, "tell them the name of the pilot and say we are caught up in cloud over the mountains and must have a bearing."

After a while he called me.

"Inverness say they cannot break regulations: no proper code word, no bearing."

"Damn," I said to myself.

What a muddle. Here I was caught up in cloud and doing the very thing that I refused to do yesterday without the help of radio. While this conversation was going on, we were being thrown about quite a bit and it took me all my time to keep the plane under proper control by instruments. It was therefore, difficult to consider our position calmly.

After a couple of minutes' intermittent thinking while trying to concentrate on the instruments, I figured the sensible thing to do would be to alter course north-east to make sure of descending over the Moray Firth at the end of the calculated elapsed time of the flight. By this time at least a quarter of an hour had passed since Jimmy told me he couldn't get a bearing on Inverness, when without warning, we suddenly flew out of cloud and there in front of us was the Beauly Firth. We were dead on course. That was a lucky break. In another quarter of an hour we landed at Longman airport – home safely – and none the worse for an extremely bad error that had been made by the officer in charge at Renfrew. He had apparently given us the code word for the following day.

Two weeks later, the air battle of Britain was at its peak. In the midst of it we had a distinguished visitor in Sir Alan Brooke. In July the Secretary of State for War recommended that General Brooke should replace General Ironside in command of Home Forces. He was now on a tour of inspection. He had with him several members of his staff, and I was instructed to fly him to Wick and Castletown, where there was only a small field to effect a landing on. On completion of his inspection, we returned to Evanton R.A.F. airfield on the Cromarty Firth and eventually to Inverness. They caught the express train back to London. Sir Alan thanked me for the speedy manner in which I had enabled him to carry out his northern survey in one day, which would have ordinarily taken three days by surface transport. My memory of the occasion is taken up with the interest Sir Alan Brooke took in our operations, for he had heard that we flew the communications on days when the Fleet Air Arm and R.A.F. were grounded. He had great charm and I took an instant liking to him.

With the fall of France, the air battle for Britain was stepped up and by 15th September the decisive battle in the air was fought. London was being savagely attacked, but in the North of Scotland we were more or less free from enemy intrusion. One night however, during that period we were awakened by air-raid sirens, but nothing appeared to happen and we went to sleep again. Next day, we were told the aluminium works at Foyers had received a visit from the Luftwaffe and had been hit. But according to reports, not much damage was done.

After September, we began to get the occasional raider sneaking along our routes and Wick airfield was attacked. I remember landing there in the autumn of 1940, and seeing a Heinkel bomber, apparently intact, on the airfield apron. I was invited to look at it. It was in a fearful mess. The gunner was riddled with our fighter bullets and slumped in the cockpit dead, and the rest of the crew were wounded. The plane was covered in blood. There had been several of them, and they were intercepted by our fighters out at sea.

An alarming incident occurred shortly afterwards. Captain

Vallance had left Inverness in a Rapide with full passenger load for Orkney. The weather was bad with low cloud flying over the Firth, north of Cromarty and it extended up to roughly 1,000 feet. Above the visibility was good. Henry Vallance, flying above the cloud, had reached the vicinity of Tarbat Ness, some 30 miles north of Inverness, on course for Kirkwall by the coastal bad weather route. He happened to glance down to his left at the swirling mist below him, when suddenly he stiffened in his seat. Without warning, a Heinkel bomber suddenly appeared climbing out of the cloud below. What was he to do? The Rapide was unarmed and even had it been otherwise, the speed and climb of our aircraft could in no way match the German raider. It was not long before the Heinkel pilot spotted the Rapide, and commenced a climbing turn to give Henry the once over and probably a burst of machine-gun fire, which would soon have finished him, his seven passengers and his radio officer. Fortunately as Henry told me afterwards, he remembered the Heinkel had no rear machine-gunner and so, if he could keep on its tail and send radio S.O.S. signals, a fighter might arrive in time to chase the enemy off.

The enemy was still 500 feet below the Rapide, and Henry acted at once. He dived at the enemy's tail and positioned himself well in the rear, and slightly below the Heinkel, which was still climbing. As he commenced to dive, Henry shouted to his radio operator to send out an S.O.S. call to Inverness advising that he was being attacked by an enemy plane and to send word to Dalcross airfield for help. During the following five minutes, Henry was having all his work cut out keeping on the Heinkel's tail, owing to the higher speed and climb of the enemy. All this time, S.O.S. messages were flowing like a stream from the Rapide's transmitter. Suddenly, for no apparent reason the Heinkel commenced to veer out to sea and made off. Henry Vallance drew a deep breath of relief and promptly returned to Inverness. Poor chap, his face was as white as a sheet and he was in no fit state to continue the service at that moment. The passengers were unloaded and were inquisitive to know why they had returned to Inverness, for they had been unable to see what was going on owing to the painted-out windows in the aircraft. When told of their narrow escape, their faces were a study. After a rest of half an hour, Henry set off again for Orkney and duly reached Kirkwall safely with his passengers. By that time, there were several of our fighters flying around the area.

On Sunday, 13th October 1940, we were requested by Air Ministry to send a plane over to Lossiemouth Naval Air Station, to transport the Duke of Gloucester and four of his staff to Wick and return to Lossiemouth with a stop at Evanton. Departure time from Lossiemouth was fixed at 10.00 in the morning, and as a director of the company I volunteered to give up my Sunday and take the flight, although I had been flying on the services every day of the week.

On arrival at the Naval Station I was taken to the Commanding Officer who presented me to the Duke and his staff of officers. The route we were about to follow was much the same as General Brooke had taken two months earlier, excepting that the point of departure and return were different, and I was not expected to fly on to Castletown as that journey was to be made by road. We took off at precisely ten o'clock in brilliant sunshine on a direct course for Wick over the Moray Firth. It was very hazy but we got above the haze at 3,000 feet. After a while, the Sutherland and Caithness coast came into view and I well remember it presented a beautiful sight with the sparkling sunshine lighting up the mountains and the deep blue sea leading to their threshold. I called His Royal Highness's attention to this scenic splendour and he got a good view by looking out of the cockpit window on the port side.

Wick was reached at 10.35 a.m. and the military were out to receive my distinguished visitors. I was requested to wait the day while the party went off in staff cars, to carry out their inspection. Time of departure for the south was said to be at 16.00 hours, so I went off to Colonel Robertson's house, which was within an easy walk of the airfield, and spent the day with them. Colonel Robertson, being ex-'War I Army' was most interested to learn who my passengers were. Mrs. Robertson and her two daughters were likewise interested in the flight and we sat and talked until lunch time. The fare in Colonel and Mrs. Robertson's house was always of the best, and that luncheon was no exception. Suffice to say, I enjoyed a short rest afterwards preparatory to continuing my journey.

Sharp on four the plane was all ready for take-off but my passengers had not arrived. It was close on 17.00 hours before we were ready to leave for Evanton. We flew down the Caithness coastline and when we picked up the Helmsdale Valley running up to Kinbrace, the Duke of Gloucester showed interest, as he told me during the pre-war shooting seasons he had frequently stayed at a lodge we could just observe. He wistfully said to me that it would be a long time before he would be able to visit that lodge again.

We spent an hour at Evanton. I was entertained in the mess while H.R.H. and his staff were closeted with the senior station officers. We left late in the evening. It was getting dusk and by the time we

209

reached Lossiemouth it was all but dark, and the ground flares were out to assist my landing.

I had to return to Inverness and after being thanked by H.R.H. for giving up my Sunday to him, I went along to the control room to phone Macrae & Dick's garage to request that they should send a couple of cars down to Longman so as to give me a flare path to land by. I was not prepared to emulate a 'Moth landing by hand torch' in a Rapide which touched down at near 70 m.p.h. against the Moth's 38 m.p.h. There was also the difficulty of the approach, as Inverness town lights, which used to be of great assistance, were now blacked out.

By the time I was in the air, it was pitch dark. There was no sign of the moon, but the coastline was dimly visible in places. On arrival over Inverness, which I could barely make out, there was not a car or light to be seen on the airfield. I flew around waiting for the cars to arrive. Fifteen minutes went by, but still no cars, so I flew as low as I dared over the garage to wake them up, but to no purpose. What was to be done? I was in a real jam. It would be no use returning to Lossiemouth, even if I could find it in the dark without radio, and the ground flares would have been retrieved long ago. There was nothing for it but to try a landing with the sole aid of my nose headlight. Flying over the airfield, I could just discern the edge of the sea which lapped alongside. I flew out on a time course and shut off the motors after making the turn for a run in. Having switched on the landing light, the sea was clearly visible, but when the shore was reached, I was too high to see distinctly. There was nothing for it, but to repeat the whole procedure. This time I got down as low as I dared over the water, and approached entirely on a compass bearing to pick up the correct direction of the airfield to land on. It was very difficult keeping my eye on the compass, the Sperry directional gyro and the water, which was not more than 25 feet below me. This time I picked up the land which was the town rubbish dump and which extended for a couple of hundred yards before the airfield perimeter was reached. I could not be too sure whether the aircraft was heading in the right direction or too much east or west of the full length of the aerodrome, which was not very large in those early days of the war. There was nothing left but to take a chance. The flaps were down and I eased the plane on to the ground. She touched, and settled down on the tail wheel. Jamming on the brakes the plane quickly came to a halt in one piece. I was sweating profusely and at the same time, cursing the attendant at Macrae & Dick's garage.

Turning the plane east and taxiing along until the fence on the eastern boundary could be seen, it did not take long to locate the hangar which was adjacent to that fence. Walking up to town and going straight to the garage, I found the attendant and asked him why there was no car to meet me? All he said was that he was alone and had no one to send.

"Why didn't you ring up Mr. Hamilton? He would have answered my call for help."

The attendant hadn't thought of that.

"How did you think I was to land on such a dark night as this, without lights?" I shouted at him, for I was seething with rage at his seeming indifference.

He looked blankly at me,

"I don't know," he replied – and he couldn't have cared less, and that was all the satisfaction that one could get from him. My neck and the aircraft could have been broken for all he cared. I was lucky to get away with that one.

CHAPTER TWELVE

WE brought the New Year 1944 in with a party at our house at 12 Mayfield Road, for our pilots and friends. It went on until the early hours. We also celebrated New Year's Day with a restricted service to the north. Only the loads affecting the war effort were dealt with. Amongst the pilots attending, I remember Captain Vallance, Captain Riley, Captain Cash and Red Haynes of the radio control at Longman Airport. We had all had a very heavy year's work and every pilot was flying the full 120 hours per month allowed by the Air Ministry, myself included. Per annum, that represented more than 1,400 hours in the air, mostly under high pressure. The engineers, under George Griffiths, must not be forgotten, for it was they who kept the aircraft running. Complete engine failure in those days with aircraft always fully loaded meant disaster under cloud-flying or sea-crossing conditions. Looking back, I don't think I ever worked with such a fine bunch of fellows. In those days, they did not have the trade union doctrines and restrictions to bother them. I was indeed proud to lead them.

On 4th January 1944, I left Inverness with Rapide G-AERN to ferry it back to Liverpool. It had been borrowed from the Associated Airways Joint Committee during the early part of the war and we had now been allocated a new plane. I attended a board meeting in Renfrew that day and planned to continue the flight to Liverpool on the morrow.

Dawn broke with shocking weather reported mostly all the way to Preston. I could not fly at altitude as heavy icing was forecast. The only way I could get through was to try and crawl underneath the low overcast. I had, my logbook informs me, 500 feet to play with, plus heavy rainstorms which cut visibility down to half a mile while flying through them. To be caught in the overcast with icing around could easily have meant my last flight. I took off from Renfrew and headed down the Clyde and around Gourock Point, following the coast past Ayr and down to Stranraer. There the weather improved a bit, insofar as the rainstorms with their bad visibility ceased. I managed to cut across the land to Luce Bay and then to the Solway Firth, picking up the Cumberland coastline at St. Bees Head which I followed to Morecambe Bay on the other side of that bit of water. Blackpool hove in sight and with it, better weather.

Arriving at Liverpool, I flew across the Mersey to have a look at Hooton Park airfield, my old joy-riding base in 1929–33. The only change I could discern was that the Pobjoys' house had been reduced to rubble. After landing at Speke Airport and handing the aircraft over to Wing Commander Measures and Captain Olley, who were operating the Associated Airways Joint Committee, I took the opportunity of paying my old joy-riding partner of days gone by, Captain Lance Rimmer, a visit. He had a wartime job working for a company who were manufacturing Halifax bombers under licence at Speke Airport. He hadn't changed much. He was surprised and glad to see me again. He and his wife lived at Hoylake, south of the Mersey.

Returning to Glasgow by train that afternoon, I went to Renfrew to stay with Captain Barclay. John Hankins was also there. I hadn't seen him since he left the Northern Section at the beginning of the war, and so my visit was doubly pleasant. We three visited the cinema in Paisley after supper. Half-way through the performance, a message was flashed on the screen for Captain Barclay. He looked agitated and uncomfortable upon his return.

"What's the matter?" I asked.

"It's a telephone message for you," he said, "from your wife in Inverness."

Some sixth sense of foreboding flashed through me.

"Is it bad news?" I asked.

David nodded his head in affirmation.

"Then keep it until the picture is finished," I asked him.

I don't now remember what was being shown, but it was an extremely good picture and I wanted to see the end of it.

When we got outside the picture house, I said,

"Now, David, what's it all about?"

The reply staggered me.

"Your wife phoned to say she had received a phone call from your brother Kenneth in London. Your mother died suddenly from thrombosis at five o'clock this afternoon."

I was stunned. I had no idea my mother suffered seriously from her heart. When David told me in the cinema that there was bad news, I thought that maybe one of my relatives or perhaps my son Richard had been taken ill.

My presence, as the eldest member of the family, was required urgently in London, my brother had added. Before I could leave for the south I had the new aircraft to deliver from Renfrew to Inverness in replacement of the plane I had just delivered to Liverpool. I phoned brother Kenneth from David's house and said I would leave on the night train from Inverness the following day, as I had to get that plane to Inverness next morning. The war effort had to go on. He agreed.

I caught the London express on Friday night, 7th January, and went straight to my mother's home at Northwood. The funeral was to take place the following week at Golders Green Crematorium. My father had died in May 1939, and so now both my parents had gone.

The first matter that required attention upon my return to Inverness, was to sort out a complaint from the Admiral in Command at Scapa Flow. In the defence of Scapa Flow against attacking aircraft, the Admiralty had erected a balloon barrage which flew at varying heights above the Flow. It was a formidable defence as each balloon was anchored by a heavy wire cable to the surface. We all took jolly good care to avoid that barrage when flying in cloud and allowed a wide safety margin to the west of our route around Hoy. Apparently, Captain Vallance had during my absence completed a trip in cloud from Inverness to Kirkwall with a strong westerly gale blowing and had not allowed sufficiently for drift. Consequently he had unknowingly flown slap through the balloons, and more amazingly, he had got away with it. A chance of one in a thousand. There was not much I could do about it after the event, but I thought it wise to call on the Admiral in person and explain how the error had occurred. I found the Admiral in poor humour.

"You know, Captain Fresson," the Admiral had said, "if it had been a pilot without much experience, some allowance might be made, but for one of your very experienced captains to err like that, there is no excuse. It's a miracle the plane was not wrecked and all the occupants killed."

I agreed with him, but expressed the opinion that no one in his right senses would deliberately fly through the maze of cables attached to that balloon barrage. I also told the Admiral that it was not easy to maintain an accurate course on the 'inland route' in cloud with a strong cross-wind blowing, as there were no radio aids to check on.

Having told Henry to steer a westerly error in future under cross-wind conditions to make sure he did not wander to the east, that was the end of the matter as far as I was concerned. No one more than Henry realised how lucky he had been and he took jolly good care not to repeat the performance.

Two months later, I had an alarming experience in Dragon

Arrival of the first air mail service to North Ronaldsay, July 1939.

The Old Man of Hoy.

The Grampians: typical view on the Inverness-Perth-Glasgow leg.

Kirkwall-Orkney : Hatston Airport site.

Stroma airfield site. The first landing in G-AAWO was made at 'X'.

North Ronaldsay landing field.

Sumburgh airfield, first constructed in 1940–41.

G-ACIT not far away from those cables. I left Inverness with a 1,000-lb. mail load and one passenger for Kirkwall. There was a 70 m.p.h. gale blowing in the Pentland Firth. To make matters worse, there was low snow cloud down to 150 feet and extremely turbulent blizzards floating around, from time to time. I caught up with the gale near Helmsdale. The trip in poor visibility across the Pentland Firth was rough and the fear always present that the high cliffs of Hoy would not be picked up in time, for in the blizzards visibility was virtually nil and the plane was being roughly thrown about. Safely reaching the south-west corner of the Hoy cliffs, we entered another blizzard. The mail was piled to the roof and the lone passenger sat just behind me. I carried no radio officer and was flying at 100 feet or so above the sea when a terrific squall all but turned G-ACIT on its back. The mail tumbled over the cabin and the left wing dropped vertically, pointing at the foam-flecked rollers only a few feet below, like some monster waiting to clutch us in its grasp. The shifting mailbags made the plane sluggish on the controls. For a few seconds it was touch and go, as we slithered down towards the white wave caps lashed in fury by the gale. At the last moment, when we had little further to drop and I thought my end had come, the left wing gradually came up with plenty of top rudder to help it.

H

We came right away up kissing the gigantic wave tops. After a terrible tussle, we rounded Hoy and flew into calmer weather. I stayed that night in Kirkwall. Nothing would induce me to risk the Hoy corner low down again under such conditions.

May was upon us and on the 24th of that month we were requested by the Air Ministry to provide a regular air service between Inverness and Stornoway, almost five years after the original date we had planned to open that service before the outbreak of war in 1939. The route was a difficult one during the winter months with the type of aircraft we were using, as icing was prevalent at the altitude we had to fly to cross the Easter Ross Mountains, which in many places topped just on 4,000 feet. We had no de-icing equipment on the Rapide aircraft or along the blades of the airscrews and the carburettor intakes were not wholly cared for under such conditions. We had, therefore, to watch carefully the meteorological icing warnings and when the red flag was out, we kept to the valley route low down whenever possible.

I flew the inaugural service and had as passengers the Provost of Stornoway, Mr. Alistair Mackenzie, and several councillors. Our chief engineer George Griffiths came along with us and our senior radio officer joined the flight. We had a pleasant trip across the mountains in fine weather and went into town for lunch which the City Fathers were giving to celebrate the air service they had been waiting for so long. The Met. Office reported before we left Inverness that there was a weather front steaming up from the south-west which was expected to reach the Hebrides during the afternoon. However, my appetite was not affected by that report, as I had radio to help me home at altitude, if necessary.

The lunch was long and excellent, and by the time we had got through all the speech-making it was getting on for half past three in the afternoon. Provost Mackenzie made an excellent address, working up through the years I had been looking for an aerodrome for Stornoway and the success that eventually came my way, only to be thwarted by the outbreak of hostilities in September 1939.

By the time we were ready to depart to the airfield for the return journey, with a full load of passengers, the weather front predicted by the Met. Office had duly arrived. The cloud ceiling was not much more than 50 feet. I planned the return flight at 5,000 feet across the mountains. At 3,500 feet we got above the first layer and I turned to my radio officer to obtain a tail bearing on Stornoway so that I could calculate the drift, if any. To my amazement, he was slumped in his seat. George Griffiths was sitting in the rear of the cabin so I asked the passenger nearest me to tell him to come forward.

"Sparks appears to be ill, will you take a look at him?"

I was worried, finding myself in the position encountered in 1931 over the Pennines and which I had made up my mind not to get into again. George Griffiths bent down to have a good look at the radio operator and in a few moments he leant into my cockpit and said,

"The only thing that is wrong with him is that he's dead drunk."

"Dead drunk," I gasped. "What the devil are we going to do?"

It was not known how far the front penetrated to the east and whether Inverness was in it. There were seven people's safety in my care, and to try and grope one's way down into Inverness Airport without accurately knowing one's position was fraught with considerable risk, as had been demonstrated to me years ago with the Moth.

There was no alternative but to brace myself for some very accurate dead reckoning flying, so I told George Griffiths

"Try and shake some life into him, you've got to get him awake somehow."

We continued climbing and were now at over 4,000 feet. George slapped the radio officer's face and shook him to no avail. Suddenly we flew over a clear chasm in the clouds, about a mile wide. I could see the sea and white horses which were whipped up by the wind quite distinctly. I made up my mind at once to duck down under it and try and get back into Stornoway airfield underneath the low cloud ceiling. At least we knew we were above water for the descent.

"Warn the passengers I am diving down quickly and returning to Stornoway," I yelled to Griffiths.

"O.K.," he replied and then came back to attend to the radio officer.

As we reached sea level, George Griffiths said

"I've got him awake at last."

"Try and make him understand that unless he can get a radio bearing on Stornoway, he's likely to lose his ruddy life along with us all," I shouted.

After a few minutes and to my relief, Sparks started to tap on his key. He came back with a mumbled bearing that I could not understand. We were now on the return course and the cliffs on Chicken Head were ahead and sticking into the murk.

"What did you say?" I yelled, "what's the bearing?"

I could just catch 320. That showed us a bit south of the course which was all to the good. He got me another bearing which was 315 and showed we were drifting north. I altered course ten degrees to the south. The visibility was only about half a mile and the gloom made our position look desperate. Five anxious minutes after, the cliffs were seen as we were almost upon them. I could only see a little way up those cliffs before they merged with the mist. Following them to the outskirts of Stornoway town we managed to pick up the road leading to the airfield. The cloud was so low that the plane was not more than 50 feet above the road. We had to be careful we did not hit any cottage roofs along the roadside, as the plane roared over them. I was thankful when suddenly a tarmac strip appeared just in front of me. We landed across wind. I had no inclination at that moment to go looking for the right strip into wind. The passengers had, of course, witnessed the disgraceful position and they were most sympathetic and thankful that they had been extricated from a difficult position and so said all of us – not least myself. We repaired to the town after phoning for transport, and we stayed the night.

Next morning, the front had gone through, and the weather was good enough to fly without radio assistance. I said nothing to my operator until we got back to Inverness, when I called him to my office and told him he was fired,

"You placed us all, including yourself, in considerable danger through becoming intoxicated during lunch and the only redeeming feature lay in the fact that you managed to get the vital bearings to locate Chicken Head."

I sent a report of the incident to Head Office at Renfrew with my reasons for the dismissal. Consequently, I was staggered to hear about two weeks later that the radio officer had been re-employed by the Renfrew boys. No notice was taken of my protest. It was an unbelievable state of affairs that the Renfrew management had condoned drunkenness when the individual was on duty and had imperilled the safety of aircraft, passengers and crew.

Two weeks to one day later, Britain invaded the Normandy coast of France. 'D' Day had arrived. We had just finished breakfast and the radio was on, waiting for the nine o'clock morning news, when the announcer came on the air to say that during the preceding night, a great armada of convoys and their escorts crossed the Channel to the Normandy coast, and that the task of landing was in progress. By October, our armies were in Holland and the end of the war was in sight. The railway companies accordingly were thinking about peacetime operations to replace the rigidly controlled wartime services. On 4th October, I received a visit from Mr. Dennis Handover who had joined the railway air company the year before as Air Adviser. He had previously held many important posts in aviation and came to the railway group from B.O.A.C. He was accompanied by his wife and they were booked to fly to Orkney that day. The weather was bad and they did not see much of the route, as we were in cloud most of the way there and back. Handover, however, managed to get an idea of our organisation in Orkney and on his return to Inverness decided to stay a few days for a post-war discussion. My wife and I found them exceedingly nice people.

He right away recognised that there were special problems in running air services in the North of Scotland, which did not exist in the south. We had long discussion and my views on past operations were noted with interest.

We took them by car over to Loch Maree, so that they might see the type of country we flew over on the Hebrides routes. Unfortunately it was pouring with rain and he couldn't see much. We had tea at the Loch Maree Hotel and returned to Garve Hotel where they were to stay the night. The road was flooded for most of the way, it was raining so hard. Miss Mackenzie, the proprietress greeted us. She was an old friend of mine and had flown on many trips to Stornoway with me. We stayed to dinner and Mr. Handover plied me with questions regarding our five years of war operations, which he appeared most interested in.

He expressed surprise when he learned of our high record of regularity.

"Never less than 97 per cent in any one year, and often more," I told him. To attain that, I explained, meant a first-class team of flying crews, and as much credit was due to the engineering staff who worked under George Griffiths, and his second-in-command Bert Farminer, whom it will be recalled was my chief engineer in my old joy-riding days. We were completely self-contained and were in a position to rebuild any aircraft, however badly it was damaged. Our stores contained a most comprehensive list of spares, sufficient for several years. I showed him our drying sheds, which gave our overhauled aircraft another 100 lb. or so of pay load, by extracting all moisture from the woodwork. In addition we carried out all complete engine overhauls and had our own engine-testing bench. He had a long talk with our chief engineer George Griffiths who had so ably welded the team into such an efficient unit. In A. McLennan, we had an expert woodworker and T. Goulden a first-class radio engineer.

He said afterwards that he was agreeably impressed with what he had seen and had little doubt we were in a first-class position to change over rapidly to peacetime operations on a profitable basis. I saw a lot more of Handover during the next two years in his London headquarters in Upper Grosvenor Street, where new offices for post-war operations had been acquired by the railway group.

January 1945 was a month of continual snow blizzards of exceptional intensity. When the snow began, the aircraft had to roll their own runways before taking-off was possible. After that, a system of rolling was put into action so as to pack the snow hard. After every fall of snow, the rolling process was continued. Inverness therefore had a runway of frozen snow as hard as concrete and it was only through that resourcefulness, and the assistance of the R.A.F. authorities at Inverness, that Scottish Airways were able to maintain the only air connections operated continuously between the mainland, Orkney and Shetland during the two Arctic weeks. The R.A.F. authorities at Longman were at first reluctant to roll the snow. It was quite contrary to their usual practice of using snow-ploughs. I had to explain that we reduced the pressure of our aircraft tyres which prevented the aircraft skidding on the rolled snow before they would act. Actually, landing and taking off were the least difficult part of maintaining operations.

The severe snowstorms which Scottish Airways' pilots were called upon to fly through day after day, and the skill that was employed to avoid dangerous icing conditions, speaks well for its pilots.

Orkney gained one over Shetland inasmuch as Scottish Airways' efforts brought their mails and newspapers regularly, whereas Scottish Airways did not hold a mail contract for Shetland. Nevertheless, we delivered a lot as the Aberdeen mail was diverted through Inverness on many occasions during that shocking fortnight. Thanks are due to the naval authorities and R.A.F. at Sumburgh and Grimsetter, and Longman, Inverness, who kept the airfields open for civil air communications.

I can now divulge an incident which occurred during that fortnight's blizzard, which was withheld from the Press at the time. Captain William Baillie left Orkney late one afternoon with a full load for Inverness, ahead of me, in a heavy blizzard extending far south. I left shortly after with a heavily loaded aircraft. We both took the east coast route. It was agreed that I would fly 500 feet lower than he, so as to avoid the risk of collision in snow cloud.

Roughly half an hour after take-off, my port engine petered out without warning. My position was roughly 15 miles out to sea off the Helmsdale coast and I was flying on radio bearings given every five minutes by the Inverness radio station. We were flying at 1,500 feet to avoid engine icing and, as I have said, we were heavily loaded. That heavy load was nearly our undoing, as I was unable to maintain height on one motor and we gradually began to lose height.

I called radio officer Stewart to come forward,

"Radio to Inverness and tell them that our port motor is out of action, and that we are losing height. Also give them our approximate position, ten to fifteen miles off the coast North of Helmsdale. Say I intend edging into the coastline, but cannot go too near as visibility is nil."

He started working his morse key as hard as he could go. He appreciated the danger, caught up as we were in heavy snow, visibility nil, and insufficient power to maintain height, with a rocky coast abeam.

I edged in nearer to the coast but was afraid of running into the cliffs which were several hundred feet high, or the mountains behind them. Gradually we sank lower. We were down to 1,000 feet when R/O Stewart told me that Inverness had acknowledged our message and had reported it to the R.A.F. Not that they were able to help us. While struggling to keep the plane on a straight course on instruments, my eye suddenly caught sight of the port motor oil gauge. It was still registering oil pressure which meant the dud motor was still turning over. That could only mean one thing, the slow running jet was functioning and I deduced from that that the main jet was choked with some foreign matter. If I could suck the foreign matter through the main jet, I would recover power. I therefore opened the throttle lever suddenly and the motor picked up for a moment. I repeated the throttle movements nearly a dozen times, moving it backwards and forwards, thus causing a heavy suction on the suspected choked jet. Suddenly the motor burst into life and kept on functioning. The trick had succeeded and it saved us.

Inverness reported clear weather, and I prayed for that motor to keep turning until we were out of that white hell. The minutes went by, the motor was still functioning when the blizzard began to get lighter. Up to then it had been a semi-dark grey colour. Within a few moments we were in the clear and Tarbat Ness was visible about five miles ahead and slightly to starboard. We landed safely at Longman airfield; none of the passengers were any the wiser about the narrow escape they had had from a watery grave.

George Griffiths and I immediately had a post mortem. I said to him

"Better change the carburettor before letting that plane in the air again if you cannot find the cause of the stopped main jet."

He agreed. Next morning I was flying the same plane. As soon as I got down to the airfield, I asked Griffiths

"Have you found the cause?"

"No," he said, "I've had the carburettor to pieces and checked all the petrol pipes from the filter to the carburettor and cannot find a trace of dirt. It must have got sucked through the jet. I have also run the motor for a good 15 minutes on the ground without loss of power."

I accepted the position without question.

The traffic officer loaded up the plane. Again a heavy load. It was that way nearly every day. It didn't appear to affect the take-off or flying, as long as the two motors kept turning over, so forgettng yesterday with the thought

"That sort of thing can't happen to me again so soon" I took-off towards the west side of the town.

I had reached above 60 feet and was just over the River Ness, when that same motor cut dead on me again. I had not attained proper flying speed, I only had around 80 m.p.h. on the clock, just ten miles over the speed necessary to keep the plane airborne. I had to turn to get back to the airfield, but turning took more power and I just hadn't got it. Quickly taking the only chance possible, I put the nose down slightly to keep what airspeed I had, thereby losing valuable height, and gingerly made a flat half turn until I was heading across the airfield, cross-wind. Dropping the aircraft down slowly we touched down on one wheel, and came to a stop. Griffiths had to send a car out to tow us in, as it was impossible to taxi on one motor. To say I was shaken by this second event, was to put it mildly. That was twice in 24 hours I had nearly been killed. Nothing like it had ever happened before on the Orkney run during the past 12 years.

The passengers were transferred to another plane, and I left again for the north after having told Griffiths,

"Change the motor if you can't find what is causing the trouble."

He agreed, being as disturbed as I was, having witnessed the whole affair.

On my return from Orkney I found Griffiths had located the trouble. The supply petrol pipe from the petrol filter was made of gut reinforced with a steel wire core. The gut had flaked and a small piece had got into the jet chamber of the carburettor. The flake was transparent and was almost invisible. Hence the reason it was missed on the previous day's examination. To prevent a repetition of that trouble, we submitted the details to de Havillands at Hatfield and they supplied a special 'banjo' filter to attach to the float chamber of the carburettor.

It was an alarming thought, that one little piece of disintegrated gut might have caused the loss of an aircraft, plus seven passengers, radio officer and pilot.

We were now ready to go into action as soon as we had been demobilised from wartime and Ministerial control. Our great headache was the lack of suitable aircraft. The civil conversion of the Douglas Aircraft Company's Dakota was of assistance on the longer routes, but we considered that type of aircraft would be too expensive to operate on the shorter haul stages such as we were faced with. What we required was a monoplane reproduction of the pre-war D.H.86 four-engined biplane, seating 14–16 passengers, with variable-pitch airscrews and de-icing equipment.

The Armistice was signed at Rheims on 7th May 1945, and the war in Europe was over. Japanese hostilities continued in the Far East but that did not affect our change-over to peacetime duties.

We had maintained an air communication service second to none during six years of war, under bad weather conditions and enemy action. Throughout that time, our continuity did not fall below 97 per cent and often we ran to 100 per cent. Together with Railway Air Services route between Glasgow and Belfast, and our Southern Section, we had flown 4,000,000 miles, carried 1,000,000 passengers and 4,000,500 pounds of mail and freight. The press, reporting these figures, went on to state:

"These impressive totals, says a statement by the L.M.S. Railway, encourage the operators in plans now being made for peace, which will bring new and greater opportunities for swift transport throughout Scotland."

That was what was thought then, but the L.M.S. Railway Administration, although they did not know it or even guess it at the time, had a second guess coming. They little knew that the deadly poison of bureaucracy within a year or two would descend all over the country, and destroy Scottish Airways and them, overnight. What, however, it could not destroy was the record of pre-war and wartime service commercial aviation gave to the country.

223

CHAPTER THIRTEEN

PARLIAMENT was dissolved on 15th June 1945, and polling day was fixed for 5th July. The wartime National Government had ceased to exist and a caretaker Government ruled until the polls.

On or about the third week in June, I received a call from Major Neven Spence, M.P. for Orkney and Shetland. Could we provide a plane to take him around the Orkney North Isles and to Fair Isle, on an electioneering campaign? He wished to leave Kirkwall on Wednesday, 27th June. I arranged to meet him in the Kirkwall Hotel on the evening of Tuesday, 26th June, and I left Inverness in Dragon G-ACIT with my wife and son Richard at noon on the Tuesday. We landed at Wick and had lunch with our good friend Harold Georgeson at his home. We set off in the afternoon for Kirkwall. In the evening, Major Neven Spence and I got down to mapping out the tour. He would require about three hours at each island. The islands to be visited were Stronsay, Sanday, Eday, where there was no known landing field, Westray, Papa Westray, also with no known landing field, and North Ronaldsay. We finished that round on the afternoon of Friday 29th.

We found a good field to land on at Papa Westray without difficulty, but Eday was a poser. We flew round and round for quite a while and were unable to locate a field which appeared anything like suitable for the Dragon to land upon. There was only one site which had the necessary length but it was situated on quite a sharp slope. It was that or nothing. The wind blew up the slope and was too strong to land down wind and up the grade. We therefore approached the downhill run gingerly. The plane touched down and effected a landing with the tail still up. The wind assisted in a quick pull up. I had a long wait there. The electorate had many questions to put and be answered.

Next morning, Saturday, Mrs. Neven Spence accompanied her husband on the Fair Isle trip. I decided to try landing on the partially constructed air strip which the naval authorities had begun at my suggestion on the side of a hill and situated in the middle of the island during the early part of the war. It was about 250 yards long and very narrow. But it looked better than the site on the south end of the island, with its attendant drop of 200 feet into the sea around most of the perimeter. After a couple of dummy runs, I managed the landing with only a few yards to go. The islanders were delighted to see me back after nearly five years and gave me a great welcome. I went to the meeting with the Major and his wife and he had a full attendance. The islanders formed a strong Liberal camp and my Tory candidate had a tough meeting. He was, however, received well. His visit by air created a first-class impression. I heard afterwards that while they did not feel inclined to betray their Liberal Party, all the same they agreed with a lot Major Neven Spence had to say to them. So in their novel way, they thought they would assist him by remaining neutral and did not vote at all.

We spent three hours on the island, and with regret took our departure from such a genuine welcome. The take-off with the light load was easy and we landed up in Kirkwall late afternoon and celebrated Orkney's first aerial election with a first-class dinner at the Kirkwall Hotel. My wife and I were the guests of the Major and his good lady.

A little over a week later, the results came in from the polls. Major Neven Spence had retained his seat in the Orkneys and Shetlands by an increased poll.

Within a week or two, the Socialists were returned to power with a very high majority. The country was stunned. To think the electorate had thrown Winston Churchill overboard, the man who had saved them from Nazi tyranny. It was said that the Forces were responsible, but that is a matter for conjecture. Whatever the reason, the country was on the verge of disastrous legislation and many were going to be hurt in the process, myself included.

Immediately after the new Government had taken its place in the House of Commons, it was announced that Lord Winster would be the new Minister for Air. I went to see him in the House of Lords and he seemed to be a friendly and reasonable Minister. He assured me that my position was secure and that Scottish Airways' services would be valued in the new organisation for operating air services in Scotland. Unfortunately, Lord Winster did not last long as Air Minister.

Soon after the election, Sir Steven Bilsland was appointed chairman of Scottish Airways. George Nicholson, who was director of the Southern Section, and myself were introduced to him prior to a board meeting which was held in the Glasgow offices of Coastline Shipping Company and of David Macbrayne Limited which operated the Western Isles' shipping routes as far north as Stornoway, and who were shareholders in Scottish Airways. We were told at that board meeting that our post-war plans were to continue as intended before the election.

However, these plans did not last long for we and Allied Airways were soon to become involved in a bitter fight with the dead hand of bureaucracy, for on 1st November 1945 the new Socialist Government declared its attitude to civil aviation, in a speech made by the new Air Minister Lord Winster. Also involved was Group Captain MacIntyre of Prestwick Airport, who had designs for running in competition with our Southern Section on the Renfrew-Belfast service. They were about to launch a Prestwick-Belfast run with a converted 25-seat Dakota, at a fare of 30 shillings single. That was roughly half of the fare we were charging. We were very much preoccupied with this threatened invasion and cut-throat competition in our territory, when Lord Winster made his announcement of nationalisation in the House of Lords.

The Press announcement of 2nd November quoted the details in the following report:

STATE TO OWN ALL CIVIL AIR TRANSPORT

Three Corporations to run Services under Ministry

"The Government's policy to bring civil aviation under State Control was outlined in the House of Lords to-day by Lord Winster. It was described by Viscount Swinton, former Minister of Civil Aviation as 'a most disappointing and damning statement for the prospects of civil aviation. The practical working plan on which we were all agreed to mobilise all our assets ready to fly at any time, is sabotaged for political theory,' he declared. 'It is a sorry day for aviation.' Lord Winster went on to say, 'The State will operate all British Air Transport Services, own all airports used for scheduled services, and provide all radio, meteorological and air traffic services. The Brabazon Committee will be retained and the existing flying companies will be free to continue only until the new organisation is established.' Prestwick was to be made an international airport."

So the rumours which had persisted for the past two months had now become reality.

Following Lord Winster's statement, he assured me that insofar as Scottish Airways were concerned, they would remain as a Scottish Division under the State Corporation to be formed for the operation of the British and European air routes, and he again told me my position would be secure in view of the valuable services Scottish

226

Airways had provided throughout the war. He requested me to do all I could to bring about successful transition from wartime to peacetime operations. I left him, thinking that perhaps after all State Control could be made to work, but I failed to take into account the scheming and jockeying for power which eventually reared its ugly head and the type of individual who would hold control against which there would be no appeal. In other words, civil aviation was to be operated under a dictatorship.

Not so long after my interview with Lord Winster, he resigned his appointment as Air Minister and the Minister who replaced him was not so appreciative of the work performed by our company over the past 14 years.

Ten days later, I received a letter from our chairman, Sir Steven Bilsland, which indicated the policy under which Scottish Airways Limited would function until the great take-over occurred by Socialism-cum-Bureaucracy. The letter is worthy of reproduction:

"I had a meeting in London last week with Sir Harold Hartley to discuss the situation created by the Minister's speech on 1st November.

"The position is that we will continue to operate our services until the new organisation has been formed. Furthermore, it is important that we should not relax our efforts in any way to develop and advertise our services and to ask for any additional aircraft that are needed to meet public demand. The Director General of Civil Aviation told Sir Harold that he would welcome any suggestions from us as to new routes.

"With regard to capital expenditure, it has been arranged that any new aircraft for which we have not already paid be hired, and the terms of hire are to be negotiated.

"With regard to other schemes of urgent development involving capital expenditure, Sir Harold has asked me to put them up to him without delay, so that they may be discussed at the Ministry.

"We will be discussing the whole position at our meeting on 30th November (namely Scottish Airways Board Meeting)."

We met in Glasgow on 30th November, and most of the time was taken up in discussing the events of the month. Our directors appeared to be under no misapprehension what it would mean being swallowed up by the Socialist octopus which had so suddenly descended upon us. We had all been under the assumption that the civil aviation plans agreed by the Coalition Government for post-war operations, and to which we had already contributed a lot of hard work and planning, would be maintained by a Socialist Government. Under nationalisation, there would be no individuality or incentive or pride in the job as we had become accustomed to under commercial enterprise.

One newspaper ably described the situation as the 'Dead Hand on Aviation', and went on to say:

"In some respects the civil flying scheme under proposed nationalisation repeats the broad lines of the Swinton scheme approved by the late Coalition. There will be three 'chosen instruments' with assigned routes of operation. But whereas the Swinton scheme did seek to make use of the experience and knowledge of pre-war and present-day operators and held out to them an inducement of financial rewards for enterprise, the Socialist Government proposals jettison such experience and kill the incentive of development.

"The North of Scotland and the Islands which are appreciative of the enterprise and the operators who serve them and who are looking for still further advantage, will note that their familiar services are to disappear. They will have to take what some large organisation, whose interests will be many, thinks is good enough for them.

"In passing, it may be remarked that the terms to be offered to dispossessed operators are 'infamous'. They are to be given only the value of their physical assets and nothing for goodwill. They have run financial risks in building up that goodwill but the Socialist Government proposes to step into their businesses and 'rob them of the fruits of their enterprise'."

We were not to feel the force and effect of those statements for another 15 months. How true that forecast was will be apparent later.

We gave a big party at our house for the New Year's festivities. Invited were all those who had taken part in the wartime air operations. Pilots, engineers, air control, plus wives, attended and the party went on well into the early hours. New Year's Day was a holiday and we only ran the mail plane to Orkney and return. It was to be the last of a series of New Year parties that we had held for the past few years, for those who did so much for the war effort. Our son was sent out to sleep, so that he would not be disturbed by the revelry.

The New Year brought serious thinking. If we could obtain a Scottish Division operated by Scottish Airways' personnel as part of the new set-up and on the lines I understood Lord Winster to be sympathetic to, then nationalisation would only mean a change in financial ownership and that should not affect us. I could not see at that period any difference between the Treasury holding the purse strings and the L.M.S. Railway Company. I certainly learned when it was too late that there was a whale of a lot of difference.

In the spring we were informed that the Corporation which was to operate the European and internal air routes, would be known as British European Airways, under the chairmanship of Sir Harold Hartley with banker Gerard d'Erlanger as managing director. Sir Harold was the late chairman of Railway Air Services, which concern had also been taken over under the new set-up and Gerard d'Erlanger was ex-Air Transport Auxiliary, which was engaged in ferrying aircraft from the factory to the squadrons of the R.A.F. during the war.

The first hint I got that British European Airways had become a reality came to me by telephone on Monday, 2nd April 1946, when our secretary William Cumming at Renfrew phoned through to say that my presence was required on Wednesday 4th, to meet British European Airways' officials who were flying up from Northolt.

They arrived just before lunch, in good style, by a Dakota aircraft which had been converted to peacetime requirements. George Nicholson, Wing Commander Measures and several others along with myself, were awaiting their arrival in the Scottish Flying Club, when they were ushered in by secretary Cumming. We were introduced individually and when it came to my turn to meet Gerard d'Erlanger, I felt he was hostile. During the speech-making after lunch, it became evident to me that the position of our company for the future was to be on an 'Overlord vis-à-vis Peasant' basis. When everyone had talked themselves to a standstill, the party left to be shown around our headquarters.

Later, they flew back to Northolt and George Nicholson, Cumming and myself discussed the future with foreboding. We sensed that we were in for difficult times ahead – and we were not far wrong. I stayed over in Ayr that night with the Nicholsons and on my return north I was engaged in an interesting survey of the North Isles with a Dr. Williamson, who was anxious to discover the location of seaweed beds. The Plastic Age was nearly upon us and it appeared that seaweed was sought after in connection with its manufacture.

We set off from Inverness in Dragon G-ACIT and flew at 400 feet around all the islands and coastlines. That appeared to be the best altitude to detect the seaweed beds. The doctor sat just behind me with a map and noted with pencil where the deposits could clearly be seen from our plane at the altitude we were flying. We spent three days on this work and the results were most satisfactory.

Dr. Williamson returned on the regular service to Inverness and I stayed over in Orkney as I had some work to do on the reorganisation of the Orkney North Isles airfields. They were too small for modern needs and required extending. Arrangements had already been made with the Orkney County Road Surveyor, Mr. John Robertson, to make a survey of the airfields at North Ronaldsay, Sanday, Stronsay and Westray and we left next morning by air to begin the work, with two of his staff equipped with theodolite and measuring equipment.

I stayed in Orkney a week, running the survey team backwards and forwards to Kirkwall each day. By the end of that time, we had four airfields mapped out, which would give us three strips of 500–700 yards on each field. Our present fields only had a maximum of 400 yards and some less. Also the surface was in its original state and rough. We intended levelling the surface on the new strips. Within a month, we received an estimate of somewhere around £7,500 to carry out the work and I laid the matter before our Board at our next meeting at the end of the month. They approved the expenditure but our chairman considered it better to submit the tender to the Minister before officially accepting. It took some months to get a reply, but in the end the proposal was shelved. The new Corporation did not appear interested in small shuttle services, no matter how much air communications meant to the islanders.

Here was our first taste of nationalised service, and we wondered what would be the fate of our other routes. Fourteen years later, the Orkney North Isles are still without the air connections they had grown to depend on for a number of years before the war.

Shortly afterwards when I was in Renfrew discussing the 1946 summer timetable with our traffic manager, I was introduced to an individual I had not seen at Renfrew before. It subsequently appeared that he was from the British European camp at Northolt, Middlesex. I had the Northern Section timetable worked out and we wished to integrate the Inverness-Glasgow section with services of the Southern Section to Ireland, Isle of Man and London. We assumed we were to carry on with the D.H. Dragon Rapide in the absence of any other and more suitable aircraft.

It turned out that the stranger was attached to the new B.E.A. Traffic Office in Northolt, and he opened up on me by saying, that the intention was to provide three different types of aircraft for the Scottish runs. They all had different cruising speeds, which would make the aircraft non-interchangeable on a given route without hopelessly upsetting the timetable. On enquiry, he admitted they had little or no spares with which to service the aircraft and, more important, no engineers qualified for maintenance and no maintenance equipment. Without any of the aforementioned prerequisites, the airline would be a shambles within a week; I told him I wouldn't look at it. He looked at me with a pained expression on his face, and replied in an aggrieved voice

"Well, Captain, it's at least a plan."

I was thunderstruck. If that was an example of the new nationalised outlook and planning, we were going to have passengers stranded all over the country.

"A plan?" I said to him, "you can take it back to Northolt. We're responsible for operations this year and Rapides we stick to."

He turned on his heel and disappeared, and unbelievable as it may seem, that was the type of mentality encountered during the first year's operations of the new Corporation.

I also learned during that visit to Renfrew that British European Airways, who were dealing with the question of post-war aircraft for Scottish operations, were negotiating with the Ministry for the allocation of a number of German Junkers Ju 52/3m monoplanes. They were to be converted to 14-seat aircraft and were powered by three 450 h.p. radial motors. The aircraft were wholly uneconomic to operate and the motors were extremely unreliable as the Germans had mass-produced those engines on the basis of 100 hours' operating life.

I suggested to Wing Commander Measures, who was acting for the purchase of these planes, that the whole proposal should be dropped and warned him about the unsuitabllity of the German wartime engines and their maximum life of 100 hours. But if they were set on purchasing these aircraft they should at least arrange to have American Pratt & Whitney Wasp radials installed and the German engines scrapped. Failure to do this, I warned him, would have disastrous results. It will be seen later how my warning came true. Apart from the technical disadvantages of using the Ju 52, I tried to impress on him that the cost in fuel alone would be prohibitive for a suggested seating capacity of 14 persons.

My advice was disregarded and a number of Ju 52s were made available the following year, at a conversion cost of approximately £12,000 apiece. Not only were the B.M.W. engines fitted, but most of them had exceeded their maximum permissible hours, with the disastrous results I anticipated after the aircraft became operational.

Soon after the war ended, it came to my notice that a new Pilots' Union was in the process of formation. By the middle of 1946 the union had a branch at Renfrew and it appeared that I had two militant 'brothers' on my staff at Inverness. One day I received a letter from Wing Commander Measures stating that he had received representations from the British Air Line Pilots Association – Pilots Executive Council, Glasgow, to the effect that they had received a letter from a member based in Scotland. It went on to say:

"The writer of the said letter refers to certain features – which he considers to be most undesirable – of the operations to and from Inverness of Scottish Airways Limited."

There were four points raised, the first three were beyond the company's control and were the concern of the Air Ministry, the last complained that pilots were expected to fly in high winds, and cancellations because of high winds were regarded with disapproval by the resident director at Inverness – which was me.

My reply to that complaint was phrased in the following terms:

"No pilot is forced by me to fly any route which he does not feel capable of doing. The question of flying in very strong winds is a necessity in this part of the world, if a high degree of regularity is to be maintained, which of course is so essential for the success of the service.

"We have flown in these high winds for the past 13 years and no pilot has ever grumbled before. If there is any pilot on this station who feels he is incapable of carrying out the high standard of flying we have maintained for so long, then he has only to say so, and his services can be dispensed with. Incidentally, Allied Airways (Gandar Dower) Ltd., match our services on such boisterous days."

My reaction to the whole four complaints that they were examples of pettiness and were merely an endeavour to stir up trouble. I went on to say in my letter that

"I think the name of the complainant should be asked for and he should be questioned by the company as to his motives in making these complaints. I should add that whoever he is, he has not been honest enough to come to me first and present his case. Instead he went behind my back and made representations to the Air Pilots Association."

I have mentioned this occurrence as it was an early pointer to the change that was maturing under the demoralising effect of nationalisation. Our engineers were the next victims. We had hitherto had a loyal and hard-working team of the highest standard. My chief, George Griffiths and myself took a personal interest in them all, and we had worked for the past ten years in perfect harmony. It was therefore with concern and sorrow that I observed the deadly poison of soulless bureaucracy permeating into one or two individuals. These happenings were additional indication of 'things to come'.

Years after, many of my old staff have remarked to me that there was nothing like the old days. They would dearly like to have them back.

"One is just a number," one individual said to me, "in a big Corporation, and of course, under the thumb of Union decisions, which, whether they like it or not, they have to follow." However, this changed outlook did not have its full impact until the fateful changeover had become effective, when further happenings crept into my daily life.

Towards the end of 1946, I noticed an ever increasing trend to 'Overlordship' on the part of my Renfrew colleagues. I found decisions were again being arrived at without reference to me. That had not been the case throughout the war. I did not pay a lot of attention to this trend in its early stages, but as the practices persisted, I began to protest, without avail. It appeared that orders, unknown to me, were being sent from our new bosses-to-be in London, and that the Renfrew Management were accepting them and putting them into effect. Later I found to my detriment the answer to this subservience. The ground was being prepared for the new management of the nationalised Scottish air routes.

On 27th September, the Southern Section had their first fatal accident. One of the Inverness aircraft, Rapide G-ADAJ was indirectly involved, piloted by Captain Hayes. Captain Hayes was making a scheduled flight from Inverness to Renfrew, and as he arrived over the airport in cloud, another Rapide, G-AFFF, was approaching from Port Ellen, Islay, off the west coast. That aircraft, Captain Hayes told me afterwards, was making heavy going in homing on Renfrew Airport and the pilot appeared to be inexperienced in the technique we employed for letting down in cloud. (I found out later that he was a pilot lent to Renfrew by the Pilots Pool and had not received specialised training on the Western Isles routes, which we considered so important for safety.) After a quarter of an hour or more of hanging around in cloud waiting for the other aircraft to get down, our pilot got fed up and asked for a priority landing, which was granted. Captain Hayes landed within five minutes of being given permission, but the other aircraft in the meantime flew into high ground some miles to the north of the airport, killing five passengers, plus himself and radio officer.

There was an enquiry held by the Air Ministry which I attended at Renfrew a month or two later. The conclusion arrived at, was that the pilot of G-AFFF, Captain Stephens, might have mistaken the bearings given to our aircraft G-ADAJ which made its final approach on Renfrew Airport from the south. Such a misconception would have headed Captain Stephens north, in cloud, towards the 1,500 feet Craigton Hill, which he flew slap into. The finding appears incorrect to me, inasmuch as the registration letters of the aircraft receiving the bearings are always prefixed by the radio station, prior to transmitting the original or subsequent bearings, excepting the final phase of approach when bearings are given in a string, that is, one bearing quickly after another. Our pilot, Captain Hayes, was blamed for crashing in on G-AFFF by asking for priority. It appeared to me at the time that if Captain Stephens was unfamiliar with the procedure and was holding up the let-down of other aircraft, he should have been given a bearing and altitude to fly on by the radio station and told to stand off for five minutes. Whoever was to blame, it was an unnecessary accident which destroyed a 12-year-old clean bill of flight. That incident proved how essential it was for pilots to receive specialised route training.

I visited Renfrew Airport the day following the accident and saw the first German Ju 52 aircraft which the Air Ministry had converted for civil use, parked on the tarmac. I was asked by the Renfrew chief pilot Captain Barclay, if I would like to fly it.

"Certainly," I said.

I was interested to see how the aircraft performed and so I flew it around for half an hour, making several landings and take-offs in order to appraise the performance of the aircraft, on our small airfields in the North.

The Junkers Ju 52 had a tremendous amount of power for the carriage of 14 passengers and as I have said was an extremely expensive and uneconomical aeroplane to operate. Further, it required a small mobile power plant to start up the motors. There were very few aircraft and engine spares available and not enough starting units to go round any of our airfields. I was not impressed and I foresaw trouble with that machine, if and when it was used in the Western Isles and on the northern air routes. I advised the Renfrew Management that they should insist on sticking to the Rapides until a suitable replacement was made available. That advice went unheeded in London, and early in 1947 the Junkers Ju 52 was operating the services from Glasgow to Stornoway, Aberdeen, Orkney and Shetland. Later we shall see the chaos which ensued.

During November, Captain Hayes was again in trouble, but this time through a different cause which was completely out of his control. For the third time since the commencement of hostilities in 1939 one of our aircraft was struck by lightning. It happened while Captain Hayes was flying the return Stornoway-Inverness service at 11,000 feet, in clear air above cloud. He was passing through two pinnacles of cloud which extended up from cumulo-nimbus cloud below, when the aircraft suddenly bridged the gap between the pinnacles. That allowed the stored up electrical energy in one of the cloud pinnacles to discharge through his plane to the other pinnacle. He was approximately half-way across the Easter Ross mountains when it happened. As usual there was a loud report and the cabin was filled with acrid fumes. The radio was put out of action, as was the compass. 'Smokey' Hayes, as he was known to his fellow pilots, fortunately kept his head, and used his Sperry directional gyro to steer an easterly course which would take him out over the Moray Firth for a let-down without radio through the cloud. Captain Hayes successfully broke the cloud off the coast by Fort George and soon landed at Longman airfield.

On examination, the usual holes in the nose were observed and the radio aerial had been burned off. It took our chief engineer George Griffiths, a week or two to demagnetise all the ferrous metal parts in the nose of that Rapide.

With the arrival of November, the first public criticism began of the nationalised airways in an article appearing in the *Glasgow Herald*, dated Monday, 4th November. It read:

Disappointment at Government's Failure to Meet Obligations

"In particular there is disappointment and hard feeling over the failure of the Government Airways Corporations to meet their obligations. None of the Scottish services listed in June, in a somewhat modest programme of development, has materialised although the target date in almost every instance was October. Doubts about the capacity of British European Airways seem to have been confirmed by suspension of services on their own main routes, caused by shortage and unserviceability of aircraft, etc."

On 16th November, an Avro Anson arrived in Inverness with the Parliamentary Secretary to the Ministry of Civil Aviation, Mr. George Lindgren, aboard. He and his party stayed at the Caledonian Hotel. A reception was laid on and I was invited to meet him.

During our conversation he told me they were planning to put 100-seater aircraft on the North of Scotland run when they could get them built. These aircraft, he told me with glee, were to carry 100 passengers at third-class railway fare. I remember looking at him in amazement. I commented that such rates would cost the taxpayer a lot of money,

"And," I enquired, "where are the airfields in the North of Scotland to accommodate such large aircraft?"

He hadn't thought about such contingencies. I let the matter drop. The whole nationalised situation was developing into a fantastic set-up.

Our last free year of commercial operations, 1946, had gone well with us. For the most part, free from political interference, we carried 28,000 passengers up to the end of September, compared to 13,200 in the corresponding period of 1945. Over 2,000,000 miles per year were then being flown by Scottish internal services. Finally, to end our year's commercial operations, we made a profit of approximately £8,000 for the year. We would have hoped to double that figure in 1947 had we been able to continue free from State interference. There was no profit the following year, or ever after on the Scottish routes. As the losses mounted, the Scottish routes were conveniently named 'social services'.

What an easy and convenient way to brush off crude inefficiency. The London set-up had been warned that the Scottish routes could not be operated at a profit on the grandiose scheme they envisaged, but no heed was given, and hence the resultant losses, which were enormous – £500,000 for the first year on Scottish routes, and considerably more in the years to follow.

CHAPTER FOURTEEN

THE first week of the New Year 1947, George Nicholson, William Cumming and myself were summoned to London for a meeting with the nationalised administrative heads of the newly formed British European Airways, who under Government charter were to operate all European routes formerly administered by British Overseas Airways and all internal British airlines operated by various commercial interests. The railway companies had considerable representation in most of the British air companies, of which Wing Commander Measures acted as the co-ordinating director under the L.M.S. chairman Sir Harold Hartley.

Sir Harold was the first chairman of British European Airways and the managing director was Gerard d'Erlanger whom I had met at Renfrew the year before. We were interviewed by these two executives. Nicholson and Cumming went in first and myself last. I was greeted by Sir Harold Hartley with a smile and handshake. I, of course, knew him well. I received a scowl from his companion,

"Sit down, Captain Fresson," said Sir Hartley, "we have brought you three down to London to acquaint you with the new set-up of Scottish Airways, which will be dissolved on 1st February, and taken over by British European Airways. Mr. d'Erlanger, as you no doubt know, will be the managing director of British European Airways and he will explain the new appointments for the Scottish Division of the new Corporation."

Gerard d'Erlanger stared at me. I was under no misapprehension of the distaste with which he viewed my presence. In a cold and pitiless voice, he told me that George Nicholson had been appointed the Scottish Divisional Director and would represent that Division at B.E.A. Board meetings. William Cumming was appointed Senior Executive Officer.

"You will be the area manager for North of Scotland and come under the jurisdiction of the aforementioned gentlemen, who will function from Renfrew headquarters. You will be given a contract for six months."

I sat there stunned – I just could not believe my ears. D'Erlanger evidently read my thoughts and remarked:

"Take it or leave it."

Sir Harold Hartley looked at me, I thought with sympathy and made some remark to try and ease the tension. I recovered my equanimity and informed d'Erlanger that I was amazed to hear that I had been placed in a junior position to George Nicholson when in fact, I was senior to him in age and operational experience. I added

"Since the amalgamation of Highland Airways with Scottish Airways, my section has been the only one that has shown a profit through the years and that surely indicated better management."

He replied,

"I am not here to argue with you," he repeated, "take it or leave it."

I had to think this serious event out in calmer water.

"How long before you require an answer?" I asked.

He stated a time (I cannot remember exactly, but it was within a few days). I undertook to let him know in writing. The meeting terminated. Sir Harold shook hands with me and wished me good luck and d'Erlanger said "Good morning," upon which I turned on my heel and left the room.

I met George and William Cumming outside, and they said they hoped that we would still work together as in the days of the recently defunct Scottish Airways. They then walked ahead of me, arm-in-arm talking seriously and looking very excited. There could be little doubt that they were delighted with the situation. For myself, I was placed in a humiliating and very insecure position.

When British Airways sold out their share in Scottish Airways to the railway company interests in 1939, Major McCrindle, one of the new directors of the reorganised British Airways which subsequently became British Overseas Airways, had said to me that if I was not treated properly in the new set-up of Scottish Airways, I could always rely on him to see that I obtained a suitable appointment with British Airways. So after my interview with Sir Harold Hartley and d'Erlanger, I at once went to see Major McCrindle and reminded him of his offer. I explained what had been said to me, and he appeared very surprised. Apparently he knew d'Erlanger well and said he would speak to him. I asked him not to do that. I would prefer it if he could arrange a transfer for me to B.O.A.C., which British Airways had been absorbed into by that time. He undertook to investigate the matter. He was not successful, so against my better judgment, I agreed to stay on with British European Airways on a six-monthly contract. Events proved that decision to be disastrous.

I returned to Inverness and as the days went on, the Press became critical of the new set-up of Scottish affairs. It appeared that along with the Renfrew appointments, there was to be an additional body to overlord our operations, under the august title Scottish Advisory Council on Aviation. Its chairman was to be Sir Patrick Dollan who was an ex-Lord Provost of Glasgow. I was unaware that Sir Patrick had any past connection with, or knowledge of the complexities of, aviation. I was told that he had functioned on different Social Boards, but that was not going to assist us much in the stormy months ahead.

The first shot came from *The Bulletin* dated 11th January 1947, which quoted the views of Lord Provost J. Ure Primrose, who had been appointed as a member to the Scottish Advisory Council on Aviation and who held constructive and knowledgeable views. His brother had held high rank in the R.A.F., and I had met him before the war when he was Air Adviser to the Postmaster General for air mail operations. I quote the report of *The Bulletin* verbatim:

"Dictation from London on the future running of Scotland's already efficient airways should be resisted," declared Lord Provost J. Ure Primrose, Perth, a member of the Scottish Advisory Council on Aviation, in a charter on the operation of nationalised Scottish air routes to be submitted to the Civil Aviation Authorities.

"The Lord Provost states that the Scottish Division proposed under nationalisation should have charge of the operation of both internal and European services operating out of Scottish airports and should enjoy powers of operational management. The Advisory Council should resist the forcing of technical matters on them by London, over the heads of the Scottish technicians. Scottish airfields, says the charter, sometimes call for different standards from those made for English and Continental airfields. The Scottish Division should not be bound in all instances to the rigid requirements laid down in the South.

"Scottish Airways, who are to be nationalised to form the base of the Scottish Division, have operated internal air services in Scotland for 13 years with almost a clean bill so far as accidents are concerned, the Lord Provost declared. At all costs the Scottish Division should avoid having a host of unwanted personnel from the South foisted upon it. Excessive centralisation should be avoided at all costs, the charter stated. The efficient management of air services requires an extreme degree of flexibility and instantaneous decisions. This cannot be attained under excessive centralisation, especially if it is situated in London. The Lord Provost said that the introduction of the Pilots Pool system in Scotland should be resisted. The system of employing and training pilots to be specialised on their routes should be continued for safety and regularity. Scottish Airways' only fatal accident occurred last September with a pilot borrowed from the South, who had not been specifically trained over Scottish routes."

Looking back on events, I must say Lord Provost Ure Primrose spoke with great wisdom and he confirmed my views which were identical and which I voiced in several public speeches early in 1946, for the safe operation of the Scottish routes at high percentage regularity. Further, a Scottish Division operated by the personnel who had learnt the special techniques required through the years would have saved the public several million pounds which were squandered on an unwieldy set-up, by men with a war operation mentality, and to whom cost meant nothing. As this story draws to its conclusion, we shall see the sorry state our well-esteemed airlines were reduced to by the central colossus of Socialist politics and inefficiency.

After my London visit, I had not been back in Inverness more than a few days when I was called upon to fly the Shetland service, owing to the indisposition of one of our pilots. The weather had been appalling, with heavy rain and many of the fields I well remembered, were flooded. In fact, Sumburgh airfield between the strips looked pretty wet. After landing at Kirkwall on my return south, I was asked by the Post Office if I would delay the southbound service and fly the mails out to North Ronaldsay, and bring in accumulated mails from the island, which had been cut off for over two weeks by storms and high seas. There was a strong wind blowing which would be of assistance as I was told that the landing ground was badly flooded and the ground very soft. I agreed to carry out the charter, provided my southbound passengers consented.

I took off from Hatston airfield around two o'clock in the afternoon on the first of three round trips, as there were many passengers who had also been marooned at Kirkwall and out in North Ronaldsay. The Press reported the relief of the marooned island in the following terms:

ORKNEY'S EPIC FLIGHT

"The finest feat in the civil flying Orkney career of Captain E. E. Fresson, O.B.E., the pioneer of Britain's internal airlines, was performed on Tuesday, 14th January, when he relieved the weather-beleaguered island of North Ronaldsay, using a land machine for a job that almost demanded the services of an amphibian aircraft. The island had been cut off from transport for 17 days. The pre-war green field aerodrome made for Captain Fresson by the men, women and children of the island, and now seldom used, was the scene of the pioneer's latest exploit.

"An island correspondent describes three landings made there on Tuesday by Captain Fresson as 'the most sensational spectacle' in Orkney's 16 years of civil aviation. The aerodrome was flooded by rain water; surrounds were covered by native sheep that normally live outside the shore dykes encircling the island. As Captain Fresson, flying a de Havilland Rapide, G-AGDG, circled overhead, the islanders cleared the sheep off the landing ground and on to the shore. The aircraft, a faster plane than the last remaining de Havilland Dragon G-ACIT so well known in Orkney, then sped down to land. The landing had to be made in a semi-circle run around the rain

lake. As the machine touched down, its wheels showered so much water out of the ground that the inhabitants feared disaster. An eye-witness said

'You would have thought he had landed in the flood water after all. It was for all the world like a flying-boat landing on the sea.'

"The plane skidded and slithered alarmingly, but came safely to a standstill.

"The Islanders crowded around to congratulate Captain Fresson and to sympathise with him for having marooned himself with them. He replied

'No fear, we shall take off all right.'

"The prophecy proved correct. The plane made, in all, three double trips that day between Kirkwall and North Ronaldsay. The three take-off performances, less spectacular but definitely more hazardous than the three landings, were accomplished with a fair margin of clearance, despite the loads carried. Each flight from Kirkwall occupied 15 minutes, return journeys requiring 20 minutes each, owing to the strong headwinds.

"The enterprise of the Post Office was responsible for the day's flying. The Post Office chartered the plane and the first flight from Kirkwall to North Ronaldsay and back again was a Post Office affair. Outward the plane carried 948 lb. of mail and no passengers. Captain Fresson flew without a wireless operator, to keep down the weight, operating the radio himself. 363 lb. of mail and two young women students were carried on the return journey. Four passengers were carried on the second outward flight and seven schoolchildren on the return journey. There were no passengers on the third outward flight. On the return trip seven adult passengers were carried.

"The North Ronaldsay flying involved some smart staff work on the part of the Post Office and Scottish Airways. The Head Postmaster in Kirkwall, Mr. David Scrimgeour, by chartering the plane for the mail flights, made the aeroplane available to the North Ronaldsay members of the general public. The Scottish Airways' Kirkwall staff, who put in a great deal of extra work on Monday night and Tuesday, were R. McKerrell, Orkney branch manager; John Watson and H. Fisher, traffic officers; Robert Bain, driver; Kenneth Wards, airport assistant and Miss I. Cooper, clerkess. Orkney ex-members of the R.A.F. and certain serving members stated to the *Orcadian* that only a pilot who had had joy-flying experience in all sorts of odd corners of the country could have effected the feat achieved by Captain Fresson in his North Ronaldsay landings and take-offs on Tuesday."

I have quoted the newspaper story of this flight in full detail, as it demonstrated the value of flying to people living in the outlying parts of Scotland – a service which I am sorry to say they have not enjoyed since the Rapides were taken away from them by nationalisation.

The day of our handover to British European Airways dawned – 1st February 1947. It was a Saturday and I was recovering from an infection which had laid me up for the past three days. I accordingly did not feel fit to fly myself down to Renfrew, more especially as there was a south-westerly gale blowing and the clouds were down to 500 feet, with rain at times. I phoned my office and asked them to get hold of the off-duty pilot, Captain Hayes and tell him I wished him to fly Rapide G-ADAJ to Renfrew with me as passenger.

We set off at ten in the morning in bad weather. Icing conditions were reported at 2,000 feet and over, and the cloud base at Renfrew around 100 feet. Accordingly, we decided to try and fly under the murk, and set off down the Caledonian Canal. After passing Fort William, the wind speed increased from the south-west and half-way down Loch Linnie we were hit by a blast, akin to the one I experienced before the war when flying the mails to Stornoway in a 70 m.p.h. gale, on a Post Office charter trip. Pilot Hayes turned round and looked at me.

"Go on a bit further," I said, "we must get to Renfrew if at all possible."

On arrival at the Crinnan Canal which we intended to follow, as all hills were well in cloud, the air became a bit calmer and we were able to reach Renfrew by circling around the coast off Ardlamont Point and cutting across the spit of land over Rothesay to the Clyde, nearly clipping off the chimney-pots in the process, we were down so low. I was glad to get out of that plane. I had received a taste of the passengers' feeling in turbulent weather and it was quite different from being in charge of the controls.

I spent the afternoon at Renfrew with Nicholson and Cumming at a meeting about the winding-up of Scottish Airways. In the evening George Nicholson drove us up to the Central Hotel, where the 'handing over ceremony' was to be held. We had hired a room where we could all change. At seven o'clock in the evening, Sir Steven Bilsland, our chairman, opened the proceedings. He said Scottish Airways Limited had passed into history, but would be reborn as a virile division of British European Airways and would contribute a wealth of flying experience and technical skill to the new company. Sir Steven went on to say that from May 1933 until January 1947, aircraft of the company had flown nearly 10,000,000 miles and had conveyed 339,812 passengers. That was a record which would compare favourably with any other airline in the world.

Sir Steven Bilsland made his first point to Mr. Lindgren. He said

"I hope that the security of the gentlemen who have spent many years in making such a profitable success of Scottish Airways will be taken over by British European Airways. I would like to know that the Government intend honouring that wish, Mr. Lindgren. I refer particularly to Captain Fresson, Mr. Nicholson and Mr. Cumming."

"Most certainly, Sir Steven," he replied, "what football club would, of its own free will, get rid of their star players. There will most certainly be a most welcome place for these gentlemen."

I have quoted those proceedings, as later it will be seen that such assurances were merely a figment of the mind, if not actually double-talk.

I hadn't been back in Inverness more than a day or two, when I learned that Inverness Town Council had received a letter from Mr. George Lindgren, Parliamentary Secretary to the Ministry of Civil Aviation, who were responsible for operating the post-war airfields, enumerating the advantages of Dalcross Airport over Longman Airport adjacent to the town. He pointed out that whereas Longman airfield had served Inverness and the Highlands well in the past, it had many grave disadvantages, in comparison to Dalcross, which outweighed anything that could be said in its favour.

The writing was on the wall: we were about to be uprooted from Longman which we had operated out of for the past 14 years without accident. Dalcross was a first-class airfield and, as I have said earlier, it was I who had recommended the site to the R.A.F. just before war broke out. Then it was my intention to move out of Longman owing to its limited size, but during the war, Longman airfield was greatly extended by the R.A.F., who used it alongside us throughout hostilities. It was as large as Renfrew, Dyce or Turnhouse (Edinburgh). The cost of operating Longman did not exceed a few hundred pounds a year, whereas Dalcross would run into many thousands of pounds. I was therefore of the opinion that we should wait and see how aviation developed in the North, before vacating Longman. Dalcross would not run away overnight, whereas Longman could easily disappear at a moment's notice for building purposes if we vacated it. I replied in a letter to the *Courier*, urging a policy of wait and see, and pointing out the heavy increased costs of operating out of Dalcross and the heavy increase in road transport costs, plus the loss of time which would be incurred.

Within a week or so, I got my knuckles rapped sharply from the British European Airways' chairman, who sent a message through Mr. Cumming, Renfrew, instructing me not to interfere, and that I was cutting directly across London policy. That was the first intimation I received that the Scottish Division was to be a 'Division' in name only, and that our experience gained over the years, was to be by-passed. In other words, we were expected to assume the role of 'yes' men.

The next jolt received was the advent in the early spring of 1947 of the German Junkers Ju 52 which I have referred to earlier. Without warning our D.H.89 Rapide aircraft were partially withdrawn, to be superseded by the Junkers aircraft. Instead of leaving us with the Rapides with high payloads around 1,200 lb. which we had gone to a lot of trouble and expense in effecting, by building a drying-out room which would extract the moisture from the wooden components during annual overhaul, we were ordered from London to dispose of these aircraft and retain a bunch of Rapides of later registration which only had a payload of around 800 lb. On enquiring into the reason for this extraordinary uneconomical action, it appeared that the decision was arrived at by an individual in the London hierarchy who considered that the aircraft with old registration letters should be the first Rapides to be disposed of.

After that order had been carried out, much against our better judgment, we were told that the Rapide was wholly uneconomical, as it only carried a limited and uneconomical load. The whole incident was completely irrational, and no doubt had been dealt with by an individual of the mentality I had met at Renfrew the year before, who dealt in 'plans'.

Having got rid of the aircraft at Renfrew, which helped us to make a reasonable profit the year before, the Junkers Ju 52 went into action. In less than a month, our Renfrew-Stornoway, Aberdeen-Orkney-Sumburgh air routes were in complete confusion and dislocation. These German aircraft were breaking down all over the outlying airfields and they could not be restarted, if and when the motors stopped, without a special power driven starting truck, which the northern stations were not supplied with. That meant that the pilot had to keep his motors running while the passengers were disembarking and embarking. In the event of a motor having stopped, a starting truck had to be ferried by air from Renfrew. That took a lot of time and was extremely costly. We had no spares at outlying stations and Renfrew headquarters were not much better off. As most of the motors were found to have exceeded their maximum permissible hours, they were extremely unreliable and spares were a vital necessity.

Passengers were kept waiting out at airfields from early morning to late evening, and were lucky if they got carried at all that day. There were no catering facilities when our base was transferred to Dalcross and no heated waiting rooms. In Aberdeen, passengers bound for London often had to wait the arrival of an aircraft coming up from London, and that plane could be anything from an hour to several hours late, even though the weather was good all along the route from London. I made it a point to find out what caused such delays and it appeared that departure of the London-Aberdeen plane was dependent on its arrival from Madrid or some other far away Continental city. Some bright individual in the London set-up had the idea of integration and utilisation of aircraft worked out on paper, without any thought being given to the possibility of the aircraft being able to operate to a strict schedule. Motor trouble which, I have said, was frequent in those days immediately after the war, together with adverse Continental weather, had not been taken into account.

By the time July was reached, the public were screaming their heads off. M.P.s were asking questions in the House, not only about the frightful inefficiency of the newly nationalised airways, but the operating losses which were mounting into millions of pounds.

In the early days of 1947, I used to attend the monthly meeting of the newly-formed Scottish Advisory Council of Aviation, but I gave it up after a couple of months as a waste of time. It involved travelling from Inverness to Glasgow, and it had become clear to me that the Council was functioning in name only. Its chairman, who knew nothing about aeroplanes, used to arrive off the night train from London, completely briefed with instructions from Northolt. Whatever we suggested from our end was rarely given any notice. Those who held high office in London headquarters mostly came from the A.T.A. ferry service which had been responsible for delivering planes from factory to dispersal fields strewn around the British Isles, or to R.A.F. squadrons during the war. They may have known about ferrying work, but they had about as much idea of operating our Scottish air services as an ape with a bad headache.

No sooner had we been taken over than our staff was increased from 75 bodies all told at Renfrew and Inverness plus outstations to something in the region of 400. Trade union rules were creeping in and demarcation of jobs being imposed, making the labour charges very costly and wholly uneconomic.

Large aircraft were being used for administration flights on a large scale, and the whole set-up was soon entangled in red tape and masses of printed orders, which were hardly issued before they were countermanded by a host of amendments true to Civil Service style.

The organisation was also engulfed with decoration schemes comprising a red line and a 'key' which had to be 'exactly so' around walls of offices and waiting rooms, plus B.E.A. crest, and other oddities of a like nature which occupied a host of wasted man hours for all concerned.

The London headquarters of British European Airways rapidly became a nest of departments with the heads of each department vying with one another as to who should have the maximum of staff, for they no doubt figured the bigger their department, the higher and more profitable status they acquired in our organisation which was already top-heavy. In Scotland we were hamstrung. We had no independence and our efforts to reorganise under the so-called Scottish Division on business-like lines were not countenanced. In fact, as events subsequently proved, we only earned black marks in our endeavour to get our services back to normal, and to make them pay.

By May 1947 it had become evident that our operations were to be conducted on a grandiose style comparable to long-distance Continental air routes. No thought was apparently given to the difference in earning power or traffic density of the two totally different operations.

Early in the spring, I wrote to the managing director of B.E.A. in London, Gerard d'Erlanger, regarding the extravagant changes that were taking place on the Scottish routes. I referred to the inadvisability of moving to Dalcross and to the operation of large aircraft on the Northern Scottish routes. I warned him that if we vacated Longman airfield and moved to Dalcross, our cost of operations would increase considerably. Our present transport cost during the winter months at Longman airfield was £25 per month. If we moved to Dalcross, the charges would be in the region of £250 in the winter and probably £350 in the summer. These increased costs applied to passenger transport. We would also be faced with additional transport for engineers and operating personnel. I added

"There are no proper waiting-room facilities at Dalcross, whereas the Air Ministry have only just completed a very nice block of traffic offices at Longman airfield. Ultimately, new buildings will have to be built at Dalcross at extra expense. At present, there are three airfields on the Inverness-Kirkwall route, within five minutes or so of the centre of the town, namely, Inverness, Wick and Kirkwall. I doubt whether there are three towns on any one route throughout the country which can boast such time-saving airfields right up against the towns they serve. It would be a retrograde step to upset this happy trinity.

I

"Lastly, the close proximity of the Longman airfield to Inverness is of great interest to visitors and as soon as the restaurant and tea-rooms are functioning on that airfield, the local traffic potential, coupled with the tourist trade, could be greatly extended. Coupled with the aforementioned facts, the publicity value must not be over-looked. Finally, the maintenance cost of Dalcross as compared to Longman will be extremely heavy.

"Regarding the larger aircraft, it is my opinion, and I have 14 years' experience to go by, that the heavy flow of traffic which would call for aircraft of the Dakota class will be from London-Edinburgh and Aberdeen via the east coast.

"The type of aircraft required on the Glasgow-Inverness-Orkney-Shetland run is a D.H.86 16-seater aeroplane, redesigned as a mono-plane which would cost a fifth of the sum required for large aircraft providing barely twice the number of seats. Also, maintenance would be considerably more economic for the smaller aircraft, and that type of plane could be run to a high utilisation figure per annum through frequency of services, thus reducing the operational costs considerably and giving better service to the public."

Finally, I suggested that to settle any doubts about the safety of Longman airfield, a Dakota should be sent up with one of our pilots to make practical tests of take-off and landing on the available air strips. Should the tests be satisfactory, then Longman Airport should be retained. After all, Dakotas were operating out of Longman throughout the war, without difficulty or danger.

I did not receive a reply to that letter. We were hustled out to Dalcross the following August. At the same time, all our maintenance was shifted to Renfrew along with our staff and substantial stock of spares. Our Renfrew friends were surprised to note how George Griffiths had catered for any eventuality. In wartime it took a long time to obtain spares. The want of a spare part could ground an aircraft indefinitely. We were never caught out.

I have gone into the outcome of nationalisation at this stage in some detail, as it will clarify and explain later events, and the appal-ling losses which were to occur before the year was through. When these losses were ultimately known, the A.T.A. boys had the temerity to describe our once profitable air routes as a Social Service and that in plain language meant the taxpayers were expected to make good the huge and totally unnecessary deficit.

We still held a number of Rapides at Inverness for our local operations, and they came in extremely handy in assisting to transport the passengers held up by Junkers' breakdowns.

248

In the spring, I took steps to improve the landing strip at the island of Stroma situated in the middle of the Pentland Firth. The island was sold immediately after the war to private interests in the south. I planned to incorporate that island in the North Isles circuit, when I could obtain permission to recommence that service. Under the Scottish Division set-up, I had not the authority to get on with the job at my own discretion, as was the case in the past. I first wrote to the new owner, explaining my proposals and suggesting that he should bear the cost of providing a small bulldozer. I added that air transport from Inverness to the island should be of assistance to him when he visited the island. He agreed to my plans and on 6th June, I flew Mr. Phillips of Wm. Tawse Ltd., well-known contractors at Aberdeen, to the island to advise on the drainage and surfacing. At that time, I was unaware that the nationalisers had no intention of recommencing the much wanted local isles service, which Kirkwall Roads Surveyor, Mr. Robertson, and myself had spent so much time surveying the previous year.

We were just on the point of ordering the small bulldozer when I got word that the island of Stroma would not be included, if and when the North Isles services were recommenced.

The third week in April, I received instructions to proceed to Aberdeen to take over Allied Airways' affairs and weld them into the nationalised Corporation. I found on arrival that Mr. Gandar Dower was away at his favourite holiday resort in Switzerland, so in his absence the take-over was effected through his representative in charge.

It was an unpleasant chore, and I would have preferred someone else to have carried out the job – but there it was. I have always felt that at that moment, 'G.D.', as he was commonly known to us all, and myself became friends in adversity. We had both been blatantly robbed of many years' hard work and effort. The Press were humming around looking for a good story. The first question they asked me when I arrived at Dyce Airport administrative block was

"How do you feel, Captain, in taking over your rival's business."

I disliked that question and answered

"No comment."

They pumped other questions at me, which I refused to answer. On completion of the necessary documentary work, I left our station officer in charge to carry on the daily working of the air services, such as they were.

On 5th July, I flew Sir Harold Hartley down from Shetland to

249

Inverness. It was raining hard most of the way, but we landed in at Longman airfield on time for his rail connection to London. He had a talk with me on the airfield apron. He thanked me for an excellent flight and said he was glad to have flown with me for the first time. I gathered from what he said that he would shortly be relinquishing the chairmanship of British European Airways for that of chairman of British Overseas Airways and that actually came about at the end of the month. He said he realised how difficult things must be for me, but told me to keep a cheery outlook on the problems which faced me. I have often thought since that he knew that his successor to the chairmanship was gunning for me, although he did not put it in so many words. I was sorry to see him go. He was the only friend I had amongst the Philistines.

Around the middle of the month, a phone call for me came through from Dalcross, from a pilot who had just landed in a Miles Hawk monoplane from London. I picked up the phone and asked what I could do for him. He said

"I have an introduction to you, Captain Fresson, from a mutual friend in London. He told me to get in contact with you as you might arrange for my transport into town." I did not place the friend who gave the introduction. He went on to say that he was touring the British Isles by air under his own steam, and that he came from Australia. I went out in my car to meet him. He was of medium height and there was nothing about his appearance much different from the average person one came up against in those days.

On the way in, I became suspicious. This visitor had steered the conversation into my relationship with the new Corporation. He asked a number of pertinent questions about British European Airways' set-up and what were my reactions to the changes which were being made. I was puzzled. If he came from Australia, why should he be interested in British European Airways or my opinions? It suddenly occurred to me he might have been sent up from Northolt. I egged him on a bit and in the end I was certain I was correct. He was no actor, and quite the wrong type to send on such a mission. I told him just what I wanted London to know, in case they had sent him.

Shortly after, another incident of a similar nature occurred and I then became certain that I was being quizzed by order of higher authority. It happened at lunch after one of our Glasgow meetings. I was placed next to the female secretary of the British European Airways Scottish Advisory Council's chairman. I had sat next to her on previous occasions. She was anxious to know my opinion on many controversial matters – what I thought about the set-up in B.E.A.? Did I like or believe in nationalisation and so on. I was then certain that the Australian 'flyer's' questioning was tied up with one and the same source.

I talked it over with George Nicholson afterwards, and he agreed it was more than likely there were 'informers' adrift in the Corporation. There appeared to be an atmosphere of being watched. Truth is lent to this supposition by Group Captain Dudley Saward, O.B.E., who in an article on British European Airways in the *Sunday Express* dated 7th December 1947 stated:

"Finally, I would like to mention an ominous aspect of a State Air Corporation. I refer to the code of disciplinary procedure set out in Northolt Station routine orders in September 1947, providing for a system of punishments up to dismissal without notice with entries on the accused's personal file. I was horrified and frightened to find such a thing in civilian commercial operation."

That smacked of the 'gestapo' outlook which calls for a system of informers for the establishment of guilt for which the personal file and disciplinary action is designed.

Early in July, I relieved a pilot on the Inverness-Orkney-Shetland run. Arriving back at my home for afternoon tea, the phone rang. On picking up the receiver, a voice said

"Hello, Fresson, is that you?"

"Yes, who's that speaking?"

"George Nicholson," came the reply. "I've rung up to tell you that I have been fired. I'm to carry on until the end of September, when the Scottish Division is to be dissolved."

"You're pulling my leg," I said.

"No, it's the truth. I was sent for yesterday to go down to Northolt, and the managing director told me I was out."

I distinctly remember saying

"I expect it will be my turn next."

"It looks like it," he said, "they seem determined to smash the Scottish Division."

"I'll be down to Renfrew soon and we will have a chat about this situation."

"Fine," he said, "let me know when you are arriving and come and stay with us."

He rang off. I turned to my wife.

"Nicholson has been sacked," I said. She looked incredulous – I told her the rest of the story.

"I'm afraid that's the beginning of the end of our so-called Scottish Division."

I went on with my job as best I could, waiting to be called to London at any moment, but no word came.

At the beginning of August, we moved from our Longman airfield to Dalcross. The Junkers were still breaking down and holding passengers up for hours. At Longman, passengers could wait comfortably in the Inverness Station Hotel and have meals when necessary. At Dalcross there was no proper waiting room, let alone a coffee bar or dining room. There also was no heating. During August, it did not matter so much, but when the winter came around, our passengers were in for a grim cold wait should the Junkers fail to appear.

Rumblings in Parliament commenced just about that time. In *The Scotsman* 3rd July 1947 the Socialist member for Tradeston, Mr. Rankin, is reported as having asked the Parliamentary Secretary for Aviation, Mr. Lindgren, how many Ju 52s had been converted, the total cost of their conversion and on which routes these machines were operating. Mr. Lindgren replied that ten Ju 52s had been converted at a cost of £125,000. These aircraft were operated by British

European Airways on five of their Scottish services, but were to be replaced in the autumn of that year.

February to October represented eight months' use of these aircraft for £125,000! How *could* the Scottish routes earn enough to pay that price? And we had been asked to do our best to operate the routes at a profit! That was just the first rumble of the financial volcano. An eruption was about to take place before the end of the year. Actually, we managed to get shot of the Ju 52s at the end of August. That arose through an incident which occurred around the first week of that month.

One of the Junkers arrived at Aberdeen from Orkney with the aircrew almost on the point of asphyxiation by carbon monoxide gas. Passengers sitting in the front seats nearest the cockpit were also affected. Half way across the Moray Firth, exhaust gases from one of the motors broke free and penetrated the cockpit and into the cabin, the door leading to the cockpit being open. The crew shut off the cabin and opened all the cockpit windows, but that was not enough. Slowly and surely, the crew were gradually getting torpid. They radioed Dyce Airport reporting what was happening. They then tried shutting down one motor at a time to find out which was the offending engine out of the three installed. By the time they had located and shut down the responsible motor, they were over Banffshire with still 40 miles to go. They only just made it.

On hearing about this grave incident, I strenuously urged Northolt to withdraw the Ju 52s at once, even though it might cut our passenger capacity, and replace them with Rapides. The Junkers aircraft had been nothing but a nightmare ever since they were put on the run after the take-over, 1st February that year.

For the first time, London responded to a request made by me. They went further, and replaced the Junkers by sending up one or two Dakota 25-seater aircraft which operated at never more than half load.

CHAPTER FIFTEEN

THE New Year 1948 was spent quietly amongst our local friends. 'Gone with the Wind' best described the celebrations amongst our staff, which over the years had been a unique and happy feature in our home at Mayfield Road. For all flying and engineering staff had been transferred to Renfrew, along with our aircraft, during the last half of 1947. They left me Dragon G-ACIT and one engineer, Archie MacDonald, to maintain it. I now had no prescribed flying duties but in the absence of any instructions to the contrary, presumed I was still expected to carry out charter flights or air-ambulance calls as they arose, otherwise why station an aircraft at Inverness? Dragon G-ACIT had been returned to Renfrew early in December for its annual overhaul, and I ferried it up on 5th February via Dyce Airport, where I was due to carry out my monthly check on operations at Aberdeen.

My first charter of the year came on 11th February, from the Ministry of Civil Aviation to transport three of their airfield inspectors to the island of Westray. The North Isles air service still appeared to be under consideration at that late date. The Westray charter was to be the last operational flight I made for the Northern section of British European Airways, as it subsequently created a storm of criticism. The flying field at Westray was some three miles away from the village. While the inspection was under way with Mr. Johnson and his party from the Ministry, a taxi arrived from the village. The driver brought a message from the hotel, asking me to return and phone surgeon McClure at the Balfour Hospital, Kirkwall, as my services were urgently wanted for a serious case ambulance flight.

On arrival at the Westray Hotel, I was connected to the Balfour Hospital without loss of time. Surgeon McClure came to the phone.

"Is that you, Captain Fresson?" he asked.

I replied in the affirmative.

"We have just received an urgent call, from the island of Stronsay, asking for an immediate air ambulance. A small boy has been crushed by a farm tractor and the island doctor says that unless he can be flown into Kirkwall Hospital for urgent attention he is likely to die. I understand an immediate operation is necessary."

I told Surgeon McClure that I was in Westray on an Air Ministry charter, but would return to the airfield and explain the urgency to my passengers and would leave for Stronsay within a quarter of an hour.

"You can tell the Stronsay doctor to have his patient on the flying field within 25 minutes."

I hurried back to the Westray landing ground, explained to the Civil Aviation Representative, Mr. Johnson what had happened. He agreed I should make the trip immediately.

"In fact," he said, "we have completed our work here during your absence, so we will come along with you, if that is all right, and it will save you the trouble of flying back from Kirkwall to get us."

Within the 25 minutes, the patient, a small boy, was being put aboard the plane at Stronsay and I landed him at Hatston airfield, Kirkwall, inside ten minutes. An ambulance was awaiting our arrival and the poor little chap, who appeared to be under the influence of a sedative, was in hospital within a few minutes. He was operated on at once, and I learnt next morning before leaving with my Air Ministry friends for Inverness that he was out of danger. They had caught him just in time.

Details have been given at some length in view of the aftermath which occurred. The Press gave the flight some publicity and within a few days I received a short terse letter from the manager of British European Airways at Renfrew, saying it was understood I had carried out an ambulance flight to Stronsay on the 11th inst., and I was requested to inform them who had given me the authority to make the flight, and that in future, I was not to carry out any further flights of a like nature. I replied, saying that I had not received any instructions forbidding me to carry out mercy flights. In fact, I understood the reason for stationing Dragon G-ACIT at Inverness was for that very purpose, plus the carrying out of any charter flights which might occur. I concluded by adding, that if I had not been near at hand and had failed to carry out that mercy flight call, the surgeon at Balfour Hospital told me the boy would most certainly have died, for he was sorely injured.

On 22nd February, the *Sunday Express* displayed in large type on the front page, an announcement:

70 B.E.A. PILOTS FACE SACKING

"H.Q. officials and Scottish Pioneers to get notices. Men who made

255

the Air Road to the Isles – Cuts caused by travel ban and £2,000,000 loss. At the same time, three pioneers of the two independent Scottish Companies which were absorbed by B.E.A. upon nationalisation, are to be dismissed."

The *Press & Journal*, Aberdeen, on 23rd February, the following day, confirmed the previous day's report, but added

"There will be no drastic changes in reorganisation or serious staff reductions in Scotland, Sir Patrick Dollan, chairman of the Scottish Advisory Council on Civil Aviation, assured a reporter of the *Press & Journal* yesterday. Many of our services have to be stepped up by 100 per cent this summer and we need all the pilots and radio officers we have, he said. Rumours of dismissal of three Scottish pioneers in aviation – Captain Fresson, Captain Barclay and Mr. Cumming, were denied by Sir Patrick.

" 'The reorganisation is bound to bring about changes and these may be in executive posts, but,' Sir Patrick said, 'should any of these three be affected, then an alternative job will be offered.' "

Sir Patrick was either pulling the wool over the eyes of the public or he was grievously misinformed, as events will confirm.

The Glasgow *Bulletin* commented very ably, in their leader on 23rd February, about the mess that one year of nationalisation had created in the country.

"If anything can shock the reluctant into a true appreciation of the Scottish position of civil aviation, surely we have it now in the news that three of our pioneers in civil flying are likely to be 'axed' by British European Airways.

"Not only have the Labour Government killed Scottish flying enterprise, but their 'chosen instrument' now seems to be in process of dealing as unceremoniously with the pioneers they took over as they did with the other pioneers who would have nothing whatever to do with a nationalised set-up which was plainly foredoomed to disaster.

"In fact, the only Scot who seems incapable of being shocked into facing the facts is Sir Patrick Dollan, chairman of the Scottish Advisory Council, who was yesterday still handing out the usual stuff about Scotland having a better deal than ever, in spite of all the official forecasts from the south about the absolute necessity for cuts in services and everything connected with them.

"These pre-war services were laid down and built up by native Scottish enterprise by people like Fresson and Cumming, for whom, we are told, there is likely to be no future under British European Airways. If those people had been given any sort of freedom after the war, they could and would have developed services far beyond anything that had been possible before, but instead Scotland was saddled with the incubus of a 'chosen instrument' which has all too plainly been finding it a struggle to maintain anything like the pre-war standard."

The Press had accurately summed up the situation. I can't say I was surprised at the turn of events in view of the lavish and stupid manner in which our well-organised business had been turned upside down. Ever since George Nicholson was fired the previous July, I knew I was on insecure ground and that it was only a matter of time. It was with grief that I gazed on the sad and chaotic state our efficient airlines had been reduced to, those airlines which it had taken us over 15 years to build up. During that time, we had served the country faithfully in peacetime and during five years of difficult wartime flying, in unarmed aircraft which were always open to attack at any moment, without the power to defend themselves or retaliate against the enemy who roamed the skies along our routes continuously.

The continual parrot cry of the politicians, that Scotland enjoyed a far better service under the chosen Government instrument, was too much for the Scottish public to swallow. For it was they who came to know, the hard way, exactly what had been going on since the airlines fell into the hands of bureaucracy in its worst form.

It would be a great loss for me to leave the air routes which had become my one ambition in life, but under the circumstances I was prepared to relinquish office, provided suitable arrangements could be worked out. I, at that time, had reached the middle fifties, and could not hope to pick up a compensating post equal to what I had built up over the years. I accordingly decided to leave for London as soon as possible and seek an interview with Gerard d'Erlanger at his home in Kensington, when I could talk to him uninterrupted about my future, for he held the final word.

I flew to Aberdeen in Dragon G-ACIT on Wednesday, 18th February, and caught the night plane down to London. I put up at the Royal Aero Club in Piccadilly, and got in touch with d'Erlanger on the phone at his house. He said he would see me on Saturday, 21st February at 10.00 a.m.

I kept the appointment punctually, and was ushered into the

drawing room. The minutes ticked by, then an hour, and still no sign of my quarry. I could hear him talking to his children who appeared to be playing in the garden. I sat waiting until after 12.00 midday. I had been there two hours or more when he suddenly appeared without any apology. His look was no more pleasant than when I had met him in January 1947 with Sir Harold Hartley. After looking through me, and still standing, he said

"You wanted to see me?"

I briefly referred to the newspaper articles reporting my impending dismissal and asked him if it were true that I was about to be dismissed from the Corporation. He said a final decision had not been taken. I suggested to him that if he wished to get rid of me, I would resign from the Corporation, inasmuch as I no longer had any authority in the operation of the Scottish air routes. I hoped the Corporation would adequately compensate me for the loss of my livelihood. He replied that he would see what could be done or words to that effect. The interview was short and at an end. He opened the door of the drawing room, I picked up my hat and coat, and was ushered out of the front door.

The following Friday in the House of Commons, Sir Basil Neven Spence, M.P. for Orkney and Shetland, had accused British European Airways of waging a cold war on Scots and the pioneers of Scotland's internal airways and declared that the services would have been better under private enterprise. The Scottish *Daily Record* in their report said that Sir Basil referred to the reported dismissal (since denied) of the three well-known Scottish airmen on grounds of redundancy. Angrily demanding

"Who created the redundancy?", he went on to say "There was no redundancy before the war. The services were organised with the correct number of people. I think it is a monstrous thing for these Corporations to create redundancy and then proceed to kick out men who have spent their lives building up these airlines. The Scottish Advisory Council on Aviation," he said, "did everything but give advice. The day after the report of the dismissals in certain papers, Sir Patrick Dollan had stated that the notices to these men were not being sent out."

Sir Basil, who uses a plane more than any other member of the House, told the Government why the Scottish internal airlines were not paying.

"I came down the other day from Aberdeen to London in a 21-seater aircraft as a sole passenger. Does it not occur to British European Airways, in running these internal airlines, that it would be far better to have 20 passengers at £10 apiece, than four at £25?"

Earlier, Mr. Lennox-Boyd (Mid-Bedford, Conservative) had re-iterated the opposition's determination to denationalise the Corporation as soon as they returned to power. In 1951, when the Tories were again in office, Mr. Lennox-Boyd failed to carry out that promise when he became Minister for Civil Aviation.

On Thursday of the following week, Mr. Cumming, Captain Barclay and myself reported to the managing director at Northolt. He appeared a kindly man, and it was apparent that he had been delegated to carry out the dirty work. Having asked me to take a seat, he said

"I am sorry having to tell you, Captain Fresson, that there is no place for you in the future set-up of British European Airways."

"I had gathered that already from the Press," I replied, and asked on what grounds I was being dismissed.

I was informed that there were no complaints. I then said, there must surely be some reason for depriving me of the business I had created and knew more about than anyone in the Corporation. He made no reply to this observation, other than that it was the Board's decision.

"Will the Corporation adequately compensate me?" I enquired.

"We have agreed to pay you £2,000," he answered.

I could hardly believe my ears,

"That amounts to the public theft of my business!!"

"Those are strong words," he answered.

"Well, doesn't it?" I retorted, "how am I going to live on the interest of such a wholly inadequate sum as that. You must surely realise that at my age, I shall be unable to obtain a commensurate job, and as for aviation – there is practically nothing left which this Socialist Government haven't seized."

He gazed at me, I thought with sympathy,

"I am only informing you of the decision of the Board."

"In that case, there is nothing more to be said," I replied.

I bid him good morning and left. As I walked along the passage, I was thinking that d'Erlanger had done nothing after my interview last week at his house to obtain just and honourable settlement, and that confirmed the suspicion in my mind that he was responsible for the situation. As I turned a corner in the passage leading to the front entrance, I ran slap into him. Before I could say a word, he glared at me, and disappeared quickly into an office on his right. I met Cumming at the Orchard Hotel, Ruislip, for lunch. He had been told exactly the same thing. David Barclay, he said, had received a last-minute reprieve. Sir Basil Neven Spence's reference in the House of Commons to 'his valuable air-ambulance work', which incidentally I had spoken to Sir Basil about previously, had caused a change in attitude. I was told that David had been interviewed and informed that he would be given the chance of organising an air-ambulance division.

We flew back to Renfrew that night. One of our pilots, whom I had always counted as one of my friends and who had been attached to the Northern routes during the war, was on the same trip. He saw us seated, but passed by although there was a spare seat at hand, and chose a place in the extreme front of the Viking aircraft. He appeared frightened to talk to Cumming and myself.

There was a battery of Press cameras and reporters to meet our plane on arrival at Renfrew. The news of our meeting and its result, had reached the Glasgow Press and we were showered with questions. The date of my departure from the Scottish airlines had been fixed for 31st March 1948, and as William Cumming and myself had not come to any decision on our future action in relation to our dismissals, we agreed to make no public statement at the moment. We merely confirmed the report that we had been sacked.

I went down to Ayr to stay with George Nicholson that night and we sat up late discussing the political theft of our business. It seemed to me like a nightmare.

I had been to see Mr. Lindgren, the Socialist Parliamentary Secretary for Air, whom I had previously met on his visit to Inverness in the autumn of 1946. He appeared pleased to see me, and called a colleague in to the discussion. I asked him if the Air Minister would take action to prevent British European Airways ruining me. After some consultation, they both eventually agreed that it would embarrass the Attlee Government should my case be brought to the House of Commons. They could or would not give any just reason for British European Airways' policy. I left, thinking that perhaps Mr. Lindgren was sympathetic, but in that I was subsequently to be proved wrong when the debate ultimately took place in the House of Commons, for he did his best to justify the B.E.A. case. Lord Winster, who I think would have befriended us, had been replaced by another Minister who did not appear to have the same degree of discrimination between right and wrong.

I returned to Inverness to work out my last month, but there was nothing for me to do. I flew up to Kirkwall in Dragon G-ACIT on the 23rd of the month to say goodbye to my staff, and on the 30th March I flew over to Dyce to bid my adieu there. They all appeared too frightened to say much but I could sense their sympathy for me.

I flew back in the afternoon, crawling along low down over the hills and moorlands south of the Banffshire coastline. I landed at Dalcross at four-thirty in the afternoon. It was my last flight in that aeroplane, which had become a trusted steed to me. Next day, unbeknown to me for I was not advised of the situation, a plane was sent up from Renfrew with an engineer and pilot, and G-ACIT was then flown to Renfrew. I did not know that it had gone until two days later. I had asked to be allowed to purchase that Dragon. I was proposing to use it for air-ambulance work in the Northern Isles, if British European Airways did not restore the facilities, and also for air charters. I was brusquely refused, and to make sure that I did not keep the plane, it was removed in a stealthy manner out of my reach.

Following the reprimand I had received in the middle of February in connection with the Stronsay ambulance flight already described, and following the removal of the Dragon from Inverness at the end of March, there occurred two calls from the Orkney County Council for ambulance flights to take an urgent surgical case from the island of Westray to Kirkwall Hospital.

"British European Airways said they could not carry out the mercy flight because they had no suitable plane available," as quoted by Doctor Bannerman, chief M.O.H. of Orkney.

And yet they had my Dragon G-ACIT in Renfrew, which we specially retained and rebuilt for that work. It can only be concluded, that it was not the aircraft they were short of, but a pilot who knew those landing fields in the Northern Isles. Having got rid of me, they at the same time got rid of the one person who could have met the ambulance contract B.E.A. had with the Orkney County Council.

With Renfrew's inability to do the job, a steamer had to be sent to Westray to bring the small patient, Inga Brown, seven years old, into the Balfour Hospital. The sea journey took six hours against the flying time of 15 minutes. The Press reported the girl was seriously ill with acute appendicitis, and the sea was very rough. The Press also quoted that it was understood that the B.E.A. pilots at Aberdeen refused to make the trip because the landing ground at Westray was not licensed. I suspect in that case, it was because none of the pilots could land a Rapide, which was the only type they had available for the job, on the small field at Westray. It was possible to do so safely, if one had the know-how, because I had frequently landed there in that type of aircraft. In any event, the law did not require a field to be licensed for a charter flight or for ambulance flights.

Meantime, a storm of protest was raised about the dismissals. The Inverness Chamber of Commerce supported by the Aberdeen Chamber and others, organised a protest meeting on 9th April in the Inverness Town Hall, which seated 400 persons. The place was packed. The Member for Inverness, Sir Murdoch MacDonald, and Lord Malcolm Douglas Hamilton, together with Mr. Eric Linklater, the famous novelist, spoke, as also did Provost Ross and certain Councillors.

The *Highland News* of 27th April 1948, described the situation created, in their leading article in the following terms:

"Indignation at the summary dismissal of Captain E. E. Fresson and the other senior Scottish Executives of British European Airways Corporation is growing throughout the country. It is certain that the question will be aired in the House of Commons, after the Easter recess, probably by Sir Murdoch MacDonald, M.P. for Inverness-shire, who is well aware of the distressed surprise that the announcement caused. Sir Murdoch has already raised the matter privately with the Under Secretary for Civil Aviation.

"This is a matter above party politics and it is more than possible that when the question reaches the floor of the House criticism will come not only from the opposition side. In the country at large, protests at the harsh and altogether stupid action of B.E.A.'s high command are being crystallised, through such democratic channels as the newspapers, Chambers of Commerce, local authorities and public societies, whose only interest is to see fair play for both these pioneers and for the air-travelling public.

"It seems possible that the 'Fresson case' will become something akin to the historic case of 'Jenkins' ear', but instead of forcing the Government to take action against a tyrant foreigner it will force an investigation into the despotic and thoroughly inefficient rule of one of the Government's most disastrous ventures.

"The word that sticks in everyone's gizzard in connection with the dismissals is that used by B.E.A. in its very self-conscious announcement 'redundant'. The only thoroughly experienced top men in the Scottish Division, the only men to reach the top the hard way, the only men with an intimate knowledge of the routes, and the public they serve, in fact, the men who planned and pioneered it all, 'superfluous'? Scottish people just won't believe it. The people of the Highlands and the Islands who 'bless' the name of Fresson, who brought the world to their door, would have a stronger word for it, a short sharp word of three letters.

"The only satisfactory answer is for the affairs of B.E.A. to be investigated by an impartial enquiry. Public opinion demands this, and the people's voice will not be stilled until such a step is taken."

Earlier in my story, I said that I would again refer to Stornoway which during the pre-war years was so reluctant to give any help in establishing an airfield. Once the air service had really got under way, the population became my staunch supporters. Their Town Council and Councillors were as demanding as any other part of the North of Scotland in their protests against my dismissal. One newspaper even reported that they were considering offering me the Freedom of Stornoway, but I never heard anything about that officially. Anyway, such an honour did not mature, either there or anywhere else.

I am afraid the demands in the last paragraph of the *Stornoway Gazette* editorial went unheeded, for the Socialist Civil Aviation Parliamentary Secretary, Mr. George Lindgren, gave no sympathy or help to public opinion. With every effort made by M.P.s to sort out the fantastic mess that British European Airways had got themselves into, plus their frantic desire to get rid of me, Mr. Lindgren's answer was always to the effect that the 'question' was a matter for the Corporation without Government interference. So having given birth to the Monster, the Socialists washed their hands of any responsibility for its deeds. A very convenient, but perhaps dishonest way of evasion.

On 31st March, I said goodbye to my Inverness staff, packed my belongings and left the office I had sat in for the past seven years. I was allowed to retain the Gipsy Moth 'Ah-WO' and Mr. Donald of Macrae & Dick, who had taken over our old hangars at Longman Airport, allowed me to house it there. Within a week or so, the Aberdeen *Press & Journal* hired me to carry out a photographic survey of the North of Scotland towns along with their photographer. We also included the Cairngorm Mountains with the small lochs to be found on their slopes. Some excellent results were obtained in 20-odd hours' flying time.

At the beginning of May, I was informed that the Conservative Party intended to raise the question of my dismissal and compensation in the House of Commons. I was later invited down, along with my wife, to stay with Colonel and Mrs. J. R. H. Hutchison (Glasgow Central, later Colonel Sir James Hutchison) at Forgandenny, south of Perth, to spend the night and to provide information for the forthcoming House of Commons debate. I was told by my host that Mr. J. S. C. Reid, M.P. for Hillhead, Glasgow, and a well-known barrister, would present the case on behalf of the Conservative and Unionist party.

That same evening, there was a big assembly, under the chairmanship of Lord Dunglass, D.L., in the Central Scotland Ice Rink, Perth, to hear Mr. Winston Churchill speak. I was invited to accompany my hosts. We were late in getting back to Forgandenny and so the notes on the debate to come were completed next morning.

I arrived at the House of Commons at two o'clock in the afternoon of Monday, 31st May 1948. I was shown into a box at floor level. Beside me sat a British European Airways' representative, who had been sent to take notes of the debate. I knew him slightly. He told me that he did not like the job he had been assigned, but it was a question of 'do as you are told or be fired'.

Mr. Hutchison had evidently been told of my arrival, for he came along and went over several points which Mr. J. S. C. Reid wanted him to check. The attack on the Minister of Civil Aviation through his Parliamentary Secretary, Mr. George Lindgren, then commenced.

Mr. Reid (later Lord Reid) was a very well-known barrister and a very skilful one, for he presented the case in masterly form. For the purpose of my story, I will content myself with referring to the more pertinent passages in his address to the House.

The case which Mr. Reid built up step by step was to prove that British European Airways had no legitimate reason for dismissing me. Scotland was, he said, disturbed and alarmed by developments in the Scottish air services. Then suddenly came an announcement that the man who had created aviation in Scotland had been dismissed. Then Scotland got really angry, and the Minister might know that there were protest meetings – large protest meetings – held in many places; there were resolutions passed by all manner of local authorities, Chambers of Commerce and the like. Indeed in one local authority in Stornoway, two Socialist members of the Council went so far to propose that Captain Fresson should receive the Freedom of the Burgh, and one said that the way Captain Fresson had been treated was no great credit to the present Government. That was a Socialist Baillie in Stornoway. Perhaps they were far enough away, so that the whip may not have reached up there. Not only that, but we had speeches and pronouncements by prominent men of all parties. We had the whole Press, local and national, up in arms and nobody had a good word to say for the Ministry.

In their first report, Mr. Reid said, British European Airways drew attention to the fact that it had been necessary for them to start speedily from scratch. That may well have been so in other departments of their work. It was emphatically not so in Scotland, but they chose to make it so, because they chose to turn things upside down when there was absolutely no need for them to do so. They chose to turn services which were practically self-supporting into services which incurred crippling losses, with the result, of course, that the Minister had to intervene. He could intervene then, why cannot he interfere now?

Then Mr. Reid went on to say

"If the Minister would accept responsibility, I should of course, confine my criticism to him. The old and good rule should hold that, where a Minister is responsible, his subordinates and others ought not to be criticised, but as the Minister disclaims responsibility, it is necessary for me to direct my criticism to the actual wrong-doer.

"The Chairman and most powerful influence in British European Airways is Mr. d'Erlanger. Whereas Sir Harold Hartley appears to have reasonable views, whereas the Minister when he saw fit to make pronouncements had more or less reasonable views, this gentleman had anything but reasonable views. I will not expatiate upon the facts of Captain Fresson's case.

"He had given 15 years of devoted service to the Highlands with universal satisfaction. He had received resolutions long before this matter cropped up. He was decorated during the war for his services and what has happened since shows the prestige which he has acquired in the Highland area."

Mr. Reid's masterly presentations of the case, plus the widespread public indignation aroused over it, failed to move the Minister of Air or his colleagues. If the full Hansard Report is read, it is not difficult to see the Party resentment which I feel was behind the stark refusal of Mr. Attlee's Government to protect me from savage persecution.

Three years later, the Conservatives returned to power. I went along to see the Minister for Air, Mr. John S. Maclay, regarding reopening the matter of adequate compensation which the Tory Party said in 1948 should be paid to me. To my utter surprise, Mr. Maclay told me that the new Conservative Government were not prepared to reopen my case. So what was honest and right for the Conservatives in 1948 appeared no longer to apply in the spring of 1952.

On 1st July 1948, I left Inverness to receive training for a three-year executive post offered in Kenya. My wife came down to Alloa with me and stayed the first week, before returning to our home in Inverness. I spent all the rest of the summer at Alloa and passed an examination towards the middle of October. I was due to leave for East Africa by flying-boat from Southampton on 23rd November 1948.

As I still had my Moth aeroplane, the *Press & Journal* contracted with me to fly their photographer over the famous Braemar Games at Ballater, which were in progress on Tuesday, 9th September. We obtained some first-rate pictures of that famous gathering. The weather was kind to us, and we were able to get low down in the valley to get the shots. Over the following week-ends I used to motor up from Alloa and return on the Monday. The *Press & Journal* photographer and I carried out a number of week-end air photo excursions. One of importance was to the Loch Cannich area which was due for post-war hydro-electric development.

In August, my wife's sister Elain Pobjoy came to stay with us in Inverness, and on 3rd November I flew her up to Orkney in my Moth 'Ah-WO' to say goodbye to my friends, the Reids, at Braebuster Farm ten miles east of Kirkwall. We landed in a tiny field alongside the farmhouse. I overstayed our time and got caught up with darkness and bad weather at Helmsdale on the return journey. I was forced to land while there was a little light left, on the same field three miles North of Helmsdale that I first used for the Avro landing in 1931. After picketing the Moth down, we returned to Inverness by the night train. It was several days before I could rescue the Moth on account of unfavourable winds.

I eventually flew it back on the Saturday, 6th November, solo.

The wind was still unfavourable, blowing from the west but at greatly reduced speed which meant a downwind take-off. The local physician, Dr. Gray, and Sandy Grigor, an old friend who owned the Belgrave Arms Hotel in Helmsdale, came along to witness the take-off. They were scared that I would not make it in the restricted downwind run. They did not understand the acceleration the down-hill take-off would give the plane, for I had no doubts the Moth would make it. In fact, it came off the ground half way down the slope. It was my last cross-country flight in that machine which had been in my possession for 17 years, since 1931. That little plane had been rebuilt two years before by George Griffiths, just after Dragon G-ACIT was similarly dealt with. The motor had also received a complete overhaul and so 'Ah-WO' had many flying years ahead of it, but not with me. I made a farewell flight around Inverness on Saturday, 13th November, and next day, Sunday, a pilot friend of mine flew 'Ah-WO' to Belado Airfield near Kinross, South of Perth. The owner of that airfield, Mr. MacDonald, said he would store it and find a buyer for me.

That last flight was like parting with an old friend and I well remember I had tears in my eyes. That little plane had flown many thousands of miles with me and was responsible for the original survey of the Inverness-Orkney route in 1931 and 1932. I just hated parting with it and had considered shipping it out to Kenya. I came to the conclusion, however, that it might be unsuitable for that type of flying, owing to the long uninhabited distance one had to fly over.

I put 'Ah-WO' back into its Longman airfield hangar that night for the last time and locked the door with a heavy heart.

CHAPTER SIXTEEN

THE 9th November dawned. At breakfast, I read in the *Daily Express* a small reminder of the function which was to take place in the Caledonian Hotel in my honour the following day. I always think newspaper leader writers are so very skilled in putting so much meaning into so few words, and the small leader article in question that day, was no exception to the rule. It ran:

"The men of the North take farewell of a pioneer tomorrow. With tiny resources and immense faith, Captain Fresson taught Scotland to fly. His small passenger planes reduced distances, once measured in days, to hours. His air ambulance on moor or beach, saved many an Island life. And he made it pay. He was taken over by the Government air monopoly, employed for a while, then ruthlessly discarded. Now he leaves for part of the Empire where there is still outlet and reward for men with the right spirit.

"He goes with the blessing and good wishes of all who admire a bonny fighter."

My eyes became misty, as I put the newspaper down. It was a marvellous little tribute and I kept the cutting for my scrap book which I am now quoting from and in fact, have been quoting from for most of this life story of mine.

All day and the next day, 10th November, the day of my farewell party, I was busy supervising the packing up at 12 Mayfield Road, in readiness for my departure a week hence. The house had been sold and that also added a tone of finality to what had descended upon my wife and myself. We had been so happy in that home and had hoped that we would have had many more years spared to us along with our young son Richard to enjoy it.

However, it was not to be and I kept on thinking as I got ready that night for the farewell dinner, which some 90 guests were to attend, what a fickle thing fate is.

On arrival at the Caledonian Hotel at 7.15 p.m. before the dinner was due to start, we went into the ballroom where the banquet was staged to take place. A wonderful sight met our eyes. There was a big rectangle of tables seating 30 guests each side with 12 seats each end. In addition there were an extra eight seats provided behind the two sides. In the middle of the rectangle formed by the tables, a striking tableau met the eye, arranged by Mr. J. S. Nairn. A scale model of the town of Inverness made by the students of Edinburgh College of Art, made up the centre-piece, and it was surmounted by an illuminated arc of fluorescent lighting, representing the sky. Model aeroplanes were suspended over the model of the town, making their way to Orkney, Lewis, Aberdeen and the south, along the air routes which I had developed. A model of the monoplane *Inverness* which commenced the service from Inverness to Orkney on 8th May 1933 topped the tableau, and the flowers which were grouped around in great profusion, made the scene most striking and beautiful. Mr. Nairn had put a lot of hard work into a lovely tableau which enchanted the guests, my wife and myself.

During the dinner, Stewart Kay and members of the Caledonian Hotel Orchestra played Highland airs. After the speeches and presentation of a beautiful antique silver tray to my wife and myself, films were shown of the inauguration of the Inverness-Orkney air service at Longman airfield in 1933 and the mail plane taking off for Orkney on the first internal air mail service in Britain at the same airport in May 1934.

Mr. Wotherspoon, one of the founder-directors and legal secretary, intimated that the original air mail pennant flown by my plane was to be presented to the Burgh of Inverness for safe custody and placed in the Museum.

I sat in the middle of the west side array of 30 chairs, on my left Sir John Gilmour, who was a director in the firm on whose behalf I was going to Kenya, on my right, Provost Hugh Ross. Three seats from Sir John Gilmour sat Sir Murdoch MacDonald, our M.P., next to him my wife's sister Mrs. E. Pobjoy, and on her left Mr. A. Trotter, editor of the Scottish *Daily Express*. Then Miss J. Ross, Mr. R. Donald, Highland Airways' chairman, Mr. N. MacArthur and Mr. and Mrs. Scott Swanson. On the right of Provost Hugh Ross sat the famous author Mr. Eric Linklater, next to him my wife, Mr. and Mrs. Wotherspoon and Mr. and Mrs. James Grigor, Mr. Wm. Hamilton, Highland Airways' secretary in the early days, and Mrs. Hamilton, Colonel and Mrs. J. Robertson, Highland Airways' Wick director, and Mr. J. South and Mrs. Lowe. There were in all 90 guests. An excellent dinner was served under the direction of Mr. B. V. Marler.

Three nights later my wife and I were entertained to another dinner given by our more intimate friends in the Station Hotel, scene of the inauguration of Highland Airways and the opening of the

Longman Airport by the Duke of Sutherland in May-June 1933. We enjoyed a novel menu, inasmuch as the first letter of each item of seven lines, was so worded as to spell our name 'Fresson'. I believe Dudley Carlin, the manager of the Station Hotel, was responsible for the clever make-up of that menu.

My last week-end was spent in helping to complete the packing at home. My wife went south with me and saw me off from Southampton, returning to Inverness to hand the house over to the new owner. On Wednesday, 17th November we left by the L.M.S. night express for London. There was a large crowd to see us off and bid me godspeed on my long air journey to Nairobi. The flying-boat was due to depart from Southampton on Tuesday, 23rd November, and we went to stay with our friend, Cecil Horne, for a few days at his lovely home situated on the bank of the Thames at Mapledurham.

He went out of his way to make our stay an enjoyable one. On the Friday, he kindly lent us his car to run over to West Downs Preparatory School at Winchester, to fetch our son Richard, who had been given special leave by Mr. Tindall, his Headmaster, to spend the week-end at Mapledurham and accompany us to Southampton to see me off on the Solent flying-boat.

Over the week-end I took ill with fever and had to send for a doctor. There was some doubt on the Saturday evening as to whether I would be fit to leave on Monday afternoon. However, I made sufficient recovery by the time the doctor came on Monday morning and was allowed to leave the house to catch the three o'clock train for Southampton.

It was a very foggy day and it took that train two and three-quarter hours to cover the 47 miles. As we neared Southampton, the fog cleared. The taxi driver who took us to the hotel told us that it had been sunny there all day. We were booked in at the Polygon Hotel which appeared to be the official hotel for B.O.A.C. passengers. My friend Whitney Straight, who held high office in B.O.A.C., had given me an introduction to the Corporation's Station Superintendents all along my long route to Africa, and I took advantage of that to call on Mr. Bingham who was in charge of the flying-boat service in Southampton. He told me to ask for him as soon as we arrived at the flying-boat landing stage next morning.

"Be along about half an hour before departure time, and we will get you through the formalities ahead of the other passengers."

I thanked him, for it gave me a chance to pick the seat in the flying-boat which I wanted. Mr. Bingham was extremely helpful and I wrote and thanked him for his courteous help while flying between stages.

Dinner in the hotel that night was not a very cheerful affair. First there was the parting from my family; next, I didn't know what was ahead of me. I was aware from experience that to clear up a mess in a business when the old management and directors held a powerful minority shareholding was to court making enemies, however tactfully the transition was put into effect. Shortly after dinner, my wife took our schoolboy son up to bed and I sat in the lounge reading my last evening newspaper in Britain. My mind would not concentrate, and I began to study the other occupants of the lounge, wondering what the morrow meant to them. Some of them might be my fellow-passengers on the Solent flying-boat *Salcombe*.

I did not sleep well that night. I just could not think how it had come about that I should be in my present position. Britain and its way of life – its conception of fair play – and just reward where it was due, just did not match up with the fact that I had been driven out by a system that was entirely foreign to my concept of British justice. The whole of Scotland had told me only too plainly that my work had been of public benefit and yet I had been treated like a criminal. In the end I gave up and started the old trick of trying to count sheep going through a gate and eventually fell into an uneasy sleep. I was glad to get up, when the bedside phone rang to tell us that the hour of 6.30 a.m. had arrived.

The morning was again free of fog. It had dawned a fine day, but with high overcast. We breakfasted, and made our way by taxi to Pier No. 50. Mr. Bingham was there to meet us and after I was through the formalities he introduced Captain Rotheram, who was the skipper of our flying-boat *Salcombe*, at the same time mentioning that I was a friend of Mr. Whitney Straight. The captain was a genial chap and invited me up to the cockpit after we had got 'on course'. I spent three to four most interesting hours, right across France to the Mediterranean and on to Sardinia, observing the technique of navigating and flying a modern aircraft. I was grateful to him as it took my mind off my recent departure.

I bade my family goodbye.

"I'll see you in three months," I said to my wife, for she would follow me out to Kenya by ship, leaving in January 1949.

Our son would return to West Downs Preparatory School, and would fly out for his summer holidays with us in Nairobi. I chose my seat amidships on the bottom deck and shortly after was greeted by a fellow-passenger, whose name was Hargreaves. He later told me that he was connected with the Calico Printers Company of Manchester. He was a most companionable passenger throughout the journey and I was truly glad of his company.

The cabin door was closed, I gave Richard and my wife, who had a handkerchief to her eyes, a final wave through the cabin porthole and we began our long taxi out into the Solent for take-off. The time was 9.00 a.m. prompt to the second of the advertised time of departure, and I recollect thinking what an efficient company B.O.A.C. were.

We taxied a long way down Southampton Water and commenced the take-off opposite Woolston, where I used to cycle down from Putney in 1906 and 1907 to stay with my Uncle Noel who was in charge of the famous racing boat *Flying Fish* and which took part in the Monaco races of that day. It was owned by the Duke of Westminster and was powered by Wolseley Motors, in which firm my uncle was a member. The boat was built by Saunders-Roe of Cowes. My mind flew back to the many exhilarating trips I had the good fortune to make in those far-off days down the Solent at 40 m.p.h. which was a high water speed for the early 1900s.

My mind came back to Mother Earth as the motors of the flying-boat were suddenly opened up. We were off the water in 45 seconds which was very good, as the ship carried a heavy load of petrol for the 1,300-mile non-stop flight to Augusta in Sicily, where we would spend the night before flying on to Alexandria next day for lunch and then on to fabulous Luxor on the Nile, for the second night stop.

We caught up with the clouds at 4,000 feet and were through and on top in brilliant sunshine at 5,000 feet. The country which had exiled me lay hidden beneath the clouds behind us.

INDEX

INDEX

A

Aberdeen 99, 105, 108, 109, 111
Aberdeen Airways 105, 120, 127, 143
Aerofilms Ltd. 37
Aircraft Disposal Co. Ltd. 25, 67
Air Ministry 119, 120, 126, 143
Air Transport Licensing Authority 176
Allied Airways 249
Anderson, Mr. 71, 72, 192
Angus, P. 52, 97
Antoinette 1
Anzani motor 1
Arbon, P. 10
Armstrong Whitworth 21, 25
Army Co-operation 181
Attlee, Clement 199
Avro 504K 19, 22, 33, 34, 54
Ayr 34

B

Baikal 7
Ballardie, A. 129
Barber, Mr. 3
Barrack, Mr. 117
Beardmore Flying School 34
Beaumont, Mr. 4, 5
Berkshire Aviation Tours 33
Berlin 6
Bilsland, Sir S. 225, 243
Bissett, R. 99, 118
Blackburn Aviation 35

Blackburn School 43
Blériot 1-4
Bradbury, Mr. 146, 161
Breguet 26
Bressay 98, 100
Brian Lewis Ltd. 90
Bristol biplane 1-4
British Airline Pilots' Association 230
British Airways 150
Brooke, A. 206
Brooklands 4, 62
Brora 97
Butchart, Mr. 31

C

California 9, 33
Cambridge School of Flying 19
Camp Borden 13, 15
Canton Hankow Railways 9
Caudron 31
Chan Tao Lin 31
Chater, B. 34
Chisholm, Mr. 65
Cirrus 31
Civil Aviation Directorate 112
Coastal Command 113
Cody, S. F. 4
Coleman, C. 88, 90, 92
Cramlington 56, 76
Croke, C. 191
Croydon Airport 67, 76, 78
Culloden Moor 84
Cumming, Dorothy 18, 19
Cumming, W. 134, 259
Curtiss JN-4 13

D

Daily Mail 1, 3
Dairen 8
Dakota 253
Dalcross 197, 203, 244, 252
De Havilland Dragon 88, 91, 92
De Havilland Dragon Rapide 118, 119, 245
De Havilland Moth 31, 41
Deperdussin 4, 5
D'Erlanger, G. 229, 238, 257, 259
De Russet 9
Director of Postal Services 53, 68, 113
Dodds, A. 55
Dollan, Sir P. 239, 256
Donald, Mr. 63, 64, 65, 72, 80, 85, 103, 263
Duncan, Mr. 132
Dunn, J. W. 1
Duxford 18
Dyce 99, 104, 116

E

Edinburgh 5, 89
Egerton, M. 1
Elgin, Dr. Alexander of 80, 103
Elliott, Sir W. 145, 174
Eve, Trustram 105
Everard, Sir L. 73
Everyman Camp 14, 15, 16

F

Fairey, R. 1
Fair Isle 100, 153, 154, 155
Farman, H. 1, 3
Farminer, B. 34, 74, 131, 219
Fort Worth 15, 16

Foula 168
Fox Moth 88
Framlingham College 10
Frances, Dr. 10

G

Gairdner, W. 92, 94
Gandar Dower, E. 104, 153, 249
Ganson, Mr. 100, 144, 191
General Aircraft Co. 67, 72, 74, 76
Georgeson, Mr. 106
Gloucester, Duke of 209
Gnôme rotary motor 3, 4
Gosforth Park 4
Goulden, T. 127
Grahame-White, C. 3
Grant, W. 63, 64
Grantown-on-Spey 46
Green motor 3
Greenshields 108
Griffiths, G. 126, 219
Groomsport 38

H

Halifax 17
Halliwell, Lt. 15
Hamilton, W. 72, 74
Handlover, D. 219
Hankins, J. 163, 180, 213
Hankow 8, 9, 23
Harbin 8
Harrogate 4, 5
Hartley, H. 227, 229, 238
Hatston 50, 70, 178, 192
Heath, Commander 168
Heinkel 208
Helmsdale 47
Hendon 3, 4, 124, 132
Heston 91
Hicks Airfield 16

Higgins, Sgt. 12
Highland Airways Ltd. 66, 161
Highland Park Distilleries 63
Holmes, Capt. 93
Holmes, F. 33
Hooton Park 34, 41, 66, 68, 213
Howe, Commander 193
Hutchinson, Mr. 263, 264

I

Inverness 53, 65, 72, 76, 77, 81, 131

J

Junkers 28, 30, 204, 231, 234, 245, 252, 253

K

Kangaroo 35
Kendal 36, 38
Kiangwan 23
Kintore 118, 127
Kirkintilloch 55
Kirkwall 41, 42, 48, 49, 52, 62, 65, 76, 125

L

Latham, H. 1, 4
Law, G. 64, 65, 82, 95
Leach, D. 21
Leathart, Connie 56, 91
Le Rhône 34, 67, 75
Lindbergh, Charles 32, 33
Lindgren, George 244, 260, 263
Linklater, Eric 262

L.M.S. 146
Loh 25
Longbranch 13
Los Angeles 9, 10, 32

M

Macbain, Willie 21, 25
McCallum, Mr. 78, 103
McClean, Frank 1
McClure, Ian 42, 43, 50, 89, 102, 254
McCrindle, Major 158, 160, 161, 236
McIntyre, Group Capt. 226
Mackenzie Capt. 16
Mackintosh Mr. 49
MacLaren S. 155
Maclay Mr. 265
McLennan A. 131
MacNider, S. 8
MacRae and Dick 72, 76, 80
Mealing, Major 112, 132, 133
Measures, Wing Co. 146, 151, 213, 229
Melbost Golf Links 111, 112, 145, 166
Monkmoore 34
Monospar 65, 87, 90, 120
Moore-Brabazon 1
Morane 3-5
Morris, D. 36
Mukden 8, 31

N

Nairn 46
Narborough 17
Nicholson, George 134, 238, 251
North British Aviation Co. 34, 36, 67, 74, 76

North Ronaldsay 101, 114, 182
North of Scotland Steam Navigation Co. 78, 90, 103
Northern and Scottish Airways Ltd. 134, 161

O

Orcadian 49
Orkney 41, 42, 49, 62, 70, 77, 116, 121
O.X. motor 13

P

Pilkington 36
Paulhan, L. 3
Pauer, Miss 41, 62, 73, 117
Pobjoy, Mr. 56, 66
Pobjoy engines 67, 73
Pugh 73, 78, 89, 126, 127

R

Railway Air Services Ltd. 146, 150
R.A.F. 18, 185
Reid, Mr. 264
Renault 22, 31
Renfrew 34, 35, 248, 254
R.F.C. 6, 9, 10, 18
Rimmer, L. 35, 56, 74, 213
Ritchie, Mr. 50, 70
Roberts, W. 129, 161
Robertson, Col. 50
Rolls, C. S. 1
Rolls-Royce Falcon 35
Ross, K. 111, 138
Rousay 114
Royal Aero Club 2, 111, 138, 257
Ryan Aircraft Co. 32, 33

S

St. Helens 36
Salmson 67
Sanday 180
San Diego 32, 33
San Francisco 9
Saunders-Roe 67, 76, 113, 134
Seaton 105, 117
Schofield, Capt. 67, 73, 76
Scotsman, The 64, 65, 82, 122
Scott, Capt. 113, 134
Scottish Airways, 94, 113, 161
Shanghai 6, 9, 20, 21, 25, 29
Shansi 23
Shearer, J. 62, 71
Shetland 98, 143, 160, 167, 184
Shih-Chia-T'swang 23
Short, Mr. 1
Simons, Gwen 56, 60, 108
Slater, Provost 111, 114
Smith Laing 66, 72
Somerville, Admiral 194
Spence, N. 224, 258
Sperry 82, 91, 125
Spooner, W. 73
Stornaway 127, 145, 164, 167, 216, 263
Stout, Mr. 155, 164, 194
Stroma 172, 249
Stromness 54
Sumburgh 98, 99, 100, 127, 203
Swanson, Capt. 51

T

Tai-Yuan-Fu 23, 24, 25, 32
Thurso 51, 53, 132, 173
Tientsin 31
Tranum, J. 86

U

United Airways 129, 132, 150

V

Valentine, J. 4, 5
Vedrines, J. 3–5
Vernon Castle 16
Voisin 1

W

Wick 41, 42, 47, 51, 76, 206
Williamson, Sir Frederick 68, 69, 113

Wilson, J. 52, 133, 173
Winster, Lord 225, 226
Woodhead Lt. 45
Wormwood Scrubs 3
Wotherspoon, Mr. 72, 80
Wright, Mr. 1
Wright Whirlwind 32

Y

Yangtze 8
Yellow Sea 7
Yen Shih Shen 23, 28
Yokohama 21
Yokosuka 21

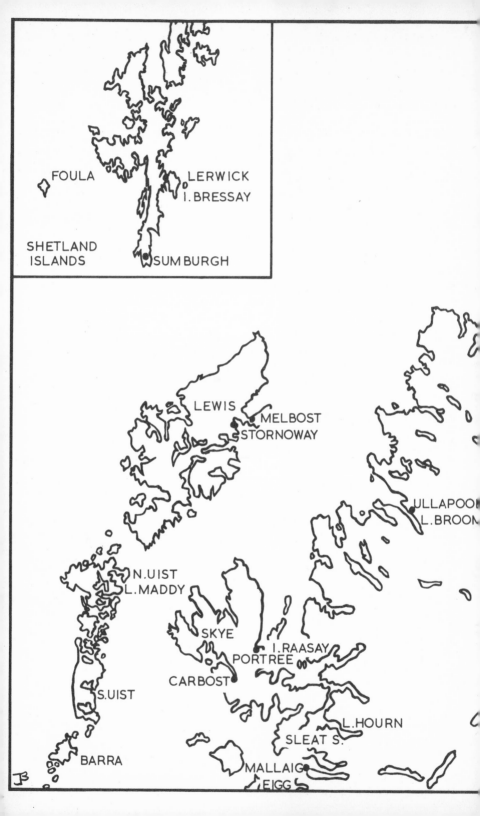